Raspb

CW00661031

RISC OS
SYSTEM

Programming
Revealed

Hands On Guide

Bruce Smith

www.brucesmith.info

Raspberry Pi RISC OS System Programming Revealed Hands On Guide

© Bruce Smith
ISBN 978-0-9923916-1-4
First edition, November 2013

Cover: Sumit Shringi, Graphic Designer (Book Cover-Design)
Typeset in 11 on 12pt Garamond by BSB using Serif PagePlus x6

Published by BSB - www.brucesmith.info.

ROSP Edition1 Final 1

Printed by CreateSpace.

Contents

4: Software Interrupts...48

5: Communications...66

6: Assembler, BASIC and C...86

17: WIMP Utilities...220

18: Font Manager..228

19: Modules..238

List of Programs

www.brucesmith.info

1: Introduction

When RISC OS was announced for the Raspberry Pi, the official RISC OS website had over a million hits. For those in the know the possibility of being able to have RISC OS running on a readily available, readily affordable computer was almost overwhelming.

As Technical Editor of *Acorn User* magazine I first encountered RISC OS when the Archimedes home computer was close to release. The first OS released with the Archimedes in 1987 was called Arthur. It was version 1.2 and two years later was replaced by version 2.0 and re-named RISC OS. It introduced the GUI on the Archimedes which ran atop of a command-line driven operating system. This owed much to Acorn's earlier MOS operating system for its BBC Micro range of 8-bit microcomputers. In fact Arthur/RISC OS was only supposed to be a stop-gap as the original OS for the Archimedes, known as ARX, was well behind schedule. Paul Fellows and his team took just five months to create Arthur.

The Late, Great Neil Raine

The ingenuity of the late Neil Raine in transforming this previously single-application-at-a-time system to one that could operate a full co-operative multi-tasking desktop for RISC OS secured its position as the OS of choice and effectively put paid to ARX.

Written in a combination of C, assembler and even BBC BASIC, it has become an enduring suite of software that has stood the test of time way beyond anyone's expectations. This is in no small part down to the team of enthusiasts who have continued to support the software and who have unwittingly created a legacy that, thanks to the popularity of the Raspberry Pi, will continue for many years to come.

Numerous versions of RISC OS have been released, but what is interesting is that the original Arthur OS core, API interfaces and modular structures remain as the heart of all versions. Not everything works on all software/hardware releases and this is certainly the case with the Raspberry Pi. For example, the Raspberry Pi videocore is very different from the graphics modes that were used to display the RISC OS Wimp on the Archimedes. A degree of emulation is therefore required and in some cases this simply isn't practical.

The PRMs

RISC OS comes with well over 4,000 pages of documentation in the form of the Programmers' Reference Manuals - the PRMs. These are a fantastic reference source and contain an incredible amount of information. They take the form of seven pdf files and you will find them in the Documents.Books.PRMs directory (folder) on the SD card.

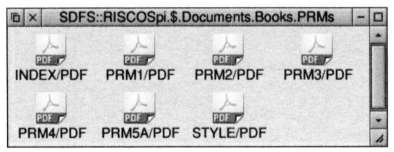

Figure 1a: The PRMs can be found in the Documents.Books.PRMs folder.

The PRMs were first released by Acorn in 1992-95 and were based on RISC OS 3 (including 3.5 and 3.6). This is still the case and while RISC OS has been released in multiple versions and upgrades since then, the fundamental information in the PRMs is still sound. It is true that some things have changed and new RISC OS releases have added more functionality and, in some cases, changed the way things work. Some of this is documented and some of it is not, but the various RISC OS forums are well supported and these changes are invariably discussed. This is certainly the case with the RISC OS Pi. This is an ongoing project and I have no doubt that RISC OS Pi will become the most popular and best supported version available.

Things that relate directly to hardware should be considered carefully as the Raspberry Pi has a very different hardware configuration to the original Archimedes. This includes video and sound related operations, as already discussed. Commands may sometimes work, but on the other hand they may only work to a degree or even not at all. Always bear this in mind and head to the RISC OS Forums to see if you can find more information, or simply to raise the question yourself.

The contents of each PRM PDF file are summarised in Figure 1b below. This will give you an overview of what you can expect to find in each PRM. Each

PRM takes a similar format and following an introduction and then explanation of any detailed technical information, you can expect to find details of all associated SWI and OS-related calls. When you find something in the PRM index you can click on the page number and the embedded link will take you directly to the referenced PRM and page directly.

File Name	Contents
PRMIX	Contains an index for just about everything you can think of, ordered in multiple ways. Use the contents list as a means of finding your way around the listings. (144 Pages.)
PRM1	Introduces the structure of RISC OS, and where components such as the Kernel, Filing System, Window Manager and System Extensions fit in. (998 Pages.)
PRM2	Provides detailed information on Filing Systems, Networking, Devices, Printing, Sound, and various aspects of the Desktop.(886 Pages)
PRM3	Introduces the Desktop and covers the Window Manager, The Shell, Colour, Font Manager, and Printer Drivers. (856 Pages.)
PRM4	Introduces the Sound system, Utilities, Expansion cards and ROMs, Floating Point Emulation, and the Shared C Library. (592 Pages)
PRM5A	This is an addendum to the PRMs and includes a lot of addition information updating all the volumes. It is also an introduction to RISC OS 3.5 and 3.6, ARM Hardware, Video interfaces, JPEG images, Parallel and Serial Devices, Internet, Boot Applications. (706 Pages)
STYLE	This manual provides all the information you need to ensure that your own work has the same look and feel as other RISC OS apps, in order to maintain consistency. (142 pages)

Figure 1b. Outline description of the contents of each PRM file.

Printed versions of the PRMs do exist, but their sheer size makes them expensive. On the other hand, printing the PDFs out is time-consuming and equally expensive, so finding your way around the PDFs and extracting any information you require is probably the best method of using them.

What You Will Learn

The information provided in the PRMs is mixed and while some is of an introductory nature much of it is only of use to programmers already experienced with using RISC OS. Parts of them could even be marked as *expert only*. Whilst there is also an element of beginner's information, this is mostly lost within the multitude of pages.

In short, the PRMs are a great resource, but the information is scattered and often requires a degree of knowledge to make sense of it. The PRMs are not a place to start learning about RISC OS, and they should be thought of as a reference point for greater detail when required.

This book is a guide to using RISC OS Pi as an operating system on the Raspberry Pi. It is aimed at those who wish to learn to program the operating system directly. It does not seek to replace the PRMs but it will hopefully go some way to making them accessible, usable and understandable. Inevitably there will be some overlap, but the material detailed in this book is provided from the RISC OS novice programmer's point of view and is therefore fundamentally less detailed. Where applicable you will also be pointed to the relevant sections and pages in the PRM for further detail.

Touching the Surface

Don't expect to see everything covered. What I have tried to include will assist with the fundamentals and will allow you to go further. For example, the Desktop could have a book to itself, so I have provided the information you need to know and then offered suggestions of how best to create your own window environments using other tools.

The 'operating system' is the name given to the fundamental software in a computer which provides the environment in which the user works. Without an OS it would not be possible to use a computer as a practical tool. The OS provides an environment where you can run applications of any sort, providing all the necessary interfacing software.

The most crucial role of RISC OS is to control the input/output devices connected to your Raspberry Pi, in particular the keyboard, the mouse, screen display and storage devices such as USB and SD Card drives. The design of RISC OS also allows it to be extended modularly and therefore provide extra functionality, for example when adding peripherals. Specific information relevant to the Raspberry Pi, such as the GPIO interface, is not in the PRMs.

RISC OS relieves you, the user, of the complexities of controlling the various peripheral devices connected to the Raspberry Pi. It allows the computer to be operated via applications (apps), by using meaningful commands or by accessing these commands from your own programs using inbuilt routines. These programs may be written in BBC BASIC, Assembly Language or C, and in fact many other languages exist.

This book will not teach you how to program in BBC BASIC, Assembler or C; I assume that you have this knowledge already. However, it will show you how to access RISC OS directly from these languages and how to take advantage of other applications to utilise them. However, that being said there is a strong bias towards using assembler and BBC BASIC.

There are specific chapters covering the use of all significant aspects of RISC OS — the Filing System, Sound and the Window Manager are some examples. These chapters and others like them are tutorials outlining how to use these modules and their associated OS interfaces. As mentioned above, it is not the intention to replace or rewrite the PRMs; these documents are after all reference works that go into much greater detail without perhaps explaining the practicalities. Thus I am seeking to make this kind of information easier to understand and in turn make the PRMs more accessible. This book also provides information not found in the PRMs. In doing so I hope to increase the usefulness of the book.

In summary, this book should help you become a proficient user of RISC OS at a system and programming level, no matter what the environment. It should provide a solid grounding into using and utilising the information in the PRMs to achieve greater things.

Assembly Language Beginners

If you have previously purchased a copy of my book Raspberry Pi Assembly Language Beginners (thank you!) then you will find this book contains a good deal of information that follows on from those pages, particularly in outlining more advanced topics such as module creation. I should also say that if you do not have a copy of Raspberry Pi Assembly Language Beginners it should not be considered a pre-requisite, although I do assume that you have the ability to program ARM machine code at some level (see Appendix B).

Compatibility

The book is equally applicable to the Raspberry Pi Model A and Model B and should not be affected by any later releases of the Pi itself. It is written with the Pi release of RISC OS in mind. The vast majority of the book also applies to other RISC OS 5 systems. As the RISC OS software is continually upgraded changes may well occur but these will not affect the underlying functionality of RISC OS. The manner in which the OS is written ensures as much backwards compatibility as possible. New versions of RISC OS Pi are more likely to add additional functionality and resolve issues that may have existed in the past.

Notation In Use

A standard notation has been adopted throughout this book. Number types and certain operations on numbers are commonplace in programming books such as this, and it is important to distinguish among them. The short list here is for reference. Their exact meaning will be described as we encounter them within the text of the book.

% or **0b** denotes that the number that follows it is in binary or base 2. For example: %11110000 or 0b11110000.

& or **0x** denotes that the number that follows it is hexadecimal or base 16. For example: &23F1 and 0xCAFE

< >Angle brackets or chevrons are used extensively to enclose a word that should not be taken literally, but read as the object to use with the command. For example, <Register> means a register name. For example, R0 might be used rather than the angled brackets and the word 'Register'.

Dest Short for destination.

Operand1 The commentary in the text often talks about Operand1 and its use. The relevant values for Operand1 as defined at that point should be used. For Operand1, this is normally a register.

Operand2 The commentary in the text often talks about Operand2 and its use. The relevant values for Operand2 as defined at that point should be used. For Operand2, this is normally either a register or an immediate value.

Op1 Shorthand format for <Operand1> when space is tight.

Op2 Shorthand format for <Operand2> when space is tight.

( ) Brackets show that the item within is optional and may be omitted if not needed. For example, ADD (S) means that S may or may not be included.

Companion Websites

Go to www.brucesmith.info and follow the directions to the book companion pages. From the site, you can download all the programs and access updates to the book and additional information and features. In addition, links to other support websites and useful downloads can be found, along with details of forthcoming Bruce Smith Books publications covering the Raspberry Pi.

I would also suggest you check out the RISC OS Open website for on-line access to PRMs and additional new information. I would highly recommend you make yourself part of the Forums there; don't be afraid to ask questions and get involved. There are a lot of practical exchanges there, some of them very amusing for the non-initiated. You will also find threads in the forums dealing with current ongoing enhancements, so that gives you a real chance to contribute.

Follow me on Twitter: **@brucefsmith** and check out my occasional blog '*Alan Turing Rocks*' which can be found on my website. To stay up-to-date with what books are in the pipeline and additional information on my writings 'Like' me at my Facebook page: **authorbrucesmith**

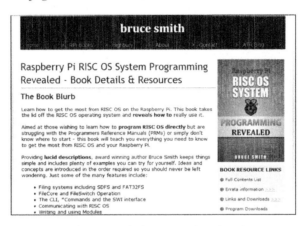

Figure 1c. The author's website contains book support pages.

This is a book of a technical nature, and amendments of various kinds are inevitable, so please do check out the website regularly for them.

Acknowledgements

I am extremely indebted to Andrew Gregson and Theo Markettos for their feedback, suggestions and additions to the original manuscript. Their extensive experience with RISC OS has certainly helped in making this a better publication.

I am also grateful to a number of people for their feedback and answers to questions via the RISC OS Open website, including Jeffrey Lee, Rick Murray, Stephen Revill, Nemo, Gavin Wrath, Trevor Johnson, Steve Drain, Colin, WPB, and Steve Pampling. Apologies to anyone I have missed out.

Thanks to Mike Ginns for the concepts of several programs listed here. Several listings originate from his book Archimedes Assembly Language which was first published by Dabs Press in 1988. (A key to how old the RISC OS actually is!). Thanks also to Alex and Nic Van Someren for the basis of several chapters and programs, originally in their book Archimedes Operating System which I also published at Dabs Press in 1991. Of course, these have been substantially revised and updated for use in this book.

2: What's It All About?

RISC OS is a clever piece of software. Considering that its first incarnation was over 30 years ago, it hasn't changed that much. This is all the more remarkable when you consider how far computers have come and have themselves changed in that same period of time.

Much of the reason for this is possibly because RISC OS was designed with the ARM chip in mind and makes use of its unique features. The ARM chip started as an innovation and has continued to be developed and innovative and to set the pace at the forefront of technology. Just about every smart phone and tablet device on sale today has an ARM chip at its core, and for example these apparently modest devices are being used to control budget satellites being placed in Earth orbit. And in theory all could run RISC OS!

In this chapter we'll look at some of the features that make RISC OS what it is on the Raspberry Pi — RISC OS Pi. Many of the concepts introduced in this simple overview form the basis of forthcoming chapters that deal with these topics in much greater detail.

Operation Process

The operation of RISC OS is based largely around the processing of interrupts and events. Take these two actions away and not a lot goes on. At the core of this RISC OS lies the Kernel (the part of the computer software that has control over everything it does) and everything that happens is directed through it. This is what holds everything together; everything else is attached to it.

Interrupts are largely driven by the ARM chip and for the most part are provided in order to deal with attached hardware, with tasks such as making sure that important peripherals such as disk drives and keyboards get serviced as quickly as possible. Because these devices are hardware connected RISC OS doesn't have to worry about looking for them; it simply has to provide the software for dealing with them. The ARM looks after interrupts right from the start, long before RISC OS is loaded.

Events are essentially sanitised versions of interrupts. They are used to inform the user whenever RISC OS performs or detects that some significant task has taken place. The user in this case may also be an application. These events may be 'captured' and acted upon. Many events are produced in response to RISC OS detecting an interrupt from the hardware and the event is 'issued' to users who can identify what it is and act accordingly.

Software and applications are written in much the same way, and use their own interrupt or polling system to manage what is going on. The Desktop that RISC OS Pi boots into provides a complete WIMP environment whereby you can use windows, menus, icons, pointers and a range of other features. This is all managed by a part of RISC OS called the Window Manager and it is continually issuing its own series of events to all the elements of the Wimp using a code number to tell or poll the various Desktop elements that certain actions have taken place. The RISC OS application programming interface (API) is extremely simple and accessible — to the point that it can be mastered by anyone with time to spare.

Routine Library

RISC OS, probably more than any other operating system available, provides an extensive library of routines which any programmer can use to interact with the hardware and applications. This means that the programmer doesn't have to spend time and effort writing their own – all that is needed is to provide the SWIs (Software Interrupts) with the relevant information and set the process in motion. This is perfect for programmers who, for example, do not have to worry about reading input from the keyboard, as there is a RISC OS routine to do just that (and just about everything else). This has the added advantage of ensuring that the interface appears standard and consistent, and for example provides an almost universal drag and drop facility for file save, file load, and operations such as copy, cut and paste. These are covered extensively.

Because RISC OS is so organised it needs programmers to be likewise when presenting information. This can be quite daunting as in some instances — thankfully few — a lot of details are required. These need to be provided in memory blocks of buffers which themselves remain consistent within applications, so it is often possible to let information run within the buffers themselves.

Extendibility

RISC OS itself is quite small and light in terms of memory usage. This is why it is so incredibly quick to boot-up. It is also infinitely expendable by adding bolt-on extras called modules. In fact RISC OS itself is largely composed of modules that provide additional functionality, making it very easy to adapt to changes and development in hardware and software. Not surprisingly, modules follow a standard format and are not difficult to write. This means that as new hardware becomes available, modules to handle their attachment can be developed very quickly.

As a programming environment RISC OS has always sought to make things as easy as possible, and in a bid to ensure everything looks and acts the same all the input/output is handled by RISC OS — programs and applications just piggy-back onto it. This is not just the keyboard and screen; it includes items such as filing systems and the opening and closing of files. Writing a filing system is simplified because RISC OS provides all the relevant i/o interfaces for the programmer to use.

The inclusion as standard of an established structured language such as BBC BASIC as part of RISC OS is a bonus. The fact that this and its built in ARM assembler are seamlessly integrated makes it amazingly simple to quickly produce effective code.

Well Supported

In addition to BBC BASIC, RISC OS Pi comes with a wide variety of compilers and programming languages — all free. Charm and Risc Lua are supplied with the standard distribution, while GCC and a variety of support libraries can be downloaded and installed simply in a matter of minutes.

There is also an abundance of educational software for a child that is easy to use, even for a person that has never touched a computer before. Scratch is a kids programming language that a four-year old would appreciate. Add to this a reasonable selection of games, both the good old ones and several new titles and you begin to understand what RISC OS really brings to the Raspberry Pi.

Programmers Tool Chest

Organising your own programming tool chest will not take too long, and you will probably already have your own likes and dislikes. Much of what you will need is already present in the Raspberry Pi RISC OS Pi distribution. If you are not sure or want to investigate other alternatives then here are a few items I would suggest you get to know. Some of these you will find on the Desktop; others in the Apps directory.

StrongEd is a full-feature programmer's text editor that is surprisingly easy to use. It can be used to edit just about anything and can do this in the context of the filetype being edited. This means that you can create a BASIC file and StrongEd will treat it like a BASIC program, saving it in the correct format. In this way you can also run the program from within the Editor so that you don't have to go to a BASIC task window, load and run it, before retreating back to make any corrections.

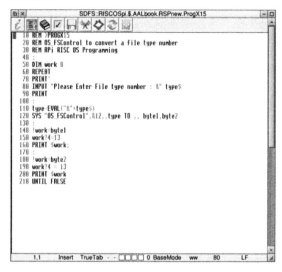

Figure 2a. A BBC BASIC program being edited in StrongEd.

PackMan is a simple, clever and easy way to add software to your set-up and ensure you have the latest releases and updates. It does this by maintaining lists of software, and you should ensure that these lists are up-to-date by selecting the 'Update Lists' option from its icon-bar menu.

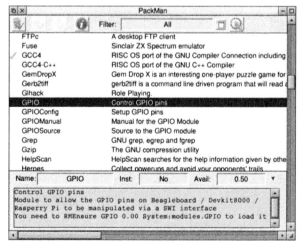

Figure 2b. The Packman window.

Once PackMan has checked their status you can choose to 'Update all' if you wish and Packman will take care of the process for you. By using Packman you should never have to download and install software by hand.

By scrolling through the alphabetical software list in Packman you can get descriptions of the programs and can see if updates are available. If you are considering C then you can get the latest version of GCC and libraries such as OSlib here too.

PackMan is based on an earlier packaging system called RiscPkg, but with a friendlier user interface (for example, the ability to move installed programs wherever you like). It is still in its infancy and you can expect to see new features as it is developed.

StrongHelp for most is an access point to StrongHelp manuals. A good majority of RISC OS software comes with hypertext manuals that invariably contain an incredible amount of information. Some examples of these are given later in this book. StrongHelp is also a simple hypertext authoring program which you can use to create your own documentation.

OS SWIs		
ADFS	FileCore	Podule
ATAPI	FilerAction	Portable
Audio	Filter	RamFS
BASICTrans	Font	RemotePrinterSupport
Buffer	FPEmulator	ResourceFS
Cache	Free	ScreenBlanker
CD	FSLock	ScreenModes
CDFS	Hourglass	SCSI
ColourPicker	IIC	SharedCLibrary
ColourTrans	Joystick	SharedSound
CompressJPEG	JPEG	Shell
Debugger	MakePSFont	Sound
DeviceFS	MessageTrans	Squash
DMA	NetFS	Super
DOSFS	NetPrint	TaskManager
DragAnObject	OS	TaskWindow
DragASprite	Parallel	Territory
Draw	PCI	Wimp
DrawFile	PDriver	
Econet	PDumperSupport	

Error block	Service Calls	Hardware vectors
Dynamic area caveats	Vectors	Deprecated calls
OS_Byte values	Image filesystems	Module format
CMOS RAM bytes	Filesystems	Upcalls

OS SWIs manual v3.35, 21 Jul 2012

Figure 2c. StrongHelp manuals abound – here OS SWI calls are arranged by function.

StrongHelp manuals are stored in the !Manuals directory in the Utilities folder on the SD Disc. The riscos.info website hosts a collection of StrongHelp manuals for everything RISC OS. A link to this can be found on the book support pages on my website.

Director can be found in Apps. It installs on the icon bar and from here you can interrogate the status of your RISC OS setup. It is a tool that allows you to customise your desktop and create quick-access menus to anything within RISC OS. With it you can create menus and place icons on the icon bar. It also provides easy access to files and a lot more. You can look at system settings and also delve into things like modules and SWIs.

Director includes a scripting system which gives you the ability to do things such as map keyboard shortcuts and custom menus to almost action.

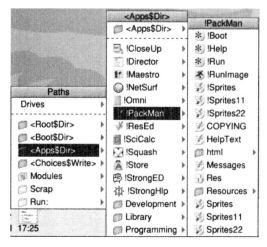

Figure 2d. Director menus allow you to interrogate features such as modules.

SparkFS is a compression filing system that gives you more disc space by saving and managing your files in a compressed — zip — format. It does so seamlessly without the need to resort to compressing and uncompressing processes – this all happens in the Filer. The bonus of this is that it maximises the use of your SD card space which can become quite tight if you are not using alternative storage options. There can be a slight overhead in some additional access time for compressed files, but for files and data that you are not accessing on a regular basis this should not be an issue. There are free and paid for versions.

!MultiTask is a multi-tasking desktop utility which allows you to examine the contents of files and to load, run and edit BASIC programs from the desktop. It is available from !Store (free of charge) and clicking on the icon installs it on the icon bar. Dragging and dropping a BASIC file onto this will load the program into its own window, from where you can type RUN to fire it up as though it was a multi-tasking program. This app is covered in more detail in Chapter 15 where it is used for a specific purpose.

This is only a small sample of my favourite apps that I consider essential for effective RISC OS *System Programming*. There are plenty of others; have fun discovering and utilising new ones.

Fitting RISC OS Together

Figure 2e illustrates diagrammatically how RISC OS slots together all its major components. We shall discuss each of these in some detail as we go forward, so you may wish to come back and refer to this figure from time to time.

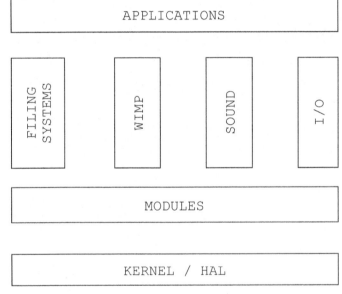

Figure 2e. RISC OS structural composition.

Holding everything together is the Kernel and Hardware Abstraction Layer. The HAL was introduced to RISC OS 5 as a way of making interfacing to different hardware setups and system chips easier. This means that RISC OS is no longer dependent on a fixed set of core chips. In the case of the Raspberry Pi the HAL has been configured to work with Broadcom's BCM2835 System-On-a-Chip. The Kernel supplies the basic core routines that make RISC OS function and interface with both the HAL and the outside world. Everything goes to the hardware via the Kernel.

Sitting on top of the Kernel/HAL are the modules. Modules provide a way of extending RISC OS giving it additional functionality. Anyone can write a Module and interface it to RISC OS by using a standard that we'll discuss later in this book. One of the first Raspberry Pi specific modules to be developed and released was one to control the GPIO port.

From the user point of view the four main operating components of RISC OS are the Filing System, the WIMP (Desktop), the Sound System and the Input/Output interfaces. These all sit alongside each other and much of their functionality is provided with module support.

Finally applications run across all these and will invariably require support from each of them. Each application will call on many of the components underneath it, indeed applications may also be implemented as modules, so it shows how integrated RISC OS is a system being

Soft Interaction

Figure 2f shows diagrammatically how the command/call hierarchy fits together in RISC OS. We shall discuss each of these in some detail as we go forward, so you may wish to come back and refer to this figure later on.

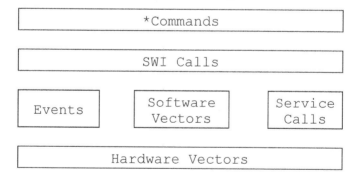

Figure 2f. The RISC OS Command/Call structure.

* Commands provide the standard CLI method of accessing operations in RISC OS. By definition they are language-independent so can operate across all software platforms. In almost all instances (but not every one) *commands have underlying SWI calls, which are provided by either the Kernel or an associated module. These in turn are supported by a trio of calls that provide three different types of RISC OS functionality. Virtually all operations are directed through Software Vectors — these provide direct control to specific locations in the Kernel or associated module. Service Calls allow RISC OS to inform all the components of RISC OS that they may need to perform

housekeeping operations. Events are actions that can be configured to occur at pre-defined times in relation to certain conditions being met.

Underlying all this are the hardware vectors; these are hard wired into the ARM chip and control access to critical operations. When you first turn on the Raspberry Pi it starts its boot-up process by accessing functions through the hardware vectors.

3: Command Line Interpreter

There are two basic methods we can use to communicate with RISC OS: * commands (pronounced 'star' rather than asterisk) and SWI calls. In general * commands allow functional operations to be executed and may require you to supply parameters with them, whereas SWI calls provide for greater individual functionality and thus more intricate control. They also allow information to be passed back to them, which is not necessarily the case with * commands. These two methods are the basic building blocks of RISC OS programming, so understanding how to use them is essential if you want to program RISC OS effectively. There are literally hundreds of each and their definitions form a large part of the PRMs. SWI calls are discussed in the next chapter; here we will concentrate on * commands.

All interpreted languages should allow you to use * commands from within them. In fact languages and software applications may also add their own * commands for you to use. These commands are often supplied in the form of modules which are added to the system software. Modules are introduced in the Chapter 7.

Although * commands can be used within programs of various types (we'll look at examples later on) and in such cases are often used to configure aspects of RISC OS before the program gets underway, they are often used directly from the keyboard in immediate mode, where they are executed as soon as you have pressed the Return key.

The Command Line Interpreter (CLI) provides direct access to * commands from the Desktop. To access the CLI press <CTRL-F12> (or select Task Window from the Raspberry Pi menu), This will display a task window. The new window will display a * as a prompt indicating you are in * command mode.

To enter a * command at this point, simply type the command. There is no need to include the * for a second time as this is taken as implicit as it is the RISC OS environment. For example, typing:

COUNTRY

This will return a message displaying the country set up in use. We can also pass a parameter with this command to change or set the country preference thus:

    COUNTRY USA

This will set RISC OS operation to USA preferences (keyboard, dollar signs, date format etc.). Figure 3a shows the Task Window with these commands executed from the CLI.

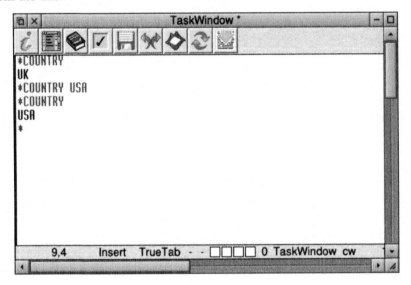

Figure 3a. * commands executed in the CLI.

If you type the * again from the CLI then it is simply ignored and the command actioned as normal. Note that * commands are keyboard case independent and thus:

    *COUNTRY

and:

    *country

Both are acceptable and are treated as identical.

This chapter looks at a number of features relating to * commands and use of the CLI. What is outlined here can be applied for use with all * commands unless otherwise stated.

CLI Command Syntax

The CLI recognises a number of characters that can be used with * commands and provides specific actions to be taken. These characters can be used as part of a command on the CLI or within programs.

* (Star)

Any additional stars entered at the start of the command are ignored. If you are running in a Task Window (where a star is the prompt) then there is no need to enter the initial star. An initial star is an absolute must when using BBC BASIC otherwise an 'Unrecognised Command' error or similar will be generated.

<Spaces>

Leading spaces are ignored. However, it is worth noting that within commands there is inconsistency in the way they are used and this is documented later.

| (Bar)

The vertical bar character is used to allow comments to be inserted. This must come at the beginning of the line — when encountered the rest of the line is ignored. This provides a good way of commenting an executable file which contains a sequence of * commands.

/ (Slash)

The slash character can be used as an abbreviation for the *RUN command. For example, the command:

```
*RUN MyFile
```

This can be abbreviated to:

```
*/MYFile
```

In fact, it can be abbreviated further to just:

```
*MyFile
```

: (Colon)

The colon character is used to allow a temporary switch in filing systems. For example, if you were operating on your local network and wished to access a file on from the SDFS filing system, you might be tempted to issue three separate command lines thus:

```
*SDFS
*EXEC $.PUBLIC.TEXTFILE
*FAT32FS
```

The first line selects the SDFS filing system. The second line EXECutes the file called 'TEXTFILE' which is located in the PUBLIC directory. The third line reselects the FAT32 (USB) filing system.

Using the colon operator we can condense this to a single line as follows:

```
*EXEC SDFS:$.PUBLIC.TEXTFILE
```

Note the use of the colon immediately after SDFS.

'<...>'

The greater than and less than characters can be used for file re-direction. When used with a filing system command, these operators specify where the output is sent (using '>') or where it is taken or read from (using '<'). These characters have an additional requirement in that the character and file address must be enclosed within curly brackets. Their position and the use of a single space either side of them is critical, otherwise an error will result.

This example will send the output of the directory *CATalogue command to a file called 'FILES' located in the home directory:

```
*CAT { > $.FILES }
```

Note the use of spaces: between the 'T' and the '{' and also between the '{' and '>' and the '$'. They are critical to the success of the command. If the named file — FILES — does not already exist then the redirection operator will create it. If a named file does exist then its contents will be overwritten. If you wish to append the contents to the end of an existing file then use two redirection operators thus (again being mindful of use of spaces):

```
*CAT { >> $.FILES}
```

The re-direction operators may be used to read input and send it out elsewhere within the same set of curly brackets. Look at this example:

```
*CAT { > FILES < OLDFILE > NEWFILE }
```

Here, FILES will be created (if it does not already exist), but nothing will be directed to it — it will be an empty file. It will be read from the file called OLDFILE and then sent to the file called NEWFILE, which will be created if it did not exist. To append the contents of OLDFILE to an existing NEWFILE, use the additional operator thus:

```
*CAT { > FILES < OLDFILE >> NEWFILE }
```

Redirection operations are quite useful tools when manipulating files and creating files of command sequences.

When you create the files they will be set as Data type files. You should reset them as Text files so that you can read them in the text editor of your choice. To do this Middle-Click on the file and select:

```
File>Set Type>
```

Then type Text over Data before saving.

C Re-direction

C compiled commands can also be programmed to send their output to a named file. Strictly speaking this is performed by the Shared C Library and not the CLI. This is done by adding '>LogName' to the end of the command line which calls the C program, where 'LogName' is the name of the output file you want to create. Using a single '>' means any existing file with that name will be overwritten each time the program starts. If you want to preserve messages from previous runs, use a pair of symbols, '>>' instead. Note that the '{}' braces around the redirection are not required (as it is not handled by the CLI)

Star Commands

The rest of this chapter details the most common general operation * commands provided by RISC OS. It is not a comprehensive list as commands relative to the filing system, for example, are discussed in the section of this book that deals with filing systems. Also many commands are added by other third-party modules and are not included. Comprehensive use of the *HELP command can be of great use when investigating these and other star commands.

When presenting the syntax of these commands the following notation is used for parameters:

<name>   A parameter to be filled in as appropriate (without the brackets)

{<name>}   An optional parameter

x | y   Two parameters, either of which but not both may be used

*Help

Syntax: *HELP {<Operand1>} {<Operand2>}

The *HELP command displays help text on topics whose keywords are provided. You will find this a quick and easy way to get initial and syntax information on any aspect of the * commands.

Try typing:

```
*HELP COMMANDS
```

This will produce a list of the modules currently available, each of which is followed by a list of keywords on which more help is available. For example:

```
*HELP MOUNT DISMOUNT
```

This lists a line or two of help on the ADFS commands *MOUNT and *DISMOUNT.

`*HELP FILECOMMANDS`

This lists all the commands relating to filing systems, while:

`*HELP SYNTAX`

This explains the format used for syntax messages.

It is possible to abbreviate keywords by terminating them with a full stop. This produces help on all the keywords beginning with the given sequence of letters, so:

`*HELP s.`

will produce help on all the available commands that begin with an 'S'.

When you issue the *Help command at the normal Command Line prompt the listing is created. You can use the scroll bars to move up and down through the listing. Alternatively you could use the redirection operators to create a text file:

`*HELP COMMANDS { > $.FILES }`

Then view the output you have created in a suitable text editor such as StrongEd.

*Configure

Syntax: *CONFIGURE {<Operand1>} {<Operand2>}

The *CONFIGURE command displays or sets the various RISC OS operating options. If it is definable then there is probably a *CONFIGURE command for it. These options are stored in memory and will be reset after a power off or reset (many of these are used as the settings that can be found in the !Boot directory on the SD Card). It is important to note that configuration settings do not take effect immediately, so it is usually necessary to issue the appropriate *FX command (or similar) if you want to change a setting right away.

When the command is issued with no parameters, all the available configuration options are listed. This is quite an extensive list. When a single operand is supplied the named option is configured. For example:

`*CONFIGURE QUIET`

This sets the configured volume for any beep to half its loudest possible volume. This change would take effect on the next reset.

When used with two (or more) parameters, the option named <Operand1> is configured to the value of <Operand2>. Where numerical values are required, several forms may be used:

nnn	A decimal number
&nn	A hexadecimal number
base_nnn	The number nnn in number-base 'base', eg, 2_1111 is the same as &F which is the same as (decimal) 15.

For example:

```
*CONFIGURE TIMEZONE -5
```

This would set the time zone in use to -5 hours from the UTC— effectively the eastern seaboard of the USA. You can use:

```
*STATUS
```

to see a list of configured options (see later).

A huge number of possible configuration parameters exist, and these definitions are throughout the PRMs so you will need to consult the index to locate the option you are looking for and its page location.

*Echo

```
Syntax: *ECHO <string>
```

This command translates the string provided as the parameter and then prints out the result. The command understands aliases and other operating system variables. Aliases are discussed later in this chapter.

```
*ECHO <Alias$.>
```

This displays the alias defined for the command:

```
*.
```

This is equivalent to *CAT unless the alias has been altered.

The string may include '|' control characters (although not all of these will work under RISC OS Pi).

*ECHO is not particularly useful on its own. In the past it has been used to define new CLI commands that are output to the VDU (screen display) by printing ASCII codes held within angle brackets. For example:

```
*ECHO <22> <0>
```

This has the same effect as MODE 0 in BBC BASIC. (VDU 22 being the code for the MODE command.) *ECHO can be usefully applied within executable files to print out strings to the screen to indicate what is happening at that point:

```
*ECHO "Configuring all settings..."
```

*Error

Syntax: *ERROR <error number> <error message>

This command generates an error whose number and associated message are supplied. This is most useful for raising errors associated with new CLI commands, for example:

*ERROR 123 That option is not supported

*Eval

Syntax: *EVAL <expression string>

This command evaluates the expression supplied and displays the result on screen. It allows string manipulation and simple arithmetic involving RISC OS variables and integers. For example:

*EVAL 255+1024

The result is an integer, value: 1279

*EVAL <count>*2

Would take the value assigned to the RISC OS variable count and double its value before displaying the result.

Logical operators may also be used by using the shift operators. Thus:

*EVAL 2 << 3

This would shift 2 left by three places to give the response:

Result is an integer, value : 12

Operators may be mixed within commands to provide more complex operations:

*EVAL 12+4*5-4

This would result in 28. Note that this arithmetical operation has the multiplication evaluated first. Brackets can be used to force the order of solution:

EVAL (12+4)(5-4)

Here the result is 16.

*FX (OS_Byte)

Syntax: *FX <Op1> {{,}<Op2> {{,}<Op3>}}

This command calls the OS_Byte routine, allowing a quick and easy way to call operating system routines from the command line or from within programs. For example:

*FX 12, 1

Here the keyboard auto-repeat rate is set to one-hundredth of a second. In assembler we could achieve exactly the same with:

```
MOV R0, #12
MOV R1, #1
SWI "OS_Byte"
```

OS_Byte definitions are scattered throughout the PRMs so refer to the PRM Index for a list of those available and their locations. The standard entry and exit conditions are:

On Entry:
R0 = OS_Byte number
R1 = Parameter one — if required
R2 = Parameter two — if required

On Exit:
R0 preserved
R1 = may contain a result if provided by action
R2 = may contain a result if provided by action

On entry, R0 contains the OS_Byte number and this will be a value in the range 0-255. R1 and R2 will contain any other values required by the call. Appendix A contains a list of OS_Byte calls.

While OS_Byte calls have one of the fundamental features of RISC OS in the past, they are becoming less useful as better APIs appear.

*Go

Syntax:*GO {<operand1>} {<argument list>}

*GO is used to execute an application located at the hexadecimal address specified by <operand1>, or at address &8000 if the address is omitted. In either case, the argument list is passed to the called program using registers. This allows an application program to be loaded at a fixed address and then called later, rather than using *RUN or similar.

```
*GO 9000
```

This calls a machine code application located at &9000. Note that *GO cannot be used to call a machine code routine stored as a file — use *RUN for this.

*If

Syntax: *IF <expression> THEN <Op1> {ELSE <Op2>}

This very useful statement allows commands to be executed conditionally on the result of an <expression>. If an <expression> is true, which is to say it yields a non-zero result, then <Operand1> is executed. Otherwise, where the 'ELSE' part of the command has been included, <Operand2> is executed. In both cases <Operand1> and <Operand2> are any valid * command.

It should also be noted that <expression> may include system variables, integer arithmetic or string manipulation if desired. For example, if there were two directories — one called '2013' and one called 'OTHER' then we could enter the appropriate one automatically by using:

```
*IF <Sys$Year>="2013" THEN DIR 2013 ELSE DIR OTHER
```

And signal the fact with:

```
*IF <Sys$Year>="2013" THEN ECHO It's 2013 ELSE ECHO It's
not
```

Note that the '*' is not required to precede the commands defined in Operand1 and Operand2 and the quotes are not required to enclose ECHO text in this case.

*Key

Syntax: *KEY <key number> {<key definition>}

RISC OS supports the action of 16 function keys. Each function key can be assigned a command line string, so that when a function key is pressed the string assigned to it is executed.

For example:

```
*KEY 1 EVAL <counter>|M
```

This sets up function key F1 to enter display a message and an evaluated value. Notice the use of |M control codes within the definition — |M will generate a <RETURN> and thus enable multiple * commands to be issued.

```
*KEY 2 *CAT|M
```

This is a much simpler definition and assigns F2 with the *CAT command so that the directory can be listed with a single key press.

Function keys are good for saving long but frequently used Key sequences — changing directories is one such useful use of them. Most keyboards have 11 functions keys which are numbered- F1 to F12. The Print key is F0 and the Insert key is F13. The other five function keys can be accessed by using:

```
*FX 4, 2
```

This will define these keys as the associated function keys:

> <COPY> = F11
> <left arrow> = F12
> <right arrow>= F13

<down arrow> = F14

<up arrow> = F15

A hard reset (cycling the power) will reset all *KEY definitions, but they should survive a soft-reset (rebooting from the task menu). Once you have established your own way of working in RISC OS you will probably find you use a standard set of calls regularly. These can be defined as *KEY settings and could be included as part of an executable file that can be run each time you boot RISC OS.

A RISC OS variable called KEY$ <key_number> exists for each key. This may be assigned using the *SET command.

*Quit

Syntax: *QUIT

*QUIT exits from the current application – that is, it returns to the previous context.

*Set

Syntax: *SET <variable name> <string>

*SET assigns the given string to the named RISC OS variable, creating the variable if it doesn't already exist. Variables can be either of type 'number' or type 'string', with obvious effects on expression evaluation as you can't multiply a string for example!

As an example of *SET:

    *SET RPI This is the Raspberry Pi

This creates and assigns the string to the variable 'RPI', which may then be displayed with *ECHO, thus:

    *ECHO <RPI>

Notice the use of angle-brackets to force * ECHO to evaluate the variable, rather than just printing the word 'RPI'.

    *SET counter 12

Here the value 12 is assigned to the variable 'counter'.

RISC OS provides a number of pre-defined built-in variables which may be altered by the user, but never deleted. They are listed in Figure 3b over.

So, to change the date and year we could use:

```
*SET Sys$Date Fri, 1 December
*SET Sys$Year 2013
```

In addition, other parts of the Operating System or other modules may add further variables of their own.

*SET can be used to pass the status of a system variables into another static variable, thus preserving their values at the time the command was executed. For example:

```
*SET xTime <Sys$Time>
```

This would save the value of Sys$Time into the variable 'xTime' as it stood when the line was executed.

Variable Name	Description
Sys$Time	Current time in the format: hh:mm:ss
Sys$Date	Current date in the format: Fri, 1 December
Sys$Year	Current year in the format: 2013
Sys$DateFormat	Sets the format in which the date is presented

Figure 3b. Predefined system variables.

*SET can also be used to create new commands and short cuts using aliases. This is discussed later in this chapter.

*SetEval

Syntax: *SETEVAL <variable name> <expression>

This command allows numeric variables to be evaluated and assigned. For example:

```
*SET counter 1
*SETEVAL counter counter+1
```

The *SET command assigns the number 1 to a user system variable called 'counter'. *SETEVAL is then used to add 1 to the value of 'counter'. Typing:

```
*SHOW counter
```

This would display the value of counter, which in this example should now be 2 and would be displayed thus:

```
counter (Number) : 2
```

*SETEVAL can also be used to concatenate strings to a string variable. For example:

```
*SETEVAL RPI "Raspberry " + "Pi"
```

Typing:

```
*SHOW RPI
```

would create the output:

```
PRI: Raspberry Pi
```

*Setmacro

Syntax: *SETMACRO <variable name> <expression>

*SETMACRO is almost the same as *SETEVAL, but the evaluation of the expression is deferred until each time the variable is accessed, so that it displays the most up-to-date information. For example, the CLI has a system variable in which it keeps the definition of the prompt displayed on the CLI — this is CLI$Prompt. Thus:

```
*SETMACRO CLI$Prompt <Sys$Time>
```

This sets the CLI prompt to display the current time help in Sys$Time each time a new line is displayed by the CLI.

Function key F1 can be set up to display the current time each time it is pressed in a similar way:

```
*SetMacro Key$1 "The time is "<Sys$Time>|M
```

*Show

Syntax: *SHOW {<variable name>{*}}

*SHOW displays the name, type and current value of system variables. When no variable name is supplied all variables are displayed; otherwise a specific variable is displayed:

```
*SHOW Cli$Prompt
```

This displays a result in the style:

```
CLI$Prompt : type String, value
```

By appending an asterisk to a partial variable name a wildcard effect is introduced, so:

```
*SHOW Sys$*
```

will display all of the system variables. Similarly, the following will display the current assignments of all the function keys:

```
*SHOW Key$*
```
And all defined aliases can be listed with:

```
*Show Alias$*
```

*Status

Syntax: *STATUS {<Operand1>}

This command allows you to examine the current setting of one or any of the options set with *CONFIGURE. When no parameter is supplied the entire list will be displayed. Otherwise, if a valid option name is supplied, its current setting is displayed.

For example, to display the configured international language setting, use:

*STATUS COUNTRY

Don't forget that the settings displayed by *STATUS are those that will come into effect next time the machine is powered-up or reset — they do not come into action immediately the *STATUS command is issued. Devious!

*Time

Syntax: *TIME

This command displays the time and date in the format defined by the system variable Sys$DateFormat. The default is of the style:

Wed, 11 Sep 2013. 21:24:53

This format can be changed by altering Sys$DateFormat.

*Unset

Syntax: *UNSET <variable name>{*}

*UNSET deletes one or more non-system variables. If an asterisk is used then all variables which begin with the characters supplied will be deleted. You cannot delete a system variable, although no error will be reported if you try to do so. For example:

*UNSET counter

will delete a previously defined system variable called 'counter'.

Aliases

The ALIAS operator can be used to create a new command or re-adjust how a particular command is used for your own needs. One simple need might be to correct an error you always make when typing. Suppose, you always type:

    *CAY

instead of:

    *CAT

An easy mistake because the Y is next to the T on the keyboard. You can create an alias so that when you type:

    *CAY

then:

    *CAT

is executed automatically for you. To create a pseudo-command called CAY that executes *CAT, you use the *SET command thus:

    *SET alias$CAY CAT

The *SET command is detailed later, but this example will ensure that when you type *CAY that *CAT is performed. (By the way, *CAT performs a catalogue of the currently set file directory and will list all the folders and files present in the directory.)

This alias method makes it possible to define command names that you personally prefer to use as alternatives for the built-in names. Note in the alias definition the star is not required and is implicit in the operation.

The syntax used to define an alias is therefore:

    alias$name

In the above line 'name' is the name of the alias you wish to add which can be made up from all alphanumeric characters and these others:

    ! `  ( )  +  −  .  ;  =  ?  @  [  ]  _  ` { } ~

The alias may also be followed by up to ten parameters which can be used to act as place holders for information that may not be known at the time of defining the alias. These pseudo-variables are labelled %0 through to %9 and are used as placeholders within the alias definition. When the alias is then called a value can be specified after it on the command line and this is substituted into the pseudo-variable:

    *SET ALIAS$ASCII ECHO |<%0>

This would print the character represented by the number stated after the alias command. So:

```
*ASCII 65
```

would print an 'A' on the screen.

(If you omit a value then you will find the brackets are printed on screen — which I would see as a bug.)

Note that you can use multiple definitions in an alias and generate new lines using '|M' with one or more variables also being used.

You can remove an alias definition at any time using the * command UNALIAS. For example:

```
*UNALIAS ASCII
```

Obey Scripts

So far the * commands we have demonstrated have been used on a one-off basis — typed at the keyboard and executed when needed. However, lists of * commands can be created and held in text files, and their commands executed en bloc when needed. This is really useful when you start a RISC OS programming session and need to define function keys, aliases and so forth. These files are called Obey Files and the *OBEY command is used to execute them.

*OBEY executes a named file which contains the * commands listed one after the other. Parameters can also be passed with the *OBEY commands and passed into the file if required.

Try the example listed below as Program 3a, by creating a new text file (in StrongEd or your preferred text editor) and save it in the root directory using a suitable filename — 'setup' might do.

Program 3a. An example *OBEY file.

```
*COUNTRY USA
*CONFIGURE TIMEZONE -5
*SET ALIAS$ASCII ECHO |<%%0>
*SETEVAL COUNTER 0
*SETMACRO CLI$PROMPT <SYS$TIME>>: *
```

These * commands should all be familiar to you as they are single line versions of examples previously used. The alert amongst you might have noticed that the alias definition in the third line has an additional '%' at the start of the pseudo-variable holder.

This is required to stop any parameters passed with the Obey file being soaked up by the alias definition at this point. The parameter is only required for this when the alias is used from the command line. So to prevent the substitution you need to change the '%' to '%%'.

An Obey file can have parameters passed to it, which can then be used by the command script. The first parameter is referred to as %0, the second as %1, and so on. You can refer to all the parameters after a particular one by putting a * after the %, so %*2 would refer to the all parameters from the third one onwards.

These parameters are substituted before the line is passed to the Command Line Interpreter. Try this example. Create a new text filed called 'details', then add the following two commands to it:

```
FILEINFO %0
TYPE %0
```

Then issuing the command:

```
*OBEY DETAILS SETUP
```

would pass the name 'setup' into the CLI and substitute it for the %0. Therefore the command would execute:

```
*FILEINFO SETUP
*TYPE SETUP
```

If the TYPE command was changed to read:

```
TYPE %1
```

then the CLI would have expected to receive a second file name. The first would be substitute for %0 and the second for %1. If a second filename was not supplied an error would be generated.

The full syntax for the *OBEY command is:

```
*OBEY {{-v}{-c} {<filename> {<parameters>}}}
```

As well as being able to pass parameters — separated by spaces — into the executing file there are two optional switches: With the -v option, each line is displayed before execution. With the -c option, the file is cached and executed from memory. For example:

```
*OBEY -v SETUP
```

There are a few other points to bear in mind regarding *OBEY files:

- An Obey file is read directly and by default will not echo the lines to the screen as they are executed.

- An Obey file stops when an error is returned, and any remaining lines are not executed.

- Using the *OBEY command will force any text file to be treated as an Obey file. This overrides the current file type, such as Text or Command. This will only have meaning if the text in the file is valid for an obey file.

- An Obey file sets the system variable Obey$Dir to the directory it is in.

The Obey$Dir variable is set to the directory from which an Obey file is being run, and may be used by commands within that Obey file.

When an obey file is run by using any of the above techniques, the system variable Obey$Dir is set to the parent directory part of the pathname used. For example, if you were to type:

```
*OBEY Top.Middle.Filename
```

then 'Top.Middle' is the parent directory of the pathname.

Note that this is not set to the full parent name, only the part of the string passed to the command as the pathname. So if you change the current directory or filing system during the obey file, then it would not be valid any more.

Ideally, you should invoke Obey files (and applications, which are started by an Obey file named !Run) by using their full pathname, and preceding that by either a forward slash / or the word Run, for example:

```
/ SDFS::ThisCard.$.Utilities.setup
```

This ensures that Obey$Dir is set to the full pathname of the Obey file.

Command Sequence

When the CLI is passed a command to execute it goes about it in a set way. It takes the following actions in sequence until such time as the * command is identified and executed. An error is generated if the * command is not found. Each step is executed in turn until one is successful.

1. A check is made to see whether the command is identified by the in the RISC OS Kernel.

2. RISC OS then passes the command to any installed modules (discussed in Chapter 7) to see if any of them wish to claim it. Modules are checked in the order of the Module List.

3. After the modules have been searched the * command is passed to the current Filing System Module in use for checking.

4. If at this stage no module has accepted, then the command RISC OS issues an 'unknown command' service call.

5. If the command is still not recognised, then a search in the current path will be made for a file matching the command name. If an executable file of that name is found it is *RUN. The result of this *RUN is passed back to the user.

So consider that when you *RUN a section of machine code all the above will be actioned before the routine gets to your code!

CLIV Vector

Finally, the software vector CLIV provides support for the OS call OS_CLI in trapping and processing * commands. Vectors are discussed in Chapter 8 whilst Chapter 19 describes the implementation of * commands within modules.

4: Software Interrupts

SWI is the common abbreviation for Software Interrupt and it is associated with one of several modes of operation with which the ARM chip may be configured; specifically, this one is called Supervisor Mode. (For this reason in other Operating Systems that run on the Raspberry Pi — typically Linux based — it is called SVC, or supervisor, rather than SWI.)

SWI commands operate at machine code level, and as such we most often utilise them in assembler programs. However, they can also be accessed using specific system calls from languages such as BBC BASIC and C, as we shall see Chapter 6.

In most instances (though not all) * commands have an equivalent SWI instruction. The converse is not true. In general SWI calls provide greater flexibility than the equivalent star commands. SWI commands also operate a lot quicker as they are acting directly with the hardware and supplying information in a format the OS can easily understand. The other benefit of a SWI call is that the data it returns can be stored and used for further use. * command actions generally act immediately and do not return information for use.

The benefit of the * command is that it is a lot quicker to use, as we do not have to write an assembly language or C routine and then decode any information that may be returned. A * command will often invoke one or more SWI calls.

Much of the documentation in the PRMs is given over to SWI calls and so you will need to refer to this frequently as you become a proficient RISC OS programmer. It is therefore important that you get to grips with using these calls, as you can do almost anything with them.

SWI Calls

Each SWI is defined by both a name and a number. Both are unique to that SWI and the SWI can be called by either of them. From a readability point of view the name method is preferred. This only affects the size of the source file (more characters to store and save) and not the assembled machine code (the assembler converts the name into a number).

As the SWI works at machine level, information is passed to the routine using a variety of the ARM registers. The more complex the SWI the more information that will need to be passed, and any information returned by the call will be passed back in the registers. In defining SWI calls it is therefore normal to define entry and exit conditions. (A quick look at SWI examples in the PRMs will confirm this!) When a SWI is called, the RISC OS Kernel locates the position of the code it relates to and jumps to the routine. This routine will carry out the required function and if necessary will interact with the Raspberry Pi hardware directly.

One of the easiest things to do with a SWI call is to print a character to the screen and this is something RISC OS does every time you interact with the Raspberry Pi. This would be a little harder and much more long winded to do in machine code without the help of RISC OS and the associated SWI.

The action to be carried out by the SWI is determined by the value supplied with the SWI instruction. Usually register R0 is involved, together with other registers depending on the complexity of the call. Sometimes R0 is used to point to a block of memory which contains information, although other registers may be used for this purpose as well.

OS_Write C

The instruction:

```
SWI "OS_WriteC"
```

will print the contents of ARM Register R0 to the screen. So, if you wanted to print the letter 'A' to the screen you would first load R0 with the ASCII value for 'A' and then call the SWI. You might do that like this:

```
MOV R0,#ASC("A")        ; Load R0 with 'A'
SWI  "OS_WriteC"        ; and output it
```

Once the SWI instruction has been completed control is handed back to the calling program. The number allocated to OS_WriteC is &00 and this can be used instead of the name, with the same effect. This is a little less clear but certainly just as effective. So,

```
SWI "OS_WriteC"
```

achieves the same result as:

```
SWI 0
```

OS_WriteC stands for Operating System Write Character. The various SWI names are known to the BBC BASIC Assembler and can therefore be used in your programs. Using the assigned system label makes the program much more readable but the disadvantage is that it makes them more complex to enter, especially as they are case-dependent. So using:

`OS_WRITEC`

would generate an error at assembly time. The exact command — including upper case or lower case letters as required — must be used. The named version must also be within double quotes. If you misspell the SWI name an error will be generated.

There is nothing to stop you defining your own set of names at the start of your program, for example:

`WRITEOS=0`

and then:

`SWI WRITEOS`

This would work fine — it's up to you. But beware — some of the SWI names are long. In such cases you may wish to define your own shorter version of the constant and document it at that point. Also, calls such as:

`SWI 0`

are used so frequently that you will know what they are, and it is just as easy to use the number value directly. (This is probably not the perfectionist's view, but the point is to do what suits your programming methods best.)

If you are using C then various veneers are provided by libraries such as OSlib which will allow you to call SWIs in a like fashion. The SYS command can be used to to call SWIs from BASIC. Chapter 6 looks at this in more detail. For the time being we'll continue with assembler examples.

PRM Example

Just to confirm that most *commands has have their own corresponding SWI call, let's look at an example of one from the PRMs. We saw how the *EVAL command can be used to evaluate an expression and display the result, let us now see how we would do this in machine code using a SWI.

Looking at the PRM index the entry for *EVAL is located at 1-497. (Murphy's Law says there may be differences between Manuals. There shouldn't be, but… So if the page numbers listed here are not exactly the same as yours don't worry as long as you get the right information.) In the index this is on page Index-6.

Looking at PRM 1, Page 497 we find the entry for *EVAL. (Note this is the page number on the PDF itself and not the one you type in at the top. There will be a slight difference so you may need to scroll to the correct page.) If you look at the heading 'Related SWIs' you will see one listed — OS_EvaluateExpression and this is the one we need. It conveniently should also state a page number: 1-472.

The entry for OS_EvaluateExpression follows a set format that is used throughout the PRMs so it is worth discussing this for a moment.

After the SWI name, the SWI number is given as part of the headline. The SWI number for OS_EvaluateExpression is &2D. Under this is a brief description of what the SWI does. Below this are the entry and exit conditions of the SWI. The entry conditions detail what the call expects to find in various registers, while the exit call details what information is returned.

When the call is made interrupts may be enabled or disabled — this information is provided. This is a non-critical call therefore there is no reason why interrupts should be disabled in this case. Exception handling is discussed in Chapter 9.

Processor Mode is SVC and this is Supervisor Mode as introduced earlier (recall that all SWIs operate in SVC Mode). The SWI is not re-entrant — this means that it cannot call itself.

The notes under 'Use' generally describe what the call does and what it returns. In reality this is normally a written summary of all the other information given on the page and may also include some additional error information. Related SWI and Related Vectors, if any, are then given.

The information provided is usually straightforward, but this is not always the case and some definitions can be a little unclear. In such instances, look at the definition for any associated * command to see if anything can be gleaned. Or just experiment!

Program 4a below is a simple BBC BASIC Assembler listing that demonstrates OS_EvaluateExpression in use.

Program 4a. Using OS_EvaluateExpression SWI as *EVAL.

```
 10 REM >Prog4a
 20 REM >OS_Evaluate_Expression
 30 REM RPi RISC OS Programming
 40 :
 50 DIM code% 256
 60 FOR pass=0 TO 3 STEP 3
 70 P%=code%
 80 [
 90 OPT pass
100 .start
110 ADR R0, string
120 ADR R1, buffer
130 MOV R2, #10
140 SWI &2D
```

```
150 ADR R3, result
160 MOV R0, R2
170 ADR R1, buffer
180 MOV R2, #10
190 SWI "OS_BinaryToDecimal"
200 MOV R4, #13
210 STRB R4, [R2, R1]
220 MOV PC, LR
230.string
240 EQUS "4*5+5-1"
250 EQUB 13
260.buffer
270 EQUS "0000000000"
280 .result
290 EQUD 0
300 EQUD 0
310 ]
320 NEXT
330 CALL start
340 PRINT $buffer
```

Let's look at what the program does. The PRM states that R0 must point to the string to be evaluated. This is done in line 110. The label 'string' is defined in line 230 and EQUS is used to assemble the string to be evaluated as a string (line 240). Note that we have terminated the string with a <RETURN> character in line 250. This is implicit in the string terminology and so is important not to forget. The result is stored in a buffer and the address of this and its length is loaded in R1 and R2 respectively (Line 120, 130, 260 and 270). The call to SWI & 2D is then made (line 140). We have performed no error checking here as we are in a closed environment.

To print the result onto the screen the program uses another SWI routine — OS_BinaryToDecimal (you may find it useful to look this up in the PRMs). Lines 150-180 set this up in a similar fashion. Before it is called the value returned in R2 by OS_EvaluateExpression is moved into R0 as required by OS_BinaryToDecimal (line 180) and the call is made. On return from the call we need to insert a 13 (<RETURN>) at the end of the string (Lines 200 and 210) — R1 has the start address of buffer and R2 has the position in the buffer of the next free spot. Inserting the <RETURN> character means that we can use BASIC's string operator to print the converted string (line 340, although we could also have used a SWI to do just that as well (SWI &46, OS_WriteN). You may wish to try that.

Inside SWIs

A SWI instruction is composed of four bytes — a word in Raspberry Pi ARM terms. The lower three bytes or 24 bits of this are the SWI identification field. This is large enough to allow just over 16 million different SWIs to be specified. In practice, this field is divided up into several groups to allow different kinds of SWI to be numbered in related ways.

Segments of bits define the group that the SWI belongs to and its position within that group. These groups are also referred to as chunks. The meanings of the individual SWI 24 bits are summarised in Figure 4a.

Bit Nos.	b23-b20	b19-b18	b17	b16-b6	b5-b0
Function	OS Identity	SWI Owner	X	SWI Chunk Number	SWI Value

Figure 4a. The meaning of the 24 bits of a SWI.

The functions of these individual bits are described below.

Bits 23-20   These four bits are used to identify the OS of which the SWI is a part. All four bits must be set to be zero to indicate that the SWI is relevant to RISC OS; other Operating Systems will use different values.

Bits 19-18   These two bits are used to indicate which piece of software is responsible for executing the SWI. The table in Figure 4b summarises the possibilities:

Bit 19	Bit 18	Meaning
0	0	RISC OS
0	1	RISC OS extensions
1	0	Third Party Applications
1	1	User Programs

Figure 4b. Bit 18 and bit 19 Functions.

Here 'Third Party Applications' refers to commercial software, whether it is free or paid for. 'User Programs' refers to definitions you may create yourself.

Bit 17   This bit, known as the 'X' bit, is used to specify how errors that occur during the execution of the SWI should be dealt with. This is discussed in more detail in the section on SWI error handling.

Generally when a SWI calls another SWI it will normally use the 'XOS' version and handle any errors.

Bits 16-6   SWIs are allocated in 'chunks' of 64 numbers. These bits identify the chunk numbers which are allocated by RISC OS Open. If you produce software which requires SWIs that will be available for general distribution (commercially or otherwise) you should apply to RISC OS Open for a chunk number. If you write your own modules for personal use you can select you own chunk number. See Chapter 19.

Bits 5-0   The bottom six bits identify the particular SWI within a given chunk. This allows up to 64 SWIs (which should be more than enough) for each application.

SWI Names

As we have seen, SWIs have unique numbers and names allocated to them. An obvious way to look these up is to use the reference manual, but RISC OS also provides SWI calls to do this!

Two calls are supplied:

```
OS_SWINumberToString
```

and:

```
OS_SWINumberFromString
```

These SWIs are used by various components of RISC OS to locate SWI numbers. For example, when the BBC BASIC Assembler encounters a SWI name, before it can assemble the code it has to convert the name to the associated SWI number. It does this by calling OS_SWINumberFromString whenever it encounters a SWI name enclosed in inverted commas.

In order to make these conversions somewhat simpler to implement, the SWI chunk 'name' followed by an underline '_' is used to prefix the SWI, so the conversion SWIs are named 'OS_...' because they are provided by RISC OS. SWIs provided by other software modules do the same, so the ADFS SWIs are all prefixed by 'ADFS_...'.

SWI numbers lower than &200 have an 'OS_' prefix to the main part, and a SWI-dependent end section (which is Undefined for unknown OS SWIs). SWI numbers in the range &100 to &1FF are converted in the form OS_WriteI+ "A", or OS_WriteI+23 if the character is not a printable one.

SWI numbers from &200 are looked for in modules. If a suitable name is found, it is given in the form module_name or module_number, for example

Wimp_Initialise, Wimp_32. If no name is found in the modules, the string 'User' is returned.

If the 'OS' is prefixed by an X, &20000 is added to the number returned — bit 17 will be set as defined above.

First, RISC OS names are checked for and if they are not found then attached modules are scanned. If the module prefix matches the one given, and the suffix to the name is a number, then that number is added to the module's SWI chunk base, and the sum returned. For example, 'Wimp_&23' returns &400E3, as the Wimp's chunk number starts at &400C0.

Program 4b below uses the OS_NumberToString routine in a BBC BASIC Assembler program to print out the first 127 SWI calls, giving their SWI number and allocated name (adjust the #127 in line 210 if you wish to increase the number printed). On entry R0 holds the SWI number for decoding and R1 has the address of buffer where the SWI string will be placed. The string is terminated with a zero byte, then OS_Write0 is used to print the string (as this is terminated by a zero byte).

Program 4b. Print SWI names using OS_SWINumberToString.

```
10 REM >Prog4b
20 REM RPi RISC OS Programming
30 REM Print first 127 SWI names
40 DIM code% 256
50 DIM buffer% 127
60 FOR pass=0 TO 3 STEP 3
70 P%=code%
80 [
90 OPT pass
100 .start
110 MOV R9, #0        ; use R9 as counter
120 ADR R1, buffer%
130 .loop
140 MOV R0, R9        ; SWI number into R0
150 MOV R2, #127
160 SWI "OS_SWINumberToString"
170 MOV R0, R1        ; move buffer address into R0
180 SWI "OS_Write0"   ; print string
190 SWI "OS_NewLine"
200 ADD R9, R9, #1    ; increment SWI number
210 CMP R9, #127
```

```
220 BNE loop
230 MOV PC, LR
240 ]
250 NEXT pass
```

As SWI commands can and do use the ARM registers to pass then return information care should be taken when issuing several SWIs in succession. Some SWIs use more registers than others. (The PRMs provide detailed information about which registers are used, preserved and corrupted by the various SWI calls.) Because OS_SWINumberToString returns information in R2, the instruction in line 150 is inside the loop as it needs to be reset each time - the maximum length of the buffer being 127 bytes in this case. An alternative could have been to use a different register, R3 for example, and this could then be placed outside the loop to save one instruction cycle per iteration.

The program uses some additional SWI calls to print out the SWI string (OS_Write0) and print a carriage return (OS_NewLine).

SWI Error Handling

Error handling is always important and provides the programmer with useful information. Two mechanisms for dealing with SWI errors are defined by RISC OS. The first and simplest is achieved through the Status Register's Overflow flag or V bit.

When a SWI is successfully executed, one of the final things it does is to clear the Overflow flag, ie V=0. If an error occurs during execution then the Overflow flag is set, V=1. Thus after a SWI call a BVS instruction (Branch oVerflow Set) will jump to an error handling routine as the flag is set indicating an error.

If an error condition exists then R0 contains an address pointing to a block of information that provides an explanation about the error. The format of the error block pointed to by R0 is:

Bytes 0-3   Error number
Bytes 4-n   Error message (ASCII text)
Bytes n+1   Zero (to terminate error message string)

Error blocks must be word-aligned and may not exceed 256 bytes in length.

X SWI Error Handling

Normally errors generated by SWIs are handled by the RISC OS error handler. However, if the X bit is set the OS returns the call for the calling routine to deal with. The X bit is set in the SWI simply by prefixing the SWI name with a capital 'X'. The default for SWI error control is the error generating state, ensuring that errors are flagged by the current error handler automatically. Error-returning SWIs use the X prefix, so the error-returning form of the name conversion SWI mentioned above is:

```
SWI XOS_SWINumberToString ; Convert SWI no to string
BVS error                 ; Routine returned error
```

However, it is often convenient to have a general purpose error handler within an application (for example, the BASIC statement ON ERROR) which deals with all errors in a consistent way. By issuing the SWI instruction with the 'X' bit clear, error control is passed by RISC OS to the currently defined error handler, which takes appropriate action. SWIs which behave in this way are known as 'error generating'. The error handler is established through the use of an OS vector call, and this and other vectors are discussed in the next section.

It is vital to remember to include software to deal with errors if the error-returning form is being used.

Error Handling Numbering

In much the same way as SWIs are uniquely numbered, so the errors which SWIs produce are numbered in a consistent manner. The error number field in an error block is 32 bits long and the bits are used as outlined in Figure 4c:

Bits	Action
Bit 31	If set, indicates a serious error from which there is no return.
Bit 30	Defined to be clear, but may be set to indicate internal errors.
Bits 29-24	Reserved
Bits 23-8	Error generator identification field (PRMs 1-42)
Bits 7-0	Error number (&00-&FF)

Figure 4c. The Error Block broken down.

The middle two bytes of the error number form a field which identifies the particular piece of software responsible for generating the error. This is similar to the SWI chunk field, but note that it has no numerical relationship with the chunk number whatsoever. Of the 65535 available error identification fields, a small number have been allocated to existing software such as RISC OS. Just as for SWI chunks, software authors should apply for an error generator field of their own.

Error Generation

As well as SWIs being able to generate errors, it is also possible for programs to generate errors of their own in order to signal unusual conditions. This is achieved by issuing the SWI OS_GenerateError with R0 pointing to the address of an error block:

```
ADR R0, Error            ;Point to the error block
SWI "OS_GenerateError"   ;Generate error
```

A good example of the need for this facility is the detection and handling of the <ESCAPE> key being pressed. All good software should check regularly to see whether the user has pressed the <ESCAPE> key, which is usually an indication that the user wishes to abandon or cancel the current operation.

To detect if <ESCAPE> has been pressed call SWI OS_ReadEscapeState, which returns with the Carry flag set if the key has been pressed. Program 4c illustrates use of OS_ReadEscapeState.

Program 4c. Using OS_ReadEscapeState to check for <ESCAPE>.

```
 10 REM >Prog4c
 20 REM RPi RISC OS Programming
 30 REM Use of OS_ReadEscapeState
 40 DIM code% 256
 50 FOR pass=0 TO 3 STEP 3
 60 P%=code%
 70 [
 80 OPT pass
 90 .escapeloop
100 SWI "OS_ReadEscapeState" ;Wait until Escape
110 BCC escapeloop
120 ADR R0,escapehandle   ;Point to the error block
130 SWI "OS_GenerateError" ;Generate an error
140 :
150 .escapehandle
160 EQUD 17 ; Error number
170 EQUS "Escape key pressed"
180 EQUB 0
```

```
190 ALIGN
200 ]
210 NEXT pass
```

Assemble and then run the machine code with:

```
CALL escapeloop
```

The program repeatedly calls OS_ReadEscapeState until the <ESCAPE> key is pressed. This sets the Carry flag so that the BCC escapeloop of line 110 does not get executed. R0 is loaded with the address of the error block (line 120 and then line 130 calls OS_GenerateError to handle the error, printing out the error message in the process).

Note that there is no return coding in this routine, ie:

```
MOV PC, LR
```

This is because this SWI does not hand control back to your program but exits directly from it to the original calling environment.

CLI SWIs

There are three useful SWIs that you should be well aware of and they relate to information we covered in the Command Line Interpreter. The first shows how we can actually call and execute a * command from within machine code and the other two allow you to set and read Operating System variables in a similar manner to *SET and *SHOW.

OS_CLI (&05)

This call invokes the CLI and is simple to use. R0 points at an area of memory that contains the * command string (without any leading asterisks) terminated by a zero or a 13 (or <RETURN>). The string will be processed as a RISC OS command and the effects it has and the result it returns is the same as if you had typed it at the keyboard. The snippet below would be one way of cataloguing the current directory from machine code:

```
ADR R0, buffer
SWI "OS_CLI"
; Other instructions a required
MOV PC,LR
.buffer
EQUS "CAT"
EQUB 13
```

OS_ReadVarVal (&23)

This call allows the existence of the type and value of one or more RISC OS variables to be established. Set-up and exit are as follows:

On Entry:
R0 = pointer to variable name, and may include wildcards (using '*' and '#')
R1 = pointer to buffer where variable value will be placed
R2 = Length of buffer, or -ve to check existence/read length
R3 = context pointer (used with wildcard names)- R3=0 for first call
R4 = 3 if an expanded string is to be converted on return

On Exit (Read value):
R0 preserved
R1 preserved
R2 = number of bytes read
R3 = new context pointer (null-terminated)
R4 = variable type (0=string; 1=signed 32-bit integer; 2=macro,
          3=expanded expression, 4=literal,
          +16=pointer to machine code.)

On Exit (Read length):
R0 corrupt
R1 preserved
R2 = NOT (length), or 0 if variable does not exist
R3 = new name pointer (null-terminated)
R4 = variable type (0=string; 1=signed 32-bit integer; 2=macro,
          3=expanded expression, 4=literal,
          +16=pointer to machine code.)

On entry, R0 should point to a zero-terminated string containing the name of the variable(s). Wildcard characters may be included for character matching: '*' to match zero or more characters and '#' to match exactly one character. R1 should point to a buffer for the SWI to use, with R2 containing the maximum size of that buffer. A special case is provided by setting bit 31 (making value held negative) of R2 which simply determines whether the specified variable(s) exist(s) by returning with R2=0 if not. On the first call to this SWI, R3 should contain zero. If wildcard matches are expected then subsequent calls should be made with the previous contents of R3 preserved, its value being updated automatically by the SWI.

The 'XOS' form of this SWI should be used where wildcard matches are expected in order to avoid the 'no more matches' error which would be generated after the last match is read. R4 should contain '3' if the result should be expanded by OS_GSTrans before returning. Other values are ignored. (OS_GSTrans is discussed in Chapter 5.)

After the first call to this SWI, the type and value of the specified variable will be returned (or those of the first match in the case of wildcard searches). R2 will contain the number of bytes which were read from the string, R3 will point to the variable's value and R4 will contain a number indicating its type (see exit conditions above).

If R4 does not contain '3' on entry, the value of the variable is returned either as an integer or as a string. If R4 does contain '3' then integers are converted to signed strings and OS_GSTrans is called to expand any variable names in macros. In the latter case, R3 points to the start of the string.

Program 4d below shows how you can test to see that a RISC OS variable exists and if so, read its value.

Program 4d: Using OS_ReadVarVal to test a variable.

```
 10 REM >Prog4d
 20 REM Using OS_ReadVarVal
 30 REM RPi RISC OS Programming
 40 :
 50 *SETEVAL counter 255
 60 DIM code% 256
 70 FOR pass=0 TO 3 STEP 3
 80 P%=code%
 90 [
100 OPT pass
110 .start
120 ADR R0, varname       ; Get addr of variable name string
130 ADR R1, varval        ; Get addr of value for variable
140 MOV R2, #valend-varval ; Calculate length of variable
150 MOV R3, #0            ; No wildcards
160 MOV R4, #1            ; Variable is of integer type
170 SWI "OS_ReadVarVal"
180 LDR R5, [R1]
190 MOV R0, R5
200 MOV PC, LR
210 :
220 .varname
230 EQUS "counter "
240 ALIGN
250 .varval
260 EQUD 0
270 .valend
```

```
280 ]
290 NEXT pass
300 result=USR (start)
310 PRINT result
```

This program starts by creating a system variable called 'counter' and sets its value at 255 (line 50). Lines 120 to 160 seed the values of registers R0-R4 with their requirements as denoted in the comments. R4 is loaded with 1 to show that we are expecting an integer value. Line 180 copies the returned value into R5, using R1 to indirectly access the location where it is stored, and this is then moved into R0, so that BASIC can transfer it to 'result' via the USR command (line 300) before printing the result.

OS_SetVarVal (SWI &24)

These calls allow RISC OS variables to be created, deleted or have their value altered. Note that not all of the possible types which may be created can be read with the previous SWI.

On Entry:

R0 = pointer to variable name, which may be wildcarded (* or #) if updating/deleting

R1 = pointer to variable value

R2 = length of value, or negative to delete the variable

R3 = context pointer (used with wildcarded names), or 0 for first call

R4 = variable type:

        0 = Value is OS_GSTransed before assignment

        1 = Value is taken as an integer

        2 = Value is taken as a string

        3 = Value is passed through OS_EvaluateExpression

        16 = Value is a piece of machine code to execute (see below)

On Exit:

R0 preserved

R1 preserved

R2 preserved

R3 = new context pointer (null-terminated)

R4 = variable type created if expression is evaluated

On entry R0 should point to the name of the variable terminated by a space or <RETURN>. R1 should point to the value to which the variable should be set, its format dependent upon the type of the variable. R2 should contain the length of the value (but see below). R3 should be set to zero on the first call and will be updated by the SWI to deal with wildcards when assigning or deleting. Finally, R4 should give a value that defines the type of the variable created. To delete a variable the top bit of R2 should be set for types 0-3, and R2 should contain 16 for machine code.

When the call returns, R3 will be updated and should be preserved for the next call if wildcards are being employed. R4 returns the type that was created if OS_EvaluateExpression was used (since it might be either a string or integer).

If the 'code' type is used you can supply your own machine code to deal with read and write operations. In this case, R1 should point to the header of the code and R2 should contain its length. The code must be preceded by a header which consists of two branches which call the write routine and the read routine respectively:

```
.start_of_code
BAL writecode
BAL readcode
```

In reality the second entry point can be the start of the 'readcode' routine and as such the branch instruction can be dropped and the routine entered directly:

```
.start_of_code
BAL writecode
.readcode
```

The code is called in Supervisor Mode so R14 should be preserved on the stack before any SWIs are used. The write entry point is called, with R1 pointing to the value to be written and R2 containing its length. The read entry point is called with no entry parameters and your code should return a pointer to the value in R0 and its length in R2. A number of errors may be generated by OS_SetVarVal according to various parameter or syntax errors in its use. Program 4e below shows how the OS_SetVarVal could be used to change the value of a variable.

Program 4e. Changing <CLI$Prompt> using OS_SetVarVal.

```
 10 REM >Prog4e
 20 REM Using OS_SetVarVal
 30 REM RPi RISC OS Programming
 40 :
 50 *SETEVAL counter 0
 60 DIM code% 256
 70 FOR pass=0 TO 3 STEP 3
 80 P%=code%
 90 [
100 OPT pass
110 .start
```

```
120 ADR R0, varname        ; Get addr of variable name string
130 ADR R1, varval         ;  Get  addr  of  new  value  for
variable
140 MOV R2, #valend-varval   ; Calculate length of variable
150 MOV R3, #0             ; No wildcards
160 MOV R4, #1             ; Variable is of integer type
170 SWI "OS_SetVarVal"
180 MOV PC, LR
190 :
200 .varname
210 EQUS "counter "
220 ALIGN
230 .varval
240 EQUD 5
250 .valend
260 ]
270 NEXT pass
280 CALL start
290 *SHOW counter
```

The code required follows a similar format to OS_SetVarVal. In this case the variable 'counter' is created and set to 0 (line 50). The value we are going to reset the variable to is defined by line 240. As before the variable type is integer (line 160). Both programs would only require minor modification to enable string variables or code to be dealt with.

*SWI Command

The *SWI command allows SWIs to be executed as * commands. Their correct format is very much like the SWI versions used in an assembler, but with the various register requirements passed on a single command line. The syntax of the command is:

```
*SWI <expr {<expr>} [TO <var> {var>} {; <var>}}
```

If you are already familiar with the SYS command used in BASIC (discussed in Chapter 6) then you will see how alike the two are.

Consider the following example:

```
*SWI "OS_ReadLine" "12345678901" 10 32 126 TO input$length
```

Executing this leaves the CLI waiting for you to enter a string at the keyboard. OS_ReadLine is explained fully in due course and this will become clearer at that point. The number string is there to create a buffer for the string to be entered. The next three values are:

10	Maximum length of string
32	Minimum ASCII value that can be entered
126	Maximum ASCII value that can be entered

The 32 and 126 are the limits on the keyboard for alphanumeric characters. When <RETURN> is pressed the entered string is placed in input$length. You can prove this by typing:

```
*SHOW input$length
```

When the command is executed the string is first GSTransed before it is read. If a string is not enclosed by double quotes then it is assumed to be a number. In the syntax, <variable> is a system variable. If a '$' is in the variable, the register is expected to point to a system variable created as a string type from that register, otherwise it is created as a number type.

An understanding of the use of how SYS works (Chapter 6), and all its options can be utilised here, will assist in the use of *SWI, with the added advantage that *SWI can be used in almost any environment.

5: Communications

Some of the most fundamental operations provided by RISC OS are those which allow the user to communicate with RISC OS — accepting input, typically from the keyboard, and displaying output, typically on the monitor display. These functions are essential to allow the user to communicate with the OS and they are also a vital component of all application software which will also utilise them — after all, there's no point in reinventing the wheel!

RISC OS provides a comprehensive set of SWI calls which allows single-character communication between the computer and the user through its display and keyboard. In addition, RISC OS provides a wide and varied range of conversion routines that assist in the process by taking the input and converting it from one format to another. This makes it possible to read an ASCII string typed at the keyboard, convert it into a number that can be manipulated by RISC OS and then perform the reverse process.

This chapter is devoted to the mechanisms for character input/output and conversion of various forms of data by using some of the many SWIs that the OS provides.

Input Selection

To allow the external world to communicate with it, RISC OS and indeed any applications programs that it is running needs to be able to deal with anything from a single key press to the input of multiple lines of text. The component that is integral to these is the character — a single unit which may be a letter of the alphabet, a number, a punctuation mark, a control code — anything that can be represented in a single byte of information and which is usually defined by the standard ASCII character set.

Sequences of one or more characters are called 'streams' (think of the flowing of characters) and historically RISC OS allows one of three possible input streams to be active at any moment. The three possible character input streams are:

- the keyboard itself
- a serial port input channel

- a *EXEC file

The serial port option is a hangover from the old Acorn days where an RS423 port was included as part of the hardware, and it is not applicable on the Raspberry Pi although it is possible in hardware to create one. A SWI call &06 (OS_Byte — discussed later in this Chapter) is provided to allow the input stream to be selected:

On Entry:
R0 = 2 — select input stream
R1 = 0 Keyboard — with serial disabled
        1 Serial port
        2 Keyboard — with serial enabled On Exit:
R1 = Previous selection
        0 Keyboard
        1 Serial

If backwards compatibility is an issue then the call should be issued prior to reading input. The default setting is keyboard and it may be that this call becomes obsolete in due course.

Character Input

OS_ReadC is the SWI that will read a character from the keyboard —its call number is &04, although no call parameters are required. The SWI returns with R0 containing the ASCII code of the character pressed on the keyboard, and the Carry flag clear if it is valid. If the <ESCAPE> key was pressed then the Carry flag is set, and R0 will contain the ASCII code &1B (<ESCAPE>). The segment below shows how you might branch to deal with an <ESCAPE> key press.

```
SWI "OS_ReadC"        ; Read keyboard
BCS escape            ; Was <ESCAPE> pressed?;
                      ; Otherwise continue with program
```

OS_ReadC will wait ad infinitum for a key on the keyboard to be pressed. If you want to put a time limit on the wait then you should use OS_Byte 129. All OS_Byte calls are calls to SWI &06, and the value specified should be loaded into R0. This call waits for a key press for a specified time limit.

On entry, R0 contains the routine number (129); R1 and R2 contain a time limit (in centiseconds) with the low byte in R1 and the high byte in R2. When the call returns, R1 contains the ASCII code of the key pressed, or &FF if no key was pressed within the specified time. Also, R2 will contain a flag indicating the result, which will be zero if a valid key was pressed, &1B if an <ESCAPE> condition occurred or &FF if a timeout occurred. Program 5a demonstrates how to implement this call (it also illustrates the use of OS_WriteS which is detailed later in this chapter.)

Program 5a: Using OS_Byte to read a key with time limit.

```
 10 REM >Prog5a
 20 REM RPi RISC OS Programming
 30 REM Wait for key in time limit
 40 :
 50 DIM code% 256
 60 FOR pass=0 TO 3 STEP 3
 70 P%=code%
 80 [
 90 OPT pass
100 .start
110 MOV R0, #129 ; It is OS_Byte code 129
120 MOV R1, #100 ; wait 1 second
130 MOV R2, #0
140 SWI "OS_Byte"
150 CMP R2, #0   ; valid character?
160 BNE escape
170 SWI "OS_WriteS"
180 EQUS "You pressed :"
190 EQUB 0
200 ALIGN
210 MOV R0, R1 ; Move ASCII char to R0
220 SWI 0
230 MOV R15, R14
240 :
250 .escape
260 SWI "OS_WriteS"
270 EQUS "Timeout or <ESCAPE> pressed"
280 EQUB 0
290 ALIGN
300 MOV R15, R14
310 ]
320 NEXT pass
330 CALL start
```

This program waits for a key press (lines 120 and 130 define exactly how long). On return, the program checks to see if R2 contains 0 which would indicate a valid response (line 150). If not then we assume that either a timeout occurred or the <ESCAPE> key was pressed. If this is the case the escape routine deals with this (lines 250-300). Otherwise, the character's ASCII code is moved from R1 to R0 (line 210) and printed to the screen. You could expand this by checking specifically for a timeout or <ESCAPE> and printing a specific message to deal with these conditions.

These single character key captures may be combined into streams of characters and allow us to get what are effectively strings of text from the user in one form or another. However, OS_ReadLine is provided specifically to do this.

Line Input

Because it is common for a program to need to input a whole line of characters at a time, OS_ReadLine (SWI &0E) is provided to do this. This routine will read a line from the keyboard into a predefined area of memory buffer.

On Entry:
R0 = Pointer to address of buffer to hold string
R1 = Max number of characters allowed for string
R2 = Lowest permissible ASCII code acceptable
R3 = Highest permissible ASCII code acceptable

On Exit:
R1 = length of string entered
       C=1 <ESCAPE> key pressed
       C=0 <ESCAPE> key not pressed

On entry, the address of the start of the memory buffer to hold the ASCII string is placed into R0. Characters will be accepted and entered sequentially, starting at the address of the buffer and then ascending through memory. The maximum number of characters that can be entered into the buffer is defined by R1. If you try to exceed this limit a beep will be issued and the character will not be accepted. The ASCII codes for the lowest and highest values that you will accept are placed in R2 and R3 respectively.

For example, this is useful if you want to limit the characters. Placing 48 in R2 and 57 in R3 would mean that only numbers would be accepted into the buffer (48 and 57 being ASCII codes for 0 and 9 respectively). Using 97 and 122 in R2 and R3 respectively would limit input to the lower case letters of the alphabet. The Delete key can be used to erase the last character from the buffer in the normal fashion. <CTRL-U> is also decoded to delete the entire contents from the buffer and the displayed line accordingly. The line may be terminated by pressing <RETURN>, <ENTER> or the <ESCAPE> key. The line returned in the buffer always has a final ASCII 13 appended to it, regardless of the way in which input was actually terminated.

On return from the call, R1 will contain the length of the string entered and the Carry flag will be clear. If the <ESCAPE> key was pressed the Carry flag will be set.

Program 5b provides a machine code equivalent of BBC BASIC's INPUT command that uses OS_ReadLine.

Program 5b. Simulating INPUT using OS_ReadLine.

```
 10 REM >Prog5b
 20 REM RPi RISC OS Programming
 30 REM Simulating INPUT using OS_ReadLine
 40 :
 50 DIM code% 256
 60 REM Define Register names
 70 pointer = 0            : REM Must use R0
 80 length=1               : REM Must use R1
 90 minASC=2               : REM must use R2
100 maxASC=3               : REM Must use R3
110 base=4
120 :
130 FOR pass=0 TO 3 STEP 3
140 P%=code%
150 [
160 OPT pass
170 .start
180 ADR pointer, buffer    ; Get line buffer start addr
190 MOV minASC, #32        ; accept all alphanum chars
200 MOV maxASC, #128       ; but no ext ASCII set
210 MOV length, #30        ; maximum string length is 30
220:
230 SWI "OS_ReadLine"      ; Input text at buffer
240 ADR base, buffer
250 .printloop             ; print string out
260 LDRB R0, [base],#1     ; Get next
270 SWI "OS_WriteC"
280 CMP R0, #13
290 BNE printloop
```

```
300 SWI "OS_NewLine"
310 MOV R15, R14
320 :
330 .buffer
340 EQUS STRING$(32, CHR$(0))
350 ]
360 NEXT
370 CALL start
```

Line 180 through to 210 set up the relevant registers to hold the required parameters before OS_ReadLine is called. The printloop segment from lines 250 through to 290 simply reprint the string that was typed in. The printloop routine is the obvious way to do this, but a smarter way would be to use the fact that OS_ReadLine returned the length of the typed string in R1. This could be used to add a 0 byte at the end of the input string and then set R0 up so that the OS_Write0 SWI can be used to output the string. You might like trying to re-write the printloop segment to use it, include some code to check for the <ESCAPE> key and issue a message to that effect if it is detected.

Keyboard Control

As well as the character and line input functions, a large number of keyboard control calls are provided to allow low-level modification of the way the keyboard operates. Almost all of these calls are provided through the OS_Byte SWI. Figure 5a lists the calls supported whilst the figures that follow detail calls that can be made to detect other key combinations.

A location known as the 'keyboard status byte' holds information on the current status of the keyboard, such as the setting of Caps Lock. Using call &CA you can read and write these settings. Note that this call does not update the LEDs. If you don't stamp this state with OS_Byte 118, then the keyboard LEDs will not be switched on or off. The keyboard status byte contains a bit pattern which represents the perceived state of the various Shift keys for the OS. These bits are arranged as shown in Figure 5b.

OS_Byte	Function
&04	Cursor key functions
&ED	Read/write cursor key function
&0B	Write keyboard auto-repeat delay
&C4	Read/write keyboard auto-repeat delay
&0C	Write keyboard auto-repeat rate
&C5	Read/write keyboard auto-repeat rate
&76	Force keyboard LEDs to mirror flags
&78	Simulate key depression
&79	Keyboard scan
&7A	Keyboard scan from 16(not for SHIFT, CTRL, ALT or the mouse)
&81	Keyboard scan for specific key
&7C	Clear ESCAPE condition
&7D	Set ESCAPE condition
&7E	Acknowledge ESCAPE condition
&B2	Read/write keyboard semaphore
&C8	Read/write BREAK and ESCAPE controls
&C9	Read/write keyboard disable flag
&CA	Read/write keyboard status byte
&D8	Read/write function key length
&DB	Read/write TAB key character code
&DC	Read / write ESCAPE character code
&DD	Read/write translation of codes &C0-&CF
&DE	Read/write translation of codes &D0-&DF
&DF	Read/write translation of codes &E0-&EF
&E0	Read/write translation of codes &F0-&FF

Figure 5a. OS_Byte keyboard SWI calls.

Bit	Value	Meaning
0	0	Reserved for keyboard handler, must be preserved when writing
1	0 / 1	Scroll Lock: off / on
2	0 / 1	Num Lock: on / off
3	0 / 1	Shift: off / on
4	0 / 1	Caps Lock: on / off
5	0 / 1	Kana lock (Hiragana entry) / Romaji lock (Latin entry in UK)
6	0 / 1	Control: off / on
7	0 / 1	Shift:: enable / disable

Figure 5b. Bit representations in keyboard status byte.

A '1' indicates that the LED is illuminated or that the specified was key pressed. A '0' indicates the opposite. If Caps Lock is on and Shift Enable off, Shift will have no effect on the letters, if Shift enable is on, you'll get lower case characters.

Calling &C9 with R1=0 will enable the keyboard. Any other value will stop the interrupt routine inserting key presses into the keyboard buffer.

The function keys along with <SHIFT>, <CTRL> and the two combined can also be written to and read from as can the <ESCAPE> key. The numeric keypad's response will vary according to whether the NumLock key is lit or not — consult the PRMs for more information if you are seeking to manipulate these keys in any way.

Output Stream

Just as there are several character input streams, so there are several output streams. The four main output streams are:

- The VDU stream, which drives the display

- The serial (RS423 port) output channel

- The printer stream

- The *SPOOL file (when activated)

The VDU stream accepts sequences of characters and either displays them, or uses them to control character output. Besides the many text and graphics functions which the VDU drivers provide, they also allow control over whether or not characters are sent to the printer stream. Many of the various VDU codes and printer control codes may not work on the Raspberry Pi simply because technology has overtaken the original RISC OS implementation which was based on old-style monitor screens and dot-matrix printers.

As for input, the RS423 port output channel is redundant unless handled directly by the user, for example to take serial output and direct it elsewhere.

Finally, the Spool file makes a copy of whatever is sent to the VDU stream in a specified file. This allows sequences of VDU codes to be recorded and subsequently replayed using *PRINT (which takes bytes from the file and sends them directly to the VDU drivers). Again, this may have limited use.

OS_Byte function &03 is used to select the output stream. By default everything is enabled so generally there is no requirement to alter this, and many of the changes available will be redundant on the Raspberry Pi.

Characters Out

There are a few SWI calls that can be used to write information to the screen. We have used several of these demonstration programs so far in this book, but they are included here for completeness. Fuller descriptions are provided here along with program segments. The XOS version of the call should be used from within modules.

OS_WriteC (SWI 0) Write Character

On entry, R0 contains the ASCII code of the character to be printed. As this will only occupy one byte of the full register word it is held in the low byte. No information is returned by the routine. Any character can be written in this way. It is possible to use the call to print out strings of text although OS_Write0 is better suited to this.

```
MOV R0, #ASC("*")        ; place asterisk in R0
SWI "OS_WriteC"          ; echo it to the screen
```

If a particular character is required to be printed to the screen, it is better to use the SWI 256+ call as this does not require the use of any registers and is therefore a quick and easy way of producing fixed characters from the ASCII set. This is described below.

OS_Write0 (SWI 2) Write Zero Terminated String

This SWI prints an ASCII string to the screen. The string can be of any length but must be terminated by a zero. On entry R0 holds the address of the string to be printed. On exit from the routine, R0 will hold an address that points to the byte after the end of the string. The string may contain any combination of ASCII codes, but will terminate on the first '0' (zero) it encounters.

This routine has been used in several previous programs, and the segment below illustrates a typical application. Note that it is important to use ALIGN on completion of the string to ensure the Program Counter is realigned at a word boundary as this is where RISC OS will reset the PC to so that the ARM can execute the next instruction.

```
.printstring
MOV R0, stringaddress
SWI "OS_Write0"
MOV R15, R14
.stringaddress
EQUS "Print this string"
EQUB 0
ALIGN
```

OS_WriteN (SWI &46) Write String of 'n' Length

This call is identical in action to OS_WriteC but allows for the printing of '0' to the screen. On entry, R0 points to the address of the string to be printed, and R1 holds the number of bytes in the string. As the string length is pre-defined by R1, there is no requirement to ensure that the string itself is terminated by a 0. If you were to run the segment below you would only see the first 10 characters of the string 'Print this'.

```
.printstring
MOV R0, stringaddress
MOV R1, #10
SWI "OS_WriteN"
MOV R15, R14
.stringaddress
EQUS "Print this string"
ALIGN
```

The notes regarding ALIGN for OS_Write0 are equally applicable here.

OS_WriteS (SWI 1) Write String that follows

This routine provides a quick and simple way to print a string of characters to the screen; the only requirement is that the string is terminated by a zero. This call is different from the others in that there are no entry or exit parameters to seed as the string as is expected immediately following the SWI call. This sounds strange but in fact is a very common way of inserting fixed messages into machine code. Indeed most error messages are dealt with in this way. On exit from the routine, the Program Counter is updated to fit to the next instruction to be fetched. This will be immediately after the string. The ALIGN directive should be used in all such instances to ensure that the next instruction is located on a word boundary.

```
.printstring
SWI "OS_WriteS"          ; Call SWI 1
EQUS "Error Message #123" ; String follows
EQUB 0                   ; Terminating byte
ALIGN                    ; Re-point to word boundary
MOV R0, #0               ; Continue with program
MOV R1, #1
MOV R15, R14
```

Another practical use of this routine is to pause your program for a key press:

```
SWI "OS_WriteS"
EQUS "Press any Y to continue"
EQUB 0
ALIGN
SWI "OS_ReadC"
CMP R0, #ASC("Y")
SWIEQ "OS_WriteS"
EQUS "Option Selected"
EQUB 0
ALIGN
```

However, this section of code, while looking perfectly acceptable, is not. The OS_WriteS instruction will write 'Option Selected' only when 'Y' has been entered at the keyboard. It is certainly true that if a 'Y' is not entered, the SWI instruction will not execute. However, in this case the Program Counter will not have been manipulated by the SWI to recommence program execution after the string. The Program Counter will therefore try to continue execution immediately after the SWI 'OS_WriteS' instruction itself. It will attempt to interpret the characters in the string as opcodes and will try to execute them! Therefore in practice a conditional execution suffix should never be added to the SWI 'OS_WriteS' instruction. Otherwise there will be a spectacular crash. The cause of this type of logical bug or failure is often hard to track down.

OS_NewLine (SWI 3) Generate a New Line

This routine simply issues a <RETURN> to the output stream. There are no entry or exit parameters.

OS_WriteI (SWIs 256-512) Write Specific ASCII Character

This routine is normally called SWI 256+. The postfix is the ASCII code of the fixed ASCII character to be printed. For example to print 'A' on the screen you would take the ASCII code for 'A', which is 65, and append it to 256 thus:

```
SWI 256+65
```

The following would also produce the same result:

```
SWI 321
```

321 being the sum of 256 and 65.

There are no entry or exit conditions, and the call does not alter the contents of any of the registers or flags. This makes it useful as a debugging tool.

Conversion Routines

So far in this chapter we have examined how to read and also print strings of ASCII characters. However, without the ability to convert data from one format to another the usefulness of these routines drops drastically. Consider a program intended to calculate a numerical value that you want to print on the screen. What you have is a binary (hexadecimal) format — your number stored in four-bytes of memory. To use one of the print routines you must first convert the value into its ASCII character equivalent. So, if the result was 65, what you want to print on the screen is '65'. But if you tried to print 65 without the conversion you would get an 'A' as 65 is the ASCII code for A. Conversely if you wanted to get a number from the keyboard you would actually get the ASCII codes for each digit and you would then need to convert it into its binary value.

RISC OS provides a whole host of SWIs to undertake these conversion processes. We'll examine them here with some examples. You will also find them covered in Chapter 18 of PRM1.

Numbers to Strings

The easiest option to use to convert a signed 32-bit integer into a string is OS_BinaryToDecimal. In fact this is one of 24 SWIs with a common calling convention that allow a wide ranging list of conversions in the format:

```
OS_Convert <Name> <Number>
```

where <Name> is the designation format of the string, for example Hex or Integer, and <Number> is the number of bytes for input. Note that OS_BinaryToDecimal is equivalent to OS_ConvertInteger4 from these SWIs, but is perhaps easier to understand. It is the only one with a specially designated call. Examples of the 'X types' are provided in Figure 5c below, where <N> is a value in the range 1, 2, 3 and 4, all apart from Hex which can be 1, 2, 4, 6 and 8:

Call	Description
OS_ConvertHex<N>	Convert hex number to ASCII String
OS_ConvertCardinal<N>	Convert to unsigned decimal number
OS_ConvertInteger<N>	Convert to a signed decimal number
OS_ConvertBinary<N>	Convert to a binary number
OS_ConvertSpacedCardinal<N>	Convert to an unsigned decimal number, with spaces every three digits
OS_ConvertSpacedInteger<N>	Convert to a signed decimal number, with spaces every three digits

Figure 5c. The range of OS_Convert routines is comprehensive.

Where it is significant the output string may be padded with zeros. This is the case with hex values and also with binary values in order to ensure that significance is retained. In all other cases padding zeros are not used.

In the case of spaced conversions, a space is inserted into the string every three digits, counting from the right as in the normal place value system. For example the value 32,123 would be returned as the string '32 123'. If commas are required then your parsing routine will need to insert them into the string before it is displayed. In the cases of signed values, a negative sign is inserted at the start of the string if the most significant bit of the bytes being converted is set.

The calls are all used in an identical fashion:

On Entry:
R0 = value to be converted
R1 = pointer to buffer for resulting string
R2 = size of buffer

On Exit:

R0 = pointer to buffer for resulting string

R1 = pointer to terminating null in buffer

R2 = number of free bytes in buffer

A couple of points to note. As R0 returns pointing to the start of the buffer, which is in turn terminated with a null, it is convenient for printing using OS_Write0. Also, with R1 pointing to the null at the end of the buffer, it is easy to add text to the end of the string should you so wish.

Program 5c below converts a single byte value into a signed decimal number before displaying the result with OS_Write0.

Program 5c. Using OS_ConvertSpacedCardinal2.

```
 10 REM >Prog5c
 20 REM Using OS_ConvertSpacedCardinaL2
 30 REM RPi RISC OS Programming
 40 :
 50 DIM code% 256
 60 FOR pass=0 TO 3 STEP 3
 70 P%=code%
 80 [ OPT pass
 90 .start
100 MOV R0,#19968
110 ADR R1, buffer
120 MOV R2, #bufferend-buffer
130 SWI "OS_ConvertSpacedCardinal2"
140 SWI "OS_Write0"
150 SWI "OS_NewLine"
160 MOV PC, LR
170 :
180 .buffer
190 EQUS "              "
200 .bufferend
210 ]
220 NEXT pass
230 CALL start
```

Strings to Numbers

Whilst there are a couple of dozen SWIs to convert values into ASCII strings of different formats, a single SWI is able to perform the reverse process and convert an ASCII string into an internally stored binary value.

OS_ReadUnsigned (SWI &21) takes a string stored in memory and converts it into a binary number for internal use. It assumes that the number is unsigned and therefore only deals with positive values. The string can be in any number base in the range 2 to 32. Base 2 would be binary;base 16 hexadecimal.

On entry, R1 points to the address of the string of digits to be converted and R0 has a value in the range 2-32 representing the base the string should be converted to. On exit, R1 points to the end of the string (if it was valid) or is unaltered if the string was invalid. R2 contains the converted value or zero if an error arose. The Overflow flag 'V' will be set if the string was not in the specified format.

The string may also contain the base to be used for the conversion in the following format:

```
<base> <number>
```

For example, to convert the string "F0FF" to a hexadecimal value, you can use the following string:

&F0FF

To convert a binary string 11110000, you would use:

2_11110000

If a base is not specified the routine assumes decimal. If a base is specified at the start of the string, this overrides any value that might be seeded into R0.

The string is analysed up to the first invalid character for the given base. So, for example, the string '92A' will return 92 if decimal was specified.

All numbers are taken as being unsigned, and no check is made otherwise. Program 5d shows how this routine can be used. The assembler also contains a routine that will check to see if you have entered a negative value as well, in other words, whether it is preceded by a '-'. For example:

-&FFFF

When RUN, Program 5d requests a string and calls the conversion routine, returning the value via the USR function.

Program 5d. Using signed numbers with OS_ReadUnsigned.

```
10 REM >Prog5d
20 REM OS_ReadUnsigned demo with signed numbers
30 REM RPi RISC OS Programming
40 :
50 DIM code% 256
55 str=1 : result=2 : neg=3: char=4
60 FOR pass=0 TO 3 STEP 3
70 P%=code%
80 [
90 OPT pass
100 .start
110 MOV neg, #0                ; clear negative marker (R3)
120 :
130 .nospaces                  ; move past leading spaces
140 LDRB char, [str], #1
150 CMP char, #32
160 BEQ nospaces
170 :
180 CMP char, #ASC("-")        ; Is it negative
190 MOVEQ neg,#1               ; Set negative marker
200 CMPNE char, #ASC("+")      ; Is it positive
210 SUBNE str, str, #1         ; If not "+" move back one
220 :
230 MOV R0, #10                ; Base is 10 — can be 2-32
240 SWI "OS_ReadUnsigned"
250 :
260 CMP neg, #1                ; Was neg marker set
270 RSBEQ result, result, #0   ; If so make negative
280 :
290 MOV R0, result             ; Return result in R0
300 MOV R15, R14
310 ]
320 NEXT pass
330 :
340 REM Pass string addr into R1 via B%
350 DIM string 100
360 B%=string
370 INPUT LINE "Enter number string: " $string
380 PRINT "String was: " USR(start)
```

The address of the string is passed into R1 via the variable B% (line 370) and the machine code starts by stripping out any leading spaces. This is good housekeeping, and you should always include a routine like this in similar situations where leading spaces might have an adverse effect on the functioning of the program. This is done between lines 130 and 160.

Lines 180 to 210 check to see if the first valid character is '-' (this is also a reason for stripping out leading spaces, so we can check the first real character for a sign). R3 is used as a flag register. If the '-' is found then a 1 is placed in R3 to signify the fact. The use of a '+' sign at the start of a positive number is also checked for in line 200. Note the conditional execution if '-' was found — we don't need to waste time looking for this. If no '+' was included then we need to move back one place so that the address in R1 is correctly positioned.

Line 230 moves the immediate value 10 into R0. This is to signify a decimal base by default. Remember, this is overridden by any base specified in the string when it is entered. The SWI routine is called in line 240. Line 260 checks to see if the negative register flag (R3) was set and if so uses the Reverse SuBtraction instruction to make the value negative. The result is moved across into R0 as this is the value returned through USR.

GS String Operations

There are three other SWI calls that are used extensively by the CLI to process strings. You will find occasional reference to one or more of these calls in these pages and certainly in the PRMs. The calls are:

```
OS_GSInit      SWI &25

OS_GSRead      SWI &26

OS_GSTrans     SWI &27
```

These three operations are a way of putting any values from 0-255 into a string using only the printable character set. OS_GSInit and OS_GSRead work together to scan a string one character at a time. OS_GSTrans performs both of these functions until the string is totally parsed. Unless you need character by character control, OS_GSTrans is easier to use as it first calls OS_GSInit and then repeatedly calls OS_GSRead.

The bar character, '|', is used by these calls to denote a special character, and it always precedes another character that will define the ASCII value to be used. Figure 5d lists the ASCII code generated by bar-character combinations.

ASCII Code	Code Characters
0	|@
1-26	|<letter> (|A=1, |b=2 etc)
27	|[or |{
28	|\
29	|] or |}
30	|^ or |~
31	|_
32-126	Keyboard character, except for: " |" | || < |<
127	|?
128-255	|!<letter> (|!@=128, |!A=129 etc)

Figure 5d. GS Control Characters.

By definition, the ASCII codes 128-255 have the most significant bit set. So inserting these codes is done by preceding the corresponding ASCII character with |! to set the top bit.

To include leading spaces in a definition, the string must be in quotation marks, "", which are not included in the definition. To include a single " character in the string, use |" or "".

As RISC OS allows values and variables to be between '<'and '>', '<'must always be preceded by a '|' otherwise results will not be as expected. As we have previously seen, a string with a name enclosed in '< >'characters will be used to look up a system variable and the value of the variable will be substituted for the name and the angle brackets using OS_ReadVarVal. A number placed between angle brackets (ie <number>) may also be interpreted by OS_ReadUnsigned as a parameter, that is, a number in any base from 2 to 36.

The *ECHO command is always sent through OS_GSTrans to parse any '|' characters within before being sent off to OS_EvaluateExpression.

OS_GSInit initialises registers for use by OS_GSRead.

On Entry:

R0 = points to a string terminated by a 0, 10 or 13.

R1 = undefined

R2 = flags how the string will be treated:

> Bit 29 = If set then a space is treated as a string terminator
>
> Bit 30 = If set control codes are not converted
> (ie '|' syntax is ignored)
>
> Bit 31 = If set double quotation marks "" are not to be treated specially, ie they are not stripped around strings.

On Exit:

R0 = value to pass back in to OS_GSRead

R1 = first non-blank character

R2 = value to pass back in to OS_GSRead

OS_GSRead should be called directly after OS_GSInit with registers R0 and R2 intact.

On Exit:

R0 = updated for next call to OS_GSRead

R1 = next translated character

R2 = updated for next call to OS_GSRead

C = 1 If end of string had been reached

OS_GSTrans is the preferred call if you wish to undertake repeated calls to OS_GSRead. The call is performed until the end of the string is reached. It gets underway by calling OS_GSInit first. Setting up for this call is done by combining elements from both OS_GSInit and OS_GSRead:

On Entry:

R0 = pointer to string, terminated by 0, 10 or 13

R1 = buffer pointer

R2 = buffer size (maxlen) and flags in top three bits

On Exit:

R0 = pointer to character after terminator

R1 = pointer to buffer, or 0

R2 = number of characters in buffer, or maxlen if the buffer overflowed

C = 1 indicates that buffer overflowed

On entry, the flags in R2 are the same as those supplied in OS_GSInit. On exit, R0 points to the character after the terminator of the source string, and R1+R2 points to the terminator of the translated string. If the C flag is set the buffer was too small for the converted string. R2 is set to the length of the buffer.

You will get a 'Bad String' error if anything causes the routine to abort. Typically this happens if there are mismatched quote marks.

MessageTrans

MessageTrans is a module that provides SWI calls to allow text files in applications to be accessed. Once located these text files can be manipulated; the most obvious would be for international markets where text files - maybe for help or instructions - many need to be translated into the local language for display.

If you click Menu on the Apps icon on the icon bar, choose Open '$' and then open the directory Resources and you'll see a directory for each module, most of them containing just a message file.

You can find out more about MessageTrans and its associated SWI calls in PRM 3-745.

6: Assembler, BASIC and C

This chapter examines how you might access specific aspects and functionality of RISC OS using either assembler, BBC BASIC or C. Essentially this comes down to the calling of SWIs and the availability of * commands from within your programs. But first we'll look at a useful feature of the BBC BASIC assembler.

Offset Assembly

The BBC BASIC variable P% is used to control where in memory machine code will be assembled. P% can be assigned to a label or an absolute address. For example:

```
P%=&9300
P% = startofcode
```

The location of P% defines how the offset to labels are calculated, how absolute addresses are referenced and other position-dependent factors calculated. It determines to a large degree where your program will be loaded and run if you are making it a standalone executable file. (These addresses can be changed post creation as we shall see in Chapter 13.)

However, there might be occasions when you will want to assemble your code so that it will load and run in another area of memory which, at the time of writing it, you can't do. For instance, in the same space as your BBC BASIC program or, if you were going to write your own machine code module or environment. This can be catered for with offset assembly. Here, P% is set to the address of where the machine code will be run and its final destination address, but O% is used to point the assembler to the area of memory where the code can be assembled — and this can be DIMed space at the top of the program.

Offset assembly is controlled by the OPT settings defined by bit 2 (below and see Figure 6a). To implement the equivalent of OPT 0 TO 3 STEP 3 assembly with offset switched you would use OPT 4-7. Program 6a shows how it works in practice.

Program 6a. Using offset Assembly with O%.

```
 10 REM >Prog6a
 20 REM Offset Assembly
 30 REM RPi RISC OS Programming
 40 :
 50 DIM C% (100)
 60 FOR OPT%=4 TO 7 STEP 3
 70 P%=0
 80 O%=C%
 90 [
100 OPT OPT%
110 .start
120 ADR R0,string
130 SWI "OS_Write0"
140 MOV R15,R14
150 .string
160 EQUS "Offset Assembly"
170 EQUB 0
180 ]
190 NEXT pass
```

Here, O% is where the code will be assembled inside the space dimensioned in line 50. P% is set to the location where we actually want to use the code. To create totally relocatable code P% should be set to &0.

Note that P% is inside the FOR...NEXT loop as it will need to be reset to its original value on the second pass through.

OPT Settings

The OPT setting is used to control how the BBC BASIC Assembler deals with errors. The Assembler is generally a two-pass assembler so that forward references can be calculated and so not generate an 'unknown label' error on the fast pass for forward references. For most purposes the first four settings — 0 to 3 — are used. However, when writing more advanced code and certainly for the generation of relocatable module code (see the next chapter) the assembly of code into non-available spaces is required, as discussed above. In such cases OPT settings of 4 to 7 are the norm. Figure 6a details the full range of OPT settings.

OPT Value	Range Check	Offset Assembly	Error Reports	Listing
0	No	No	No	No
1	No	No	No	Yes
2	No	No	Yes	No
3	No	No	Yes	Yes
4	No	Yes	No	No
5	No	Yes	No	Yes
6	No	Yes	Yes	No
7	No	Yes	Yes	Yes
8	Yes	No	No	No
9	Yes	No	No	Yes
10	Yes	No	Yes	No
11	Yes	No	Yes	Yes
12	Yes	Yes	No	No
13	Yes	Yes	No	Yes
14	Yes	Yes	Yes	No
15	Yes	Yes	Yes	Yes

Figure 6a. The full range of OPT settings.

If you substitute No and Yes for 0 and 1 respectively in the table, you should see a direct correlation between the OPT number and a binary representation. OPT 15 relates to 1111 in the table. Effectively if the option is off then the bit is 0, and if it is on then the bit is 1. As you can see from the table, you can use OPT to decide if in fact you want an assembly listing produced. If no OPT directive is used, then the default value is OPT 0.

BBC BASIC

RISC OS Pi is supplied with BBC BASIC, which is an excellent implementation of the BASIC language. Indeed parts of RISC OS were written in BBC BASIC and the original ABC (Acorn BASIC Compiler which I commissioned for Dabs) was written in BASIC and compiled itself!

BBC BASIC is entered by typing:

```
*BASIC
```

at the CLI in a Task Window. At this point BBC BASIC is in interactive mode and as such anything typed at the prompt will be executed immediately <RETURN> is pressed. All BBC BASIC commands are available for use, but also all * commands remain available. However, the '*' of the command must be entered otherwise it will not be passed to RISC OS and an error will most likely occur. At this point all * commands should have the same effect as if they had been entered directly at the CLI.

To exit BBC BASIC type:

```
*QUIT
```

And you will return to the CLI '*' prompt.

RISC OS * commands may also be included in BBC BASIC programs as illustrated in Program 6b.

Program 6b. *commands can be included in BBC BASIC programs.

```
10 REM >Prog6b
20 REM Simple demo of * commands in BBC BASIC
30 REM RPi RISC OS Programming
40 :
50 *COUNTRY USA
60 *CONFIGURE TIMEZONE -5
70 *SET ALIAS$ASCII ECHO |<%0>
80 *SETEVAL COUNTER 0
90 *SETMACRO CLI$PROMPT <SYS$TIME>>: *
```

When RUN this program performs the same set of commands that we saw demonstrated in the section on Obey files earlier on. This illustrates that their operation in BBC BASIC is (and should be) nearly identical. I say 'nearly' because there is a slight difference in that for the Alias definition (line 70) we only need to use the one '%' and not two as we do for in the Obey file. Note also that the time will not be shown at the prompt unless you *QUIT out back to a task window and the CLI.

Note that BBC BASIC allows more than one of its own keywords to be used on a single line, so multiple commands can be packed in separated by colons (:). This is not the case for * commands where you should limit each command to a single line as illustrated.

The SYS Call

SWI commands can be issued from BBC BASIC by use of the SYS command. SYS, short for system, can be used from the BBC BASIC prompt and also in programs. The lines of code can look a little complex at times, but this is dependent on the amount of information that has to be supplied to the call and what might be passed back from it. With complex calls, care needs to be taken to make sure that all parameters are passed and in the right order.

The format of the command is:

```
SYS Expr1 {,{exprn}...}{TO{var1}{,{var2}...}{;flags}}
```

Expr1

This is required and may be evaluated to a number which relates to the RISC OS SWI routine to be called. It may also be a string which is the name of a routine. BBC BASIC uses the SWI OS_SWINumberFromString to convert from a string to number, so the case of the letters in the string must match exactly that of the SWI name.

exprn

This is the optional list which may contain up to eight expressions. These are placed in order in the ARM registers R0 through to R7 respectively. If the expression evaluates to a number, it is converted to an integer and placed directly in the relative register. If the expression evaluates to a string, the string is placed on the BBC BASIC stack, beginning at a word boundary and terminated with a null character. A pointer to it is put in the relative register. Any expressions not given must be accounted for by the use of commas, unless the expressions are at the end of the command line. Thus:

```
SYS "OS_Name", 1,2,3,,,6,,8
```

Indicates that there is nothing to go into slots '4', '5' and '7'. This is important otherwise data will not be ordered correctly. A 0 is placed in the vacant slot so the above example might also be written:

```
SYS "OS_Name", 1,2,3,0,0,6,0,8
```

TO

This is optional and allows information to be passed back from the SWI to the calling SYS command. A variable list must be provided to take the values of the registers R0 to R7 respectively. If the variable is numeric, the integer in the register is converted to an appropriate format and copied into it. If the variable is a string, the register is treated as a pointer to a string terminated by ASCII 0, 10 or 13 and this string is assigned to the variable. As with the input expressions, output variables may be omitted, using adjacent commas in the list.

An optional existing variable you can use is 'flags', into which RISC OS will pass the four main Status Register flags. The value returned is a binary value structured in such a way that the lower four bits represent the N, Z, C and V flags respectively. Note that the 'flags' variable is separated from the others by the use of a semicolon.

Here are a couple of SWI examples of SYS calls:

```
SYS "OS_WriteC", ASC ("A")
SYS "OS_ReadMonotonicTime" TO time%; flags
```

Program 6c is a BBC BASIC version of Program 4b, presented earlier in Chapter 4, which uses the SYS command to print out the first 256 SWI names.

Program 6c. Using SYS to print out SWI names.

```
 10 REM >Prog6c
 20 REM Print details of first 256 SWI calls with SYS
 30 REM RPi RISC OS Programming
 40 :
 50 DIM buffer% 127
 60 FOR swi%=0 TO 255
 70 PRINT swi% "    ";
 80 SYS "OS_SWINumberToString", swi%,buffer%,127
 90 SYS "OS_Write0",buffer%:PRINT
100 NEXT
```

OS_SWINumberToString returns each SWI name at the location called 'buffer%' and this name is printed using OS_Write0. Both the BBC BASIC SYS command and the BBC BASIC Assembler perform this conversion automatically whenever they encounter a SWI name enclosed in inverted commas.

Program 6d illustrates how SYS can be used to call an actual SWI number, rather than a named SWI. It takes a string and then for each of the characters within it calls SYS $100+the ASCII value of the character.

Program 6d. Using a number to define the OS call with SYS.

```
10 REM >Prog6d
20 REM Use SYS with number
30 REM RPi RISC OS Programming
40 :
50 a$="RPi RISC OS Programming"+CHR$13+CHR$10
60 FOR char%=1 TO LEN(a$)
```

```
70 SYS &100+ASC(MID$(a$,char%,1))
80 NEXT
90 END
```

Even if you are not using assembler, the SYS version of a SWI call is often more useful than using the equivalent * command as the information return by the SYS call can be captured and saved in variables for further interrogation and use. So SYS provides a very compelling tool for the BBC BASIC programmer.

USR Calls

Another way of calling machine code programs is the USR command. This is similar to CALL. However, it allows you to pass a result back from your machine code. It takes the format:

<variable>=USR <address>

As you can see the address, which may be a variable, is used to identify where the machine code is located. On the left of the command a variable is specified into which a value will be returned. For example:

```
Result=USR start
Value=USR &9300
```

The value returned is taken from the contents of R0 when the program was exited.

Because of this and the fact that when you call your machine code from BBC BASIC the values of the integer variables A% through to H% are passed into the registers R0 to R7 respectively, you can conveniently seed values that might be needed for SWI calls. This may be easier and more obvious than the method required with SYS.

For example if your program included:

```
A%=&FF
B%=&FF0000FF
```

then when you call the machine code from BASIC, these two values would be loaded in registers R0 and R1 respectively.

Calling XSYS

If the X form of the SWI is being used then the ON ERROR statement can be used to process errors within BBC BASIC programs and interrogated by accessing the flags variable.

For example:

```
:
SYS "XOS_Write0", "RPI RISC OS Programming"+CHR$0 TO
block;flags
IF (flags AND 1) = 1 THEN PROCdisplayerror(block)
PROCcarryon
:
```

The error block consists of a 4 byte error number followed by a zero terminated error string. Calling the non-X version of the SWI will leave it up to BASIC to alter the program flow, such as

```
:
ON ERROR PROCdisplayerror(ERR, REPORT$) : END
SYS "OS_Write0", "RPI RISC OS Programming"+CHR$0
PROCcarryon
:
```

So in this example PROCcarryon will never be reached.

C Code

As C is a compiled language and we will always be using the machine code it generates to operate with, there is no sense in using * commands. These can be called via a SWI call if required, but it is more efficient to use the full SWI version of the call.

Provision for calling SWI is made in all versions of C implemented under RISC OS. Indeed at a deeper level all C functions (such as printf) use these Kernel calls to achieve their own output. They all go about it in a slightly different way, but the common point is that you should try to use a tried and tested library that works with RISC OS.

If you need to call a SWI, then you can use the _swix and _kernel_swi functions provided by SharedCLibrary and Unixlib which come as standard with most versions of C available for RISC OS. These are relatively straghtforward to use, but do not do any error checking for you. Details on how to use these are provided below.

If you are planning to program in C regularly then I would suggest that the preferred option is to install and use OSlib, which has a couple of added bonuses. Firstly, OSlib provides an interface to SWIs where function veneers are defined for most SWIs if not all, with all the parameters typed and,where necessary, supplied with struct definitions to represent the data blocks. This will minimise any potential mistakes. Secondly, as you will come to realise as you work through this book, RISC OS uses data blocks extensively, especially in dealing with the Desktop Wimp environment and icon data. OSlib makes dealing with this almost seamless and there is very little programming translation required by the user.

Two other pluses are that OSlib works with most compilers and associated assemblers and is regularly updated. Linking details are explained on the product website, and OSlib comes with an extensive help via StrongHelp manuals. As the figure below shows, the depth of detail that they go to is excellent.

```
os_convert_cardinal4

OSLib: os_convert_cardinal4

Defined in:   oslib/os.h
Declaration: extern char  *os_convert_cardinal4
                          ( int value,
                            char *buffer,
                            int size
                          );
Description: Converts a 4-byte number into an unsigned decimal string

Entry:   value   (R0)
         buffer  (R1)
         size    (R2)
Returns: end     (R1)
```

Figure 6b Examples of OSlib StrongHelp windows.

Downloading OSlib, support library and manuals can be done straight from the Desktop via PackMan, which will also handle installation and future updates for you.

_swi, _swix and _kernel_swi

These options work in a fashion more similar to BASIC's SYS function covered above, in that they expect you to pass the relevant data and in the correct order. For example, these two examples achieve the same "OS_File" call.

```
_kernel_swi_regs regs;
regs.r[0]=5;
regs.r[1]=filename;
_kernel_swi (OS_File,&regs,&regs);
r4=regs.r[4];
```

and:

```
_swi(OS_File,_IN(0)|_IN(1)|_OUT(4),5,filename,&file_size);
```

Both call OS_File with R0=5, R1=filename and on exit, the length of the file is returned in R4. In the _swi example the use of IN and OUT with values in brackets helps to order the information being passed. With SYS the use of commas was required to ensure that values were in the correct order. In the example above IN(0) and IN (1) denote that the first and second tems are input and that only only items is passed back(out) and this will be in the fourth parameter — OUT(4).

The X SWI version of the call would be:

```
_swix(OS_File,_IN(0)|_IN(1)|_OUT(4),5,filename,&file_size);
```

where file_size has previously been defined as 'int' to denote it as a pointer.

These SWI calls require the non-ANSI header file swis.h which exists in both GCC (inside !Unixlib) and in Acorn C/C++. This header file creates the SWIs used by the machine but be aware that the SWI numbers in the files might not contain the most recent additions. For this reason alone OSlib is preferred.

7: Modules

In the early days of home computers memory was at a premium and expensive and so system software was burned permanently into Read Only Memory. ROM chips were fitted making the OS available immediately on start-up. As modern manufacturing techniques have dramatically reduced the cost (and size) of volatile memory (RAM), the use of burned-in memory has become almost redundant. Operating Systems can be loaded into RAM in a matter of seconds. If you have tried using one of the RISC OS Emulators on a PC or Mac, RPCEmulator for example, you will be aware that you need to obtain and install ROM images to use the emulator.

RISC OS Pi is a memory-based operating system. On start-up the RISC OS ROM image stored on the Raspberry Pi SD card is loaded into the memory on your Raspberry Pi. This provides the basic operating system and is to a large extent unchanged down the years, at least from a user's point of view.

However, RISC OS has been enhanced and extended, no more so than with the release of RISC OS Pi. The additional functionality has been provided by supplying extra system code in the form of Relocatable Modules.

Relocatable Modules

Modules allow RISC OS to be extended and enhanced. Modules can add applications, services or functionality to RISC OS and the Raspberry Pi in general in a well-defined and structured way. These additions can be in the form of new command sets, languages or software to control hardware connected to the Raspberry Pi. Something like the GPIO Module is a good example of this. It can be downloaded and installed using PackMan and allows easy access to the GPIO - the General-Purpose Input/Output interface on the Raspberry Pi to which you can connect and control external devices.

One of the most important things about modules is that they do not need to be physically installed in the computer; they are supplied as software and RISC OS maintains an area of memory exclusively for them. This is called the Relocatable Module Area (RMA). Modules can be added as required and also removed when not required. Because they take advantage of the ARM's instruction set they are also fully relocatable and can be added in any order and independent of any other modules.

Modules can also be used to provide enhancements to existing functions by the use of hardware and software vectors.

Module-related commands are detailed below. Figure 7a shows an edited list of some of the standard modules installed on a Raspberry Pi. Use the:

*MODULES

command to display the list for your own Raspberry Pi. This is an edited list and just shows some examples.

No	Position	Workspace	Name
1	FC01EF1C	00000000	UtilityModule
2	FC040000	20000014	PCI
3	FC041F08	200001D4	FileSwitch
4	FC04EF04	20000E74	ResourceFS
5	FC04FBEC	20000EB4	TerritoryManager
6	FC0520E0	00000000	Messages
7	FC148DAC	20000FB4	UK
8	FC14A19C	20002D94	WindowManager
9	FC14BDAC	20003334	Desktop
:			
98	FC39C268	20147A94	AcornURI
99	FC39EC08	00000000	!Edit
100	FC3A16EC	00000000	!Draw
101	FC3CB354	00000000	!Paint
102	FC3E1848	00000000	!Alarm

Figure 7a. Typical part-listing of Modules installed in RISC OS Pi.

Your list may be different or it may be identical. Either way do not worry as installed modules come and go depending on the software and hardware that you are using. If you examine the list you will see a lot of names that are probably familiar to you. Note how applications such as !Paint and !Draw are implemented as modules.

The listing consists of four columns, the first and fourth of which are fairly self-explanatory. The 'Position' column is the hexadecimal address where the module starts in memory. High values starting &FF are called ROM-based modules. Those with low memory addresses typically starting with &2 are RAM-based modules.

The 'Workspace' addresses define the start address of the memory used by the module as its workspace. Workspaces addresses given as &0 generally indicate that the module uses no module workspace — however, it may still use other memory.

Each of these modules has specific functions, many of which you can guess at from their name. Many provide *commands and SWIs of their own relative to the functions that they add. Much of the additional support provided by modules for the Raspberry Pi has yet to be fully documented. By investigating the modules you can glean a lot of what they do.

You can use the *HELP command to find out more about each module. Figure 7b shows a typical response for the information on the SoundDMA module.

```
*Help SoundDMA
==> Help on keyword SoundDMA
Module is: SoundDMA    1.7(09 Nov 2012) HAL version

Commands provided:
Audio  Speaker   Stereo   SoundGain

Configuration keywords:
SoundSystem
*
```

Figure 7b Getting help on a module.

So from this we can see that the SoundDMA module provides the following commands:

```
*AUDIO
*SPEAKER
*STEREO
*SOUNDGAIN
*CONFIGURE SOUNDSYSTEM
```

*HELP can then be used to investigate these commands further. Some modules will also list the SWI commands that they provide and may also list *HELP information if you request it.

Another way to investigate what functionality a module adds is to look at a disassembly of it. As we know for the start address of modules we can use the *MEMORYI command provided by the Debugger module to examine its code.

To do this requires a working knowledge of ARM Assembly Language plus knowledge of the structure of relocatable modules. The structure of modules and writing module code is examined in Chapter 19 and this will help your reverse engineering process.

ROM Modules

The command:

    *ROMMODULES

lists details regarding current System ROM modules that are present. By definition the ROM Modules never go away, but this listing does show whether they are active or not. Figure 7c shows some sample output by the use of this * command.

No	Position	Name	Version	Status
1	System ROM	UtilityModule	5.19	Active
2	System ROM	PCI	0.11	Active
3	System ROM	FileSwitch	2.81	Active
4	System ROM	ResourceFS	0.25	Active
5	System ROM	TerritoryManager	0.54	Active
6	System ROM	Messages	1.10	Active
7	System ROM	MessageTrans	0.49	Active
8	System ROM	UK	0.56	Active
9	System ROM	WindowManager	5.19	Active
10	System ROM	Desktop	2.74	Active
11	System ROM	SharedCLibrary	5.75	Active
12	System ROM	TaskManager	1.41	Active
13	System ROM	BASIC	1.53	Active

Figure 7c. Output produced by the command *ROMMODULES.

The command:

    *HELP MODULES

will produce a listing of System ROM modules. Figure 7d overleaf shows a sample output from this command:

Name	Version	Date
MOS Utilities	5.19	(27 Jan 2013)
PCI Manager	0.11	(02 Feb 2012)
FileSwitch	2.81	(13 Jan 2013)
ResourceFS	0.25	(19 Jan 2010)
Territory Mger	0.54	(16 Oct 2012)
UK Messages	1.10	(20 Mar 2012)
MessageTrans	0.49	(26 May 2012)
UK Territory	0.75	(23 Feb 2013)
WindowManager	5.19	(09 Oct 2012)
Desktop	2.74	(08 Sep 2012)
C Library	5.75	(17 Jan 2013)
Task Manager	1.40	(31 Oct 2012)
BBC BASIC V	1.53	(31 Oct 2012)

Figure 7d. Sample output from *HELP MODULES

This information is useful to see what modules have been updated, by examining the date column, and the module's current version number.

Module-Related Commands

A number of module-related * commands exist to handle the installation, removal and use of the relocatable module system. Each of these is detailed below. These commands are provided by RISC OS and take advantage of the module interface which we will be examining later on.

*Modules

Syntax: *MODULES

The *MODULES command displays a list of all the modules which are installed in the computer (see earlier Figures). No distinction is made between modules that are supplied in ROM and those that have been installed into RAM from a filing system. For each module present, a one-line entry appears that details the module's name (for use with other commands), the base address in memory where the module appears and the address of where the module's private workspace begins.

*RMkill

Syntax: *RMKILL <module name>

The *RMKILL command removes an individual module from the RMA, freeing its code space and workspace. System modules murdered in this way revive themselves after a hard reset or upon receipt of the *RMREINIT command (see below).

*RMload

Syntax: `*RMLOAD <filename> {<initialisation string>}`

This command loads and initialises the specified file, which must be a valid piece of module code and must be of filetype 'Module', ie, with filetype code &FFA. After initialisation in this way the module will respond in the usual way both to its commands and to others such as *HELP.

The initialisation string is optional and specific to the module being loaded — it can be used to request a particular amount of workspace for the module or for whatever other purpose the author of the module requires.

*RMreinit

Syntax: `*RMREINIT <module name> {<reinit string>}`

The *RMREINIT command is used to resuscitate modules which have been *RMKILLed or *UNPLUGged (see below). It is effectively the same as the initialisation part of *RMLOAD, but the module must already be present in the machine (which is usually only the case for system modules).

*RMrun

Syntax: `*RMRUN <filename> {initialisation string}`

This command executes modules in the same way as *RUN executes machine code programs. The file must have a filetype of &FFA and is loaded and executed if it is valid. *RMRUN is usually reserved for starting large applications rather than just system extensions.

*RMTidy

Syntax: `*RMTIDY`

This command tidies up the relocatable module area. It compacts the RMA and maximises the free memory available. Because modules need to be warned when this is happening (they may be running) certain modules will initiate their own tidying up, so sounds may cease and files may be ensured onto the appropriate storage medium.

*ROMmodules

Syntax: `*ROMMODULES`

The *ROMMODULES command displays a list of all the modules which are installed in the computer, (see earlier Figures). It also lists the version number and the execution status of the ROM Module.

*Unplug

Syntax: *UNPLUG {<module name>}

*UNPLUG allows a system module (in ROM) to be excluded from the initialisation process, rendering it completely inoperable until *RMREINITed again. Because this command alters configuration memory, the module will not reappear even after switching the power off and on. It is therefore important to remember the module's name, and for this reason entering *UNPLUG on its own will give a list of the modules which are unplugged.

OS_Module

The SWI OS_Module (SWI &1E) is used for module management and as might be expected it can be used to perform the * commands detailed in this chapter. It also deals with other functions vital to the operation of the module system. For that reason we'll look at this SWI in Chapter 19 when we look at how to write module code.

8: Vectors

Extensions to RISC OS are made possible by the use of special locations called vectors. A vector is a known location in memory that is exactly one word wide. There are two types of vectors — hardware vectors and software vectors.

Vectors are useful to the programmer for a couple of reasons. First, they allow programs to access a standard routine without directly calling the physical address where the code for the routine is stored.

In the early days of computers operating systems were small and everything was hard coded, meaning addresses were used in absolute terms. The problem with using absolute addressees (and by this I mean a real physical address rather than a branch offset for example) is that you are always tied to that address. If the OS is updated then a pound to a pinch of salt that address will change! Now any external or third-party code that uses that absolute address might be snookered. Using vectors if the code is updated and its execution point is changed, all that needs to happen is for the address in the vector to be changed. Also, if the code is hard coded to memory locations, bang goes relocatable code!

The second advantage in using vectors is that as programmers we can also change the address in the vector and by doing so we can intercept it. By intercepting or claiming vectors we can modify and even change the way the user operates in a RISC OS environment.

Vectors are a fundamental feature of both the ARM processor and RISC OS. Virtually every significant operation that RISC OS processes will start off by being directed through a vector.

Hardware Vectors

Hardware vectors control the ultimate flow of information and are a set of memory addresses that are known to the ARM chip. The term 'known' here means that they are physically hard-wired and are thus termed hardware vectors. When the Raspberry Pi first boots, some of the first operations it performs are to jump to hardware vectors associated with its initialisation process.

Hardware vectors typically control the flow of abnormal events which the chip itself cannot deal with. They are often referred to as exception vectors and they reside right at the start of the memory map from &00000000 to &0000001C. Figure 8a lists the hardware vectors.

Address	Vector
&00000000	ARM reset
&00000004	Undefined Instruction
&00000008	Software Interrupt (SWI)
&0000000C	Abort (pre-fetch)
&00000010	Abort (data)
&00000014	Address exception
&00000018	IRQ
&0000001C	FIRQ (or FIQ)

Figure 8a. The ARM Hardware vectors.

For example, when an IRQ interrupt occurs it ultimately goes via the IRQ vector. This location is 32 bits wide (a word), and is just big enough to contain an instruction that facilitates an instruction to branch to another memory location.

SWI Example

Whenever you execute a SWI, the SWI handler routine jumps to the hardware vector location &00000008. Located here is a PC relative instruction. Typically, this might look like this:

```
LDR      PC,&000002C8
```

This instruction means load the Program Counter with the address stored at &2C8. The addressed stored at &2C8 might be:

```
&20284F44
```

Therefore the code to handle SWI calls starts at this location.

This code effectively saves information onto the stack and then sets about calculating what SWI number is being used, and then branching to the absolute address in memory that handles the particular SWI called. Of course, this is only a very short piece of the code that deals with it. The code itself contains absolute references as they are accurate for this version of the OS. Chapter 19 contains more detail on this.

By changing the destination address that a vector is pointing to, we can in effect take control of what happens in a variety of situations by pointing it directly at our own machine code. However, this is a very risky occupation, and there is usually an easier to use facility provided by RISC OS. For example, to add extra SWI instructions we do not need to replace the SWI hardware vectors as the OS provides an Unknown SWI software vector. (That said, it is much easier just to use a module to add more SWIs.) These are handled through the software vector set. This is the preferred option to maintain compatibility and is detailed shortly.

Software Vectors

RISC OS contains a whole series of vectors to provide access to its own internal routines. These are grouped by type and are listed in Figure 8c overleaf

For example, whenever the OS_WriteC routine is used it is accessed through the WrchV vector (number &03). Equally, the OS_ReadC routine is accessed through the RdchV vector.

Several of these vectors are described in more detail towards the end of this chapter.

Vector Lists

There are two SWI calls that are specifically designed to help in the interception of software vectors. These are OS_Claim and OS_Release. Although we could actually enter the address of our own routine into any of these vectors, and process any call to the vector ourselves, only in extreme circumstances would we want to do this. In normal circumstances RISC OS maintains a vector user list. It you want to claim use of a vector, RISC OS will add your code's details to the list for the particular vector. Whenever the vector is accessed, RISC OS will pass the call through the list associated with the vector, starting with the most recent caller, before finally ending up calling the original RISC OS address. It uses a stack for the addresses and is therefore organised as a last-in/first-out structure.

If you write a routine that uses a vector, it must obey the same entry and exit conditions as the corresponding RISC OS routine. For example, a routine on WrchV must preserve all registers, just as the SWI OS_WriteC does. If you fail to do this it could have significant effects on the operation of RISC OS.

No	Name	Vector Function
&00	UserV	User Vector
&01	ErrorV	Error Vector(OS_GenerateError)
&02	IrqV	Interrupt Vector
&03	WrchV	Write Character Vector(OS_WriteC)
&04	RdchV	Read Character Vector (OS_ReadC)
&05	CliV	Command Line Interpreter Vector (OS_CLI)
&06	ByteV	OS_Byte indirection Vector
&07	WordV	OS_Word indirection Vector
&08	FileV	Read/Write File Vector(OS_File)
&09	ArgsV	Read/Write File Arguments Vector (OS_Args)
&0A	BGetV	Read Byte from File Vector(OS_BGet)
&0B	BPutV	Write Byte to File Vector(OS_BPut)
&0C	GBPBV	Read/Write Byte Bock to/from File Vector (OS_GBPB)
&0D	FindV	Open File Vector (OS_FSControl)
&0E	ReadLineV	Read a line of Text Vector (OS_ReadLine)
&0F	FSContr olV	Filing Control Vector (OS_FSControl)
&10	EventV	Event Vector (OS_GenerateEvent)
&14	InsV	Buffer Insert Vector n(OS_Byte)
&15	RemV	Buffer Remove Vector (OS_Byte)
&16	CnpV	Count or Flush Vector Buffer
&17	UKVDU23V	Unknown VDU23 Vector (OS_WriteC)
&18	UKSWIV	Unknown SWI Vector (SWI)
&19	UKPLOTV	Unknown VDU 35 Vector (OS_WriteC)
&1A	MouseV	Mouse Vector (OS_Mouse)
&1B	VDUXV	VDU Vector (OS_WriteC)
&1C	TickerV	100Hz Vector
&1D	UpCallV	Warning (OS_UpCall)

Figure 8c. A selection of RISC OS software vectors.

RISC OS will only allow you to claim a vector once. If you try to claim it a second time, it will remove the first instance and add the most recent to the vector. Routines are defined to be identical if the values passed in R0, R1 and R2 are the same. As one of these will be the address of where your code is, it is unlikely this would be duplicated by another claim.

In practice each vector is the head of a chain of structures, each one in turn pointing to the next routine to have claimed it. From a user's point of view this is seamless and is handled by RISC OS. The routines are called in the reverse order to the order in which they called OS_Claim, so the last routine to call OS_Claim will be the first one called.

You also have the option of fully claiming the vector by pointing it at your own code and taking full control of the process dealing with any operation that comes through it. You should save the default address and direct control to it when your own routine has finished.

Joining the Vector List

There are two SWI calls that are used to add and remove your vector routines to a routines vector list.

OS_Claim (SWI &1F)

This call is issued when you wish to intercept a vector for your own purposes. There are three register conditions that must be set up before the call is made.

On Entry:
R0 = Number of the vector
R1 = Address of the routine to be added to the list
R2 = Address of workspace to be used, if any.

The R2 value enables the routine to have a workspace pointer set up — this being passed into R12 by RISC OS. If the routine using the vector is in a module, this pointer will usually be the same as its module workspace pointer. Here is a segment of code that could be used to claim the RdchV (OS_ReadC):

```
MOV     R0, #RdchV
ADR     R1, MyownRdchV
MOV     R2, #0
SWI     "OS_Claim"
```

No results are returned by this call.

OS_Release (SWI &20)

This SWI removes the specified call from the vectors users list, therefore preventing subsequent calls to it.

On Entry:

R0 = The number of the vector

R1 = Address of the routine to be added to the list

R2 = Address of workspace to be used, if any

Here is a segment of code that code be used to release the call from the RdchV list:

```
MOV     R0, #RdchV
ADR     R1, MyownRdchV
MOV     R2, #0
SWI     "OS_Release"
```

No results are returned by this call.

Writing Vector Routines

There are some important points to bear in mind when you are writing any type of vector intercept routine, regardless of whether it actually intercepts the vector or utilises the vector list.

If you write a routine that uses a vector, it must obey the same entry and exit conditions as the corresponding RISC OS routine. For example, a routine on WrchV must preserve all registers, just as the SWI OS_WriteC does.

Registers may be preserved on the stack while they are used. For example:

```
STMFD R13! {R0-R12}
```

would save the contents of all registers except the PC, LR and SP itself on the stack. This could be retrieved using:

```
LDMFD R13!, {R0-R12}
```

An intercepting routine will be entered in SVC, IRQ or FIQ mode depending on the type of vector.

If your own vectored routine calls a SWI while you are in SVC mode, you will certainly corrupt the return address held in R14. Consequently, your routine should use the full descending stack addressed by R13 to save R14 first.

When exiting from an intercept routine use:

```
MOV PC, LR
```

This will enable the OS to enter the next routine detailed in the vector user list (if any), or return if the end of the list has been reached. This routine should always be used if the default routine is to be entered after the intercepting one.

If you pass the call on, you can deliberately alter some of the registers to change the effect of the call. However, if you do so you must arrange for control to return again to your routine so that you can restore the register values that the old routine would normally have returned, before finally returning control to the calling program. This is because some applications might rely on the returned values being accurate.

There are some vectors which should not be intercepted — they must always be passed on to other claimants. This is because the default owner, ie the routine which is called if no one has claimed the vector, might perform some important action. A perfect example of this is the error vector, ErrorV. This vector points to the OS error-handling routine and if this is intercepted the error handler might never be called and therefore would not be dealt with properly.

Program 8a below is a trivial example of a program that intercepts a vector. It claims the RdchV vector which is called each time a character is read from the input stream — typically from the keyboard. Each time RdchV is called an asterisk is printed. The call uses SWI 256+ so no registers are altered in any way.

Program 8a. Intercepting the ReadC vector.

```
 10 REM >Prog8a
 20 REM Intercepting the ReadC vector
 30 REM RISC OS Programming
 40 :
 50 DIM vector 100
 60 P%= vector
 70 [
 80 .vector
 90 STMFD R13!, {R14}
100 SWI 256+42
110 LDMFD R13!,{R14}
120 MOVS PC,R14
130 ]
140 *KEY 1 SYS "OS_Release",4,vector,0|M
150 SYS "OS_Claim",4,vector,0
```

Press Function Key F1 to remove the intercept from the vector list.

Although this is a trivial example, care needs to be taken because if we return to the desktop without releasing the vector then the Raspberry Pi will crash (because the app slot will be swapped for another app and the vector will call random code inside that app!).Remember that this BASIC example is in the app slot (BASIC is supplied as a module) and will get paged out when Wimp_Poll is called. (Wimp_Poll is discussed later in this book.)

Vectored SWI Calls

Not all SWI calls pass through vectors. When you call a SWI, RISC OS uses the SWI number to decide what to do. It uses the SWI number as an index into a table of addresses and jumps to that address to perform the requirements of the SWI. In some instances this address will be that of an associated vector and so a jump through this is made.

For example, a call to SWI 'OS_WriteC' will be directed through the WrchV address.

Vector Related SWIs

There are a number of SWI calls that are directly associated with vectors and vector lists. These are outlined below.

OS_CallAVector (SWI &34)

This SWI will call a vector directly. It is frequently used by the OS itself including extension modules.

The call is also used to call vectored routines that don't otherwise have an entry point; this is some instances of InsV, RemV and CnpV. This routine should never be used to call ByteV, as the vector handlers expect entry conditions that cannot be accommodated by the call.

On Entry:
R0-R8 = vector routine parameters
R9 = vector number (see page 1-78)

Exit conditions are dependent on the vector called.

The SWI is re-entrant, but not all vectors that it calls are re-entrant, so always check first to avoid any disasters.

OS_AddToVector (SWI &47)

This call adds the routine whose address is given in R1 to the list of routines claiming the vector, and it benefits by being the first routine to be used when the vector is called. Unlike OS_Claim, any earlier instances of the same routine remain on the vector list and are not removed. Thus it is a useful way to first to set-up a vector and then process it then, or later in the list.

On Entry:
R0 = The number of the vector
R1 = Address of the routine to be added to the list
R2 = Address of workspace to be used, if any

The R2 value enables the routine to have a workspace pointer set up. If the routine using the vector is in a module, this pointer will usually be the same as its module workspace pointer.

On Exit:
R0 - R2 preserved

The SWI cannot be re-entered as it disables IRQ.

OS_DelinkApplication (SWI &4D)

This call will remove any vectors that an application is using. This is an important call if your module is about to be deactivated or a routine removed from memory. If you don't release the vectors then they will still be called; the chances are that they will have a terminal effect on your OS operation if they are called.

On Entry:
R0 = pointer to buffer
R1 = buffer size in bytes

On entry R0 points to a buffer. This is used to store details of the vectors used, so that they can be restored afterwards. Each vector requires 12 bytes of storage and the list is terminated by a single byte.

On Exit:
R0 preserved
R1 = number of bytes left in buffer

If the space left returned in R1 is zero, then you must allocate another buffer and repeat the call as the buffer that you have contains valid information. When you relink you must pass all the buffers returned by this call.

The SWI is not re-entrant because interrupts are disabled

OS_RelinkApplication (SWI &4E)

Restore from a buffer any vectors that an application is using. When an application is going to be swapped in, all vectors that it uses must be restored.

On Entry:
R0 = pointer to buffer

R0 on entry points to a buffer, which has previously been created by OS_DelinkApplication.

On Exit:
R0 preserved

The SWI is re-entrant

Post-Vector Calls

In some cases it will be useful for a vector to be intercepted after the default RISC OS routine has been called. This is not directly possible, but can be achieved by using some tricky coding. The following code fragment serves this purpose:

```
.intercept_code
STMFD R13!, {R9}
ADR R9,continue_after
STMFD R13!,{R9,R12}
MOV PC,R14
LDMFD R13!,{R9,R12}
.continue_after
;
; < Code to execute after default routine has been
; called should be placed here >
;
LDMFD R13!,{PC}
```

The code should be linked to the vector by intercepting it in the normal way.

The routine places a dummy return address on the stack and then calls the default vector routine. This routine would normally return directly to the main program which called the vector in the first place. However, because we have modified the stack, it actually returns back into our code. We can then perform any processing required before returning directly back to the vector caller ourselves.

Remember that the default routine may return results in the registers or flags. These are available to our routine to modify before passing them back to the caller. Care must be taken to preserve any results required. This is particularly easy to overlook if the results are returned in the status flags.

Vector Details

Details of the more commonly used vectors and their actions can be found below. This is by no means a comprehensive list — for the more esoteric vectors please refer to the PRMs. The vectors &03 through to &0F are in every case exactly the same as the default routines called and both the entry and exit requirements relating to register values. They work as though you had called the associated SWI routine.

[&01] ErrorV: Error Vector

This vector is called every time an error occurs. Normally it will link to the error-handling routine which reports the error. As stated earlier, it is considered bad programming practice to intercept and use this error as an unclassified or un-identified error may not be dealt with correctly. One reason for intercepting the error is for the user's routine to be informed of the error.

On Entry:
R0 = Pointer to error block

On Exit:
No information returned.

[&02] IrqV: Interrupt Request Vector

This vector will be called in response to the ARM being informed of an interrupt. As such it will normally be passed at some point from the associated hardware vector. It can be thought of as the first-level interrupt handler for decoding by RISC OS. The default routine will try to establish what has happened and then call the appropriate handling routine. For example, the keyboard will cause an IRQ error and ultimately the interrupt software will parse it and hand it over to OS_ReadC through RdchV.

If this vector is intercepted (as opposed to claimed) then the routine must be able to handle calls generated by every possible device. Alternatively, the user routine will perform any information gathering and processing it needs to before passing the call on. Needless to say, any routines that do claim this vector must exit it with all registers preserved. This vector should never be called using OS_CallAVector.

On Entry:
No information passed

On Exit:
No information returned

[&03] WrchV: Write Character Vector

This vector is used every time a character is printed.

On Entry:
R0=ASCII code of character to be written

On Exit:
No information returned

[&04] RdchV: Read Character Vector

This vector is used every time a character is read. The ASCII value of the character is expected in R0. An example of using this vector is given as Program 8a earlier in this chapter.

On Entry:
No information passed.

On Exit:
R0=ASCII code of character read

[&05] CliV: Command Line Interpreter Vector

All calls to OS_CLI are directed through this vector. The call will execute the * command pointed to by R0. The star command line must be less than or equal to 1024 bytes long, including the terminating character. If it is not, the error 'Too long' is returned. This routine should be claimed and used by modules that may have implemented additional * commands. It is a simple, albeit lazy way, of issuing * commands from within machine code programs.

On Entry:
R0 = Pointer to string terminated by 0, 10 or 13

On Exit:
R0 = preserved

[&06] ByteV: OS_Byte Vector

All OS_Byte calls (*FX) are indirected through this vector. When OS_Byte is called the OS disables interrupts. This means that if you claim this vector you need to complete your code as quickly and economically as possible. As a rule of thumb if you are going to hold the processor for more than 100ms then you should be prepared to re-enable interrupts and be re-entrant.

On Entry:
R0 = OS_Byte number
R1 = Information as required
R2 = Information as required

On Exit:
R0 = Preserved
R1 = as returned by individual OS_Byte
R2 = as returned by individual OS_Byte

R0<128: Only R1 is used to pass further information. These calls set a status variable, and may also perform some other task. R2 is corrupted unless stated otherwise.

R0=128-165 (inclusive): Both R1 and R2 are used to hold parameters, and both registers may contain information on exit from the call.

R0=166-255 (inclusive): R0 acts as an index to a status variable, which is altered using the contents of R1 and R2.

[&07] WordV: OS_Word Vector

All OS_Word calls are directed through this vector. When OS_Word is called the OS disables interrupts. The points made for OS_Byte above are as important here.

On Entry:
R0=Reason code
R1=pointer to parameter block

On Exit:
R0=Preserved

[&08] FileV: OS_File Vector

FileV is used to direct all calls to OS_File.

On Entry:
R0 = reason code
Other registers dependent on reason code

On Exit:
R0 corrupted

The action taken by OS_File is given by the low byte of the reason code supplied in R0. OS_File is discussed further in Chapter 13.

[&09] ArgsV: OS_Args Vector

ArgsV is used to direct all calls to OS_Args which can be used to read or write an open file's arguments, or return a value indicating the filing system type in use.

On Entry:
R0 = reason code
R1 = file handle, or 0
R2 = attribute to write, or not used

On Exit:
R0 = filing system number or preserved
R1 preserved
R2 = attribute that was read, or preserved

OS_Args is discussed further in Chapter 14.

[&0A] BGetV: OS_BGet Vector

All calls to OS_BGet are directed through this vector, the function of which is to read a single byte from an open file at the position of the sequential file pointer, which is then incremented. If the sequential file pointer value equals the end file extent pointer, the end of the file has been reached. Then the EOF-error-on-next-read flag is set, and the call returns with the carry flag set to signify the fact. If the call is issued and the EOF-error-on-next-read flag is set, then an End of file error is given. Otherwise, the sequential file pointer is incremented and the call returns with the carry flag clear. This mechanism allows one attempt to read past the end of the file before an error is generated.

An error is generated if the file handle is invalid; also if the file does not have read access.

On Entry:
R1 = file handle

On Exit:
R0 = byte read if C clear, undefined if C set
R1 preserved

OS_BGet is discussed further in Chapter 14.

[&0B] BPutV : OS_BPut Vector

All calls to OS_BPut are directed through this vector, the function of which is to write a single byte to an open file at the position of the sequential file pointer, which is then incremented, and the EOF-error-on-next-read flag is cleared. An error is generated if the file handle is invalid, locked against deletion, or does not have write access.

On Entry:
R0 = byte to be written
R1 = file handle

On Exit:
Registers preserved

OS_BPut is discussed further in Chapter 14.

[&0C] GBPBV: OS_GBPB Vector

All calls to OS_GBPB are directed through this vector. This call reads or writes a group of bytes from or to an open file. If an error should occur then the read or write is aborted and no bytes are read or written at all. The call can only be completely successful.If there is an error the entire call fails.

On Entry:
R0 = reason code

Other registers depend on reason code

On Exit:
R0 preserved
Other registers depend on reason code

OS_GBPB is discussed further in Chapter 14

[&0D] FindV: OS_Find Vector

All calls to OS_Find are directed through this vector. This call opens and closes files. When a file is opened a unique file handle (identifying value) is returned to you. This is needed when using calls to OS_Args, OS_BGet, OS_BPut and OS_GBPB. It is also ultimately needed again by OS_Find to close the file.

On Entry:
R0 = reason code
Other registers depend on reason code

On Exit:
Depends on reason code

OS_Find is discussed further in Chapter 14

[&0E] ReadLineV: OS_ReadLine Vector

All calls to OS_ReadLine routine are directed through this vector. OS_ReadLine reads a line of text from the current input stream using OS_ReadC at the same time echoing them to OS_WriteC (so you can see what is being typed).

On Entry:
R0 = Pointer to the text buffer (see note below)
R1 = Maximum size of line
R2 = Highest permissible ASCII character
R3 = Highest permissible ASCII character
R4 = Alternate ASCII character to be echoed

On Exit:
R1 = Length of buffer
C = 1 <ESCAPE> terminated entry

The top two bits in R0, b30 and b31 have significance. If b31 is clear then ASCII values outside the range specified in R2 and R3 are echoed (but not read). If b30 is set then the ASCII character is read but the ASCII value in R4 is echoed in its place. This is useful for password masking on screen.

If the number of characters exceeds the limit specified in R1 then they are echoed but excluded. The Delete key along with the other editing keys has the desired effect.

[&0F] FSCV: OS_FSControl Vector

All calls to OS_FSControl are directed through this vector which controls filing systems and the filing system manager.

On Entry:
R0 = reason code
Other registers depend on reason code

On Exit:
R0 preserved
Other registers depend on reason code

OS_FSControl is discussed further in Chapter 12

[&10] EventV: Event Vector

All calls to OS_GenerateEvent are directed through EventV. This vector is called whenever an event occurs. Events are provided to indicate that something specific has occurred, as defined by a reason code. User events may also be defined and acted upon. To reduce process time, events are nominally disabled. Like Interrupt events must be claimed and released using OS_Claim and OS_Release. The restrictions that apply to interrupts (IRQ and FIQ) apply to event handlers. OS_Byte 13 must be called first to disable an event before OS_Release can be finalised to release the EventV.

On Entry:
R0 = Number of Event
R1-R4 = Dependent on event

On Exit:
No information returned

Events are covered in Chapter 9.

[&14] INSV: Insert Character into Buffer Vector

InsV is called to place one or more bytes (ASCII characters) in a buffer. OS_Byte 138 and OS_Byte 153 direct their actions through this vector and it may also be used by OS_CallAVector. If the latter is used then interrupts must be disabled prior to the call. OS_Byte does this automatically.

On Entry:
R0 = ASCII code of character to be inserted
R1 = Buffer number

On Exit:
C = 1 is insertion failed

Bit 31 of R0 is used to define if the operation is for a byte (b31=0) or a block (b31=1). The above parameters define the entry and exit conditions of a byte operation. See the PRM 1-88 for the full block details.

[&15] REMV: Remove Character from Buffer Vector

RemV is called to remove one or more bytes from a buffer. OS_Byte 145 and OS_Byte 152 direct their actions through this vector. It may also be called using OS_CallAVector and it may also be used by OS_CallAVector. If the latter is used then interrupts must be disabled prior to the call. OS_Byte does this automatically.

On Entry:
R1 = ASCII code of character to be inserted
Overflow flag set = Buffer to be examined only
Overflow flag clear = character to be removed

On Exit:
R0 = Next character to be removed
R2 = Character actually removed from buffer
C= 1 if buffer was empty

This vector can also be used to remove a block of information; again the PRMs have the full detail.

[&16] CnpV: Count/Purge Vector

This vector is called by OS_Byte 15, OS_Byte 21 and OS_Byte 128. The default action is used to either count the number of entries in a buffer or to flush (clear) the contents of a buffer. It may also be called using OS_CallAVector and it may also be used by OS_CallAVector. If the latter is used then interrupts must be disabled prior to the call. OS_Byte does this automatically.

On Entry:
R1 = Buffer number
V = 1 Purge buffer
V = 0 Count characters in buffer
C = 1 then return number of buffer entries
C = 0 then return amount of space in buffer

On Exit:
R1 = Number of paces/entries if counting

[&17] UKVDU23V: Unknown VDU 23 Vector

This vector is called in response to an unknown VDU 23,n command where n is in the range 18-24 or 28-31. This vector is a useful way to add additional commands or enhancements to BBC BASIC. If the vector is not claimed then an unknown VDU 23 command is normally ignored. Up to nine parameters can be sent with the VDU 23,n command.

On Entry:
R0 = VDU 23 number

On Exit:
R1 = Pointer to the VDU queue

The nine parameters sent after the VDU 23 command are stored in the VDU queue. R1 points to the byte holding n, with any other parameters stored in memory after it, 0 being the default. If you claim this vector and intend to pass additional parameters your routine should extract them from the VDU queue and store them in workspace.

[&18] UKSWIV: Unknown SWI Vector

This vector is called in response to an unknown SWI command. By claiming this vector the user can add new SWIs to the system. This vector is called after SWI numbers are passed to modules for processing. If a module recognises a SWI as its own, then this vector will not be encountered However, the module mechanism only allows for the addition of 64 SWIs for an individual module — therefore this vector could also be claimed to allow additional SWIs to be claimed by a module. (The module mechanism for adding SWIs is much more efficient then UKSWIV and should always be used in preference to it.)

If the SWI is not recognised a 'No such SWI' error is issued by RISC OS.

On Entry:
R0-R8 = As defined by user
R11 = SWI number

On Exit:
No information returned

The process of adding SWIs via modules is discussed in Chapter 19.

[&19] UKVDU25V: Unknown PLOT Vector

VDU 25 is graphics plot command. This is normally followed by a byte-sized value defining the action to be taken. If the value supplied is not known then this vector is called. As with UKVDU23V this is a simple way of adding plot functions to the system.

UKPLOTV is called when a VDU 25,n (Plot) or a SWI OS_Plot n command is issued with an unknown value of n.

On Entry:
R0 = PLOT number

On Exit:
R0 = Preserved

[&1A] MouseV: Mouse Vector

All calls to OS_Mouse are directed through this vector. The default routine returns the position of the mouse and its button status. This vector could be used to add a joystick interface to the system, thus ensuring any application that used a mouse would work with a joystick.

On Entry:
No information passed

On Exit:
R0 = X position of mouse
R1 = Y Position of mouse
R2 = Button status

The mouse x and y positions are values between -32768 and 32767. This is assumed to be the screen area unless the graphics origin has been changed. The low bits or R0 have significance as follows:

b0 = 1 Right button down
b1 = 1 Middle button down
b2 = 1 Left button down

If there is no entry in the mouse buffer, the current status is returned.

[&1B] VDUXV: Special VDU Vector

This vector allows the user to create and maintain the VDU output stream and it is controlled by OS_Byte 3 (*FX 3). With b1=0 and b5=1 both VDU and VDUXV are enabled — however, all characters that would usually be sent to the VDU drivers are sent instead to the routine on the VDU extension vector.

This allows you to replace the VDU drivers, usually temporarily. For example, the Font Manager uses this facility. The character sent to VDUXV can be sent to the printer stream by setting the carry flag on return from the vector.

On Entry:
VDU Option requested

On Exit:
No information returned

Note that this only affects the display driver; other output streams such as the printer and *SPOOL file are called as usual, even when VDUXV is used for screen updating. OS_Plot can be used to write to the VDU directly rather than going through the stream system, and it is much faster.

[&1C] TickerV: 100Hz Pacemaker Vector

This vector is called every centisecond (100 times a second) by the OS. If claimed this vector can be used for timekeeping functions. There are no entry or exit conditions.

[&1D] UpCallV: Warning Vector

All calls to OS_UpCall are directed through this vector which is called when a filing system error occurs. The OS processes the call last of all, therefore it provides any applications that have claimed the vector with an opportunity to take corrective action if they identify the error. There are no entry or exit conditions.

9: Interrupts and Events

This chapter provides an overview of exception handling, the various modes of ARM operation and interrupts. This is a fundamental design aspect of the ARM chip and combined with good vector use, provides a clever and versatile way to customise the manner in which RISC OS works.

Modes of Operation

The ARM uses individual bits in it's Current Program Status Register (CPSR) as flags to denote certain conditions shown in Figure 9a.

31	30	29	28	27...8	7	6	5	4	3	2	1	0
N	Z	C	V		I	F	T		MODE			

Figure 9a. The Status Register configuration.

The Mode bits are the ones we are concerned with now are held in the low byte of the register in bits 0 to 7, and are located from 0 to 4 (five in total). The combined state of these bits determines which of the six operating modes the ARM operates in. Figure 9b summarises these modes. Any of them can be entered by changing the CPSR. Except for User Mode and Supervisor Mode all modes can be entered when an exception occurs.

User Mode is the one used by default by programs and applications. This is the environment we work in, and in truth, we as programmers never have to leave it, unless we are looking to be more adventurous and take over total control of the ARM chip itself, maybe write a Module or Utility which are run in Supervisor Mode.

Referring back again to Figure 9a, bits 7 and 6 are used for enabling and disabling IRQ and FIQ interrupts respectively. If a bit is set the associated interrupt is disabled. If the bit is clear then the interrupt is enabled. Bit 5 is the Thumb mode bit, but for all interrupts this bit is clear and the processor is operating in ARM State.

Mode	Description
FIQ	Entered when a high priority (fast) interrupt is raised
IRQ	Entered when a low priority (normal) interrupt is raised
Supervisor and Reset	Entered on reset and when a Software Interrupt instruction is executed
Abort	Used to handle memory access violations
Undef	Used to handle undefined instructions
User	Unprivileged mode under which most tasks run

Figure 9b. The ARM's six modes of operation.

Register Arrangements

Each of the modes has an associated set of registers available to it. The registers available to the programmer vary according to the current CPU operating mode and are illustrated in Figure 9c.

When executing in User Mode the full set of registers, R0 to R15, are available for use. However, when the CPU switches into another operation mode this all changes. Figure 9.c shows the register arrangement depending on the mode of operation. All modes have dedicated stack pointers and link registers associated with them. Whilst all modes except for User Mode have a new register, the Saved Program Status Register, available to them, only FIQ mode has several dedicated registers from R8-R12. Otherwise registers remain unchanged.

The SPSR is used to hold a copy of the User Mode Status Register when one of the other modes is entered. The User Mode does not have and it does not need an SPSR. An important point to note here is that the CPSR is only copied into the SPSR when an exception or interrupt is raised; it is not changed if you physically write to the CPSR to change mode.

The idea behind this banked register system is that each processor mode has some private registers which it can make use of without affecting the values of the normal registers, thus ensuring that the programmer does not have to worry about saving the contents of their own User Mode registers when an alternative mode is entered.

User	FIQ	IRQ	SVC	UND	ABT
R0					
R1					
R2					
R3					
R4					
R5					
R6					
R7					
R8	R8_fiq				
R9	R9_fiq				
R10	R10_fiq				
R11	R11_fiq				
R12	R12_fiq				
R13 SP	R13_fiq	R13_irq	R13_svc	R13_und	R13_abt
R14 LR	R14_fiq	R14_irq	R14_svc	R14_und	R14_abt
R15 PC					

CPSR					
	SPSR_fiq	SPSR_irq	SPSR_svc	SPSR_und	SPSR-abt

Figure 9c. The ARM programmer's model.

Figure 9d shows how the low byte of the CSPR looks when one of the modes is invoked. With the exception of User Mode, all modes are privileged. When power is first applied to the ARM chip it starts off in Supervisor Mode.

	I	F	T	MODE			
	7	6	5	4	3	2	1	0
Abort	1	1	0	1	0	1	1	1
FIQ	1	1	0	1	0	0	0	1
IRQ	1	uc	0	1	0	0	1	0
Supervisor	1	uc	0	1	0	0	1	1
System	1	1	0	1	1	1	1	1
Undefined	1	uc	0	1	1	0	1	1
User	0	0	0	1	0	0	0	0

Figure 9d. Bit settings for Mode changes in CPSR.

Interrupts can be enabled and disabled very easily in ARM -- using masking. Bits 7 and 6 enable or disable IRQ and FIQ interrupts respectively. If either bit is set then the associated interrupt is disabled and will not be processed. When an exception or interrupt occurs, the interrupt mask bit will normally be set by the chip. For a number of modes the FIQ bit remains unchanged (uc).

Exception Handling

An exception is a condition that requires the halting, temporary or otherwise, of whatever code is executing. A segment of code called an exception handler is called at this point. It identifies the condition and passes control to the appropriate route to handle the exception. When an exception causes a mode change the following sequence of events needs to happen:

- The address of next instruction is copied into the appropriate LR

- The CPSR is copied into the SPSR of the new mode

- The appropriate mode is set by modifying bits in the CPSR

- The next instruction is fetched from the vector table.

- When the exception has been dealt with, control can be returned to the code that was executing when the exception occurred. This is done as follows:

- The LR (minus an offset) is moved into the PC

- The SPSR is copied back into CPSR and by default this automatically changes the mode back to the previous one

If set, the interrupt disable flags are cleared clear the interrupt disable flags to re-enable interrupts.

Figure 9e. Swapping registers on at a privileged exception.

The illustration in Figure 9e shows what happens at a register level when a SWI call is made. The concept is the same for any of the privileged mode exceptions.

The SP and LR of the accessing Mode are switched in over the User Mode ones to allow the exception to be serviced, whilst preserving the status of the interrupted program. The return address is copied from the User Mode PC and stored in the LR of the privileged mode being invoked. R14_svc in the example above.

By preserving the status of the three User Mode registers shown, the status quo of program execution can be maintained when the SVC Mode call has been serviced simply by swapping them back. As stated earlier the CPSR is only saved into the requesting mode's SPSR when an exception occurs. It does not happen when the mode is changed by flipping the Mode bits.

MRS and MSR

There are two instructions which can be used directly to control the contents of the CPSR and SPSR and they can be used on the whole contents or at bit level.

The MRS instruction transfers the contents of either the CPSR or SPSR into a register. The MSR instruction works the opposite way and transfer the contents of a register into either the CSPR or SPSR. The instruction syntax is as follows:

```
MRS (<suffix>) <Operand1>, <CSPR|SPSR>

MSR (<suffix>) <CSPR|SPSR|Flags>, <Operand1>

MSR (<suffix>) <CSPR|SPSR|Flags>, #immediate
```

Some examples will make their operation clearer. The following three lines of code could be used to enable IRQ Mode:

```
MRS R1, CPSR
BIC R1, R1, #&80
MSR CPSR_C, R1
```

First the CPSR is copied into R1 where it is then masked with 10000000 to set the bit at b7 -- the position of the I flag. R1 is then written back to CPSR. Note the use of the _C as an addition to the CPSR operand. For the purpose of programming, the CPSR and SPSR are divided into four different sectors. These are illustrated below in Figure 9f.

Flags (F) [24:31]				Status (S) [16:25]				Extension (X) [8:15]				Control (C) [0:7]			
N	Z	C	V									I	F	T	Mode

Figure 9f. The CPSR/SPSR segments to control updating.

No	Event Cause	Vector Function
0	An output buffer is empty	R0=Event Number R1=Buffer number
1	Input buffer full	R0=Event Number R1=Buffer number R2=Character which couldn't be added
2	Character place in input buffer	R0=Event Number R1=Buffer number R2=ASCII value of new character
4	Vsync scans has reached bottom of screen	R0=Event Number
5	Interval timers crossed zero	R0=Event Number
6	ESCAPE detected	R0=Event Number
7	Serial device error	R0=Event Number R1=Serial device status R2=Character received
8	Event generated by Econet	R0=Event Number
9	Event generated by user	R0=Event Number
10	Mouse button changed	R0=Event Number R1=Mouse X co-ord R2=Mouse Y co-ord R3=Mouse button state R4=Lower 4 bytes of real time centi second value
11	Key pressed/released error	R0=Event Number R1=1 - if key pressed R1=0 - if key released R2=Key matrix number
12	Sound system reached start of a bar	R0=Event number **R1=2** **R2=0**
13	PC Emulator event	
14	Econet receive complete	
15	Econet transmit complete	
16	Econet OS remote procedure called	

Figure 9g. Operating System Events [Continued over]

No	Event Cause	Vector Function
17	MIDI system event	R0-Event number R1=Event reason code: 1-Byte received into previously empty buffer 2-Background MIDI error occurred 3-Scheduler queue about to empty, add more data
18	Reserved for developers	
19	0	
20	Reserved for developers	
21	Expansion event	R0=Event number R1-Reason code
22	Device overrun eve	R0=Event number R1=Device driver's handle R2=File handle R3=0
23	Reserved for external developers	
24	Driver received frame for Internet (DCI 2 only)	
25	Driver completed Internet transmission request (DCI 2 only)	
26	Copy of the Econet_Rx	
27	Copy of the Econet_Tx	
28	Portable Battery Management Unit event	R0=Event number R1=Battery Management Unit status flags

Figure 9g. Operating System Events.

By using the correct adjunct(s) on the appropriate instruction we can ensure that only the correct bits of the associated register are updated. The F, S, X and C suffixes may be used in like fashion.

To disable the IRQ, the following segment of code would suffice:

```
MRS R1, CPSR
ORR R1, R1, #&80
MSR CPSR_C, R1
```

The same commands can be used to effect a mode change thus:

```
MRS R0,CPSR            ;    copy the CPSR
BIC R0,R0,#&1F         ;    clear mode bits
ORR R0,R0,#new_mode    ;    select new mode
MSR CPSR,R0            ;    write CPSR back
```

In User Mode you can read all the bits of the CPSR but you can only update the condition of the field flag, ie, CPSR_F.

Interrupts When?

Interrupt Request Mode (IRQ) and Fast Interrupt Mode (FIQ) are called when an external device pages the ARM chip and demands its attention. For example, the keyboard generates an interrupt whenever a key is pressed. This is a signal to the CPU that the keyboard matrix should be scanned, and the ASCII value of the key entered into the keyboard buffer. If the ASCII value is 13 (<RETURN>), the keyboard buffer must be interpreted.

When the ARM chip receives an interrupt signal it saves what it is doing in line with what we have already discussed and then hands control to the calling interrupt routine by invoking the appropriate mode of operation. When the interrupt has finished its work (in the keyboard example this would be reading the key press and placing the ASCII code in the keyboard buffer) it hands control back to the ARM which restores all its previously saved information and returns to User Mode, picking up where it left off.

So here the interrupt is a function of the ARM chip itself, but how it is dealt with and what happens thereafter is a feature of the software handling it -- RISC OS in this case.

Without an effective interrupt system, RISC OS would have to spend a lot of its time checking all attached components just to see if anything has happened, taking up time and resources. Think of all the connections to your Raspberry Pi keyboard, mouse, USB ports, disk drives... They all require servicing, and often.

Fast Interrupts (FIQs) are deemed to be ones that have the highest priority and are the ones that must be serviced first. For example, any disk drive connected, otherwise data might be lost. The only time a FIQ is not serviced first is when another FIQ is in the process of being serviced. The Interrupt Request (IRQ) line is deemed to be of lower priority where a slight delay will not create any problems.

The need for speed in processing an FIQ interrupt is signified by its position in the hardware vector table. It is the last in the list. This is because it actually begins executing right at that point -- the other vectors all perform other branch instructions further into the system software. The FIQ code resides in the space between the vector at &1C and address &FC so as not to corrupt the RISC OS workspace beyond &FC. It is then the job of the appropriate interrupt coding to identify which device caused the interrupt and process it accordingly and as quickly as possible.

Your Interrupt Decisions

When dealing with interrupts you need to make the decision about other interrupts. For example what happens if a new interrupt occurs whilst you are handling an existing interrupt? The easiest method is to invoke what is called a non-nested interrupt handling scheme. In this all interrupts are disabled until control is handled back to the interrupted task, The downside of this is that only one interrupt can be serviced at a time, and if a succession of interrupts are occurring you may lose some of the requests. This could have consequences.

A nested interrupt scheme allows more than one interrupt to be handled at a time and in this case you would look to re-enable interrupts before fully servicing the current interrupt. This is more complex but it solves the problems that can occur with interrupt latency, which is the interval of time from an external interrupt signal being raised to the first fetch of an instruction of the raised interrupt signal.

For an FIQ, the IRQs are disabled as the FIQ is deemed critical in relation.

In all cases the implementation of a stack for interrupt handling (interrupt stack) should be considered essential for context switching between the modes and preserving information. If several interrupts occur at the same time the details need to be stored somewhere for processing as the sequence is dealt with.

Returning From Interrupts

When the interrupt service routine has been performed, the operating system must return to the original program which was interrupted by the FIQ or IRQ. This is done by using the following instruction:

```
SUBS R15, R14, #4
```

This restores the program counter so that the interrupted program can be resumed from exactly the point at which it was suspended. The 'subtract 4' calculation is required to correct for the effects of pipelining. Providing that the interrupt handling routine has not corrupted any shared registers or workspace, the program will continue executing as if the interrupt had never happened. On the Raspberry Pi, interrupts are occurring and being serviced all the time without the user even realising it.

Writing Interrupt Routines

Usually, you will not need to create interrupt service routines of your own because the OS provides a well-defined system for doing so.

If you intend to write direct interrupt handling routines, you should observe the following rule to avoid potential disasters:

- Do not re-enable interrupts in the handling routine. If this is done, a second IRQ/FIQ could interrupt the processor before it has finished handling the first. Sometimes this may be permissible, but you could be walking on thin ice if you do it. Be very aware!

- The interrupt routine must be written as economically as possible. Processing the interrupt at maximum speed should be a major goal. If it keeps interrupts disabled for too long, then the normal Raspberry Pi background activities will grind to a halt. The keyboard will lock, various software clocks will lose time, and the mouse pointer will freeze.

- All shared processor registers should be preserved. They should contain the same values on exit from the interrupt routine as they did on entry to the interrupt. This is absolutely vital if the interrupted task is to be resumed correctly.

- The interrupt handling routine should limit the calling OS routines - see below for details.

SWI Calls during Interrupts

Many interrupt or event driven routines (specifically IRQ ones) may need to make use of some SWI routines. Great care must be taken to use this feature carefully. It is possible that one of these routines would be only half executed when it is interrupted by IRQ/FIQ. If re-entered in the interrupt routine, workspace could be disturbed, causing the routine to corrupt when resumed. Only operating system routines which do not suffer from this problem (re-entrant routines) should be used in interrupt handling. (Refer to the PRMs to find out if a SWI is re-entrant or to the developer's notes if it is post-PRMs.)

When a SWI instruction is used it is implicit that the contents of R14_SVC are overwritten by a new value. This can create a problem. When in User Mode, this corruption of R14_SVC does not arise. If we are operating in SVC Mode we can guard against the problem by pushing the Program Counter onto the stack. Unfortunately processing of interrupts or events takes place in IRQ or FIQ mode, so one or the other is going to get corrupted by being overwritten.

To get around this it is necessary to switch from IRQ or FIQ Mode into SVC Mode, preserve R14_SVC, execute the SWIs, restore R14_SVC and then return to the interrupt processor mode. Care also needs to be taken to ensure that the effects of processor pipelining are catered for, allowing the processor to fill-up. This can be done without any effect with:

```
MOV R0,R0
```

This instruction has no implication other than allowing the pipeline to sync.

Because of the requirement for maximum speed when processing FIQ interrupts, the calling of SWIs should be avoided at these times as it rather defeats their purpose of being quick!

Enabling and Disabling Interrupts

It is possible to disable and enable prompts via an OS call using the following SWIs:

```
SWI "OS_IntOff"
SWI "OS_IntOn"
```

They both function as-is and do not require any entry parameters; nor do they pass any parameters back. They simply act as a switch. In practice the use of either of these SWIs should be avoided unless they are used for a very specific purpose.

Program 8a demonstrates the use of the calls and the effect on the system clock which is slowed by a factor of two.

Program 9a. Disabling interrupts.

```
10   REM >Prog9a
20   REM Disabling Interrupts
30   REM RPi RISC OS Programming
40   :
50   SYS "OS_IntOff"
```

```
 60   T%=TIME
 70   FOR x= 1 TO 100000
 80   REM  Just do nothing
 90   NEXT
100   :
110   SYS "OS_IntOn"
120   PRINT "That took: ";(TIME-T%)/100;" seconds."
```

The Primary Interrupt Vector

It is very unlikely that you will need to intercept the IRQ interrupt system at a lower level than that provided by the normal Operating System vector. However, if it is vital that your routine is called before any other when an interrupt occurs, then the primary interrupt vector can be intercepted.

This vector is a kind of intermediary between the hardware interrupt vectors and the Operating System. It is located in memory at address &100. When an IRQ interrupt occurs the OS branches to a routine the address of which is stored at location &100.

Normally, the default routine jumped to from this vector is the Operating System's first level interrupt handler (FLIH). This is responsible for determining the source of the interrupt and for calling an appropriate handling routine in the OS.

If users place the address of their own code at location &100, then whenever an IRQ interrupt occurs that code will be executed instead of the default routine.

It is obviously a drastic action to try to replace the entire OS interrupt handling routine. For this reason, most intercept code will perform its function and then jump on to the default routine. Therefore it will have to save the default address which was stored at location &100 when it was initialised.

Events

Events are essentially sanitised versions of interrupts. They are used to inform the user whenever RISC OS performs or detects that some significant task has taken place. For example, when a key is pressed, a buffer becomes empty or a timer expires.

The user may specify that they are interested in a particular event and wish to be advised each time that event has taken place. RISC OS will then inform the user when the event occurs by jumping via the event vector to a section of code supplied by the user. A full list of the events recognised by the system is given in Figure 9g.

Many events are produced in response to RISC OS detecting an interrupt from the hardware. They allow the user to take action when these significant happenings occur, without having to intercept the interrupt system and deal with the hardware itself.

Using An Event

In order to make use of an event, we must first intercept the event vector (&10) by using SWI "OS_Claim". The routine will now be called when an event occurs. To allow it to differentiate between events, the routine is entered with the event identifying number in R0. Other parameters are passed in various registers as described above. To enable an event so that when it occurs the event vector is called, we use the following *FX command.

```
*FX 14,<n>
```

where n is the number of the event which we want to enable. Similarly to disable an event again, use:

```
*FX 13,<n>
```

The OS_Byte SWI could be used. For example, to enable event number four we could use the following code:

```
MOV R0,#14    \ Using OSBYTE 14
MOV R1,#4     \ Event number 4
SWI OS_Byte   \ Call OSBYTE
```

On exit from either OS_Byte, R1 indicates the previous condition of the event in the following way:

R1 = 0 Event was previously disabled
R1 > 0 Event was previously enabled

Most events are triggered by RISC OS when it detects an interrupt. The same rules concerning the writing of interrupt handling routines also apply to writing event handlers.

To return after an event routine is completed, we simply use:

```
MOV PC,LR
```

This is possible as the OS will have set up a return address in R14 for use. It will then deal with the more complex problem of returning to the interrupted code. Note that, like interrupt routines, event handlers must preserve R14_SVC before using a SWI instruction, as illustrated earlier.

Because RISC OS does not keep track of who or what is enabling a particular event, it keeps a count of how many requests have been made to enable it. At each disable event request it decrements the count, so while the count remains above zero it keeps the event enabled. This simple but effective method ensures that the system always generates the event if at least one task requires it. On reset, the event counters are set to zero, although some modules may need an event and hence increment the appropriate event counter.

As with interrupts, the routine dealing with events must do so very quickly, so that it can continue with the previous task as quickly as possible. If a routine cannot deal with an event quickly, it should re-enable interrupts (as they are always disabled when entering a routine), but it must then be disabled before passing on or intercepting the call and it must ensure that the processing of one event is complete before starting to process another. The routine is always entered in a non-user processor mode.

Routines that handle events must only call the error-returning SWI calls. That is, SWI calls that have their X bit set.

OS_GenerateEvent [SWI &22]

Users can generate their own event by using the OS_GenerateEvent SWI.

This event happens in SVC Mode and not IRQ Mode.

On Entry:
R0 = Number of event to be generated
R1 (and others) = hold parameters as required

On Exit:
All registers preserved

Event number 9 has been specifically reserved as a User Event. R1, R2, R3 etc can contain event parameters to pass to the event handling routine through the event vector. The event vector will only be called if the event number given in R0 has previously been enabled using OS_Byte 14. This is because Events are disabled by default, which prevents RISC OS from generating them. and in turn, this is because there is a significant processor overhead involved in dealing with them.

If you intend to release software that uses Events then you should contact RISC OS Open to have an event number allocated officially for your purposes.

10 : The Filing System

The filing system is arguably the most used function of any computer. This is certainly the case under RISC OS because everything we do with it generally calls filing into action. Under RISC OS even peripheral devices such as the printer are treated as filing systems.

Filing systems are the parts of the Operating System which are responsible for the storage and retrieval of large amounts of information collectively known as files. Without their effective organisation and manipulation use of the Raspberry Pi would fall apart. From the moment power is applied to the Raspberry Pi and RISC OS starts to boot into life the filing system is active as it loads everything it needs from the SD Card.

The Raspberry Pi can deal with a variety of storage mediums. Each needs to be dealt with differently as they are all physically implemented differently, so each different storage medium has its own filing system to deal with the housekeeping and hardware control necessary for the device concerned. Because many of the operations that the filing systems perform are common to all devices, RISC OS Pi divides the management of files into two sections: a generic part, concerned with all filing systems, and a specific part which deals with a specific kind of device.

All this stems from two modules — FileSwitch and FileCore. These two modules provide most of the functionality required for a RISC OS filing system. The key to this is that they are both device-independent and are generic in operation. Hardware specifics are added by modules supplied for the appropriately named filing system. The data format of a filing system is not defined by the FileSwitch module — it only specifies what the user interface must look like.

The display of files and directories (folders) on the desktop, and also the functionality to interact with them is provided by The Filer module. This uses a standard set of calls to do so and hence will work with any filing system — indeed it is used for all filing systems. Each filing system Filer provides an icon on the icon bar. Filing system specific filers can also provide other operations which are not sufficiently generic to be provided by the Filer. (Chapter 15 FileCore - has more detail on this.)

This approach has many advantages, not least that it keeps the command syntax consistent, and further it reduces the amount of software required to implement a new filing system. These filing system components are implemented as modules, and you would be surprised how many there are on RISC OS Pi. You will find that there is one FileSwitch module that services all generic filing system requirements and then individually personalised FileCore modules for each of the main filing systems. However, each implements the same subset of commands. In summary FileCore concerns the structure of data on a disc, and FileCore filing systems implement the disc access itself.

In addition the individual filing system modules often supply addition controls specific to their own requirements. We'll examine each of these in the next few chapters.

Filing Systems

As you may have gathered, there are a large number of filing systems in place for use with RISC OS on the Raspberry Pi. Some of these are well established while some are relatively new and in continual development. No doubt others will become available. For this reason it is important to ensure that you keep your software up-to-date and that you have the latest distribution available. It is not possible to cover all filing systems here, so we will concentrate on the main systems in use on the Raspberry Pi. The fundamentals will remain the same while the variations will be particular to the hardware and delivery mechanisms.

The filing systems which are most intensively used on RISC OS Pi are the SD Filing System (SDFS) and the FAT32 Filing System (FAT32FS). These two filing systems deal with the SD Card and with any flash drives or external drives that you might plug into the USB ports. (FileCore formatted devices (such as a SD Card in a USB reader will show as a SCSI device.)We'll be looking at these in much more detail in due course. Others that you might come across include the ShareFS, the Network Filing System (NFS), DOS Filing System (DOSFS) and the Advanced Disk Filing System (ADFS). There is also CDFS which you'll use if you come into contact with a CD drive. (Use PackMan to download any additional modules that you might require.) All of these filing systems operate in fundamentally the same way, but each will have its own specific subset of commands provided by its relevant FileSwitch Module.

RISC OS also provides a RAM Filing System (RAMFS) — a RAM disk — and this is useful for quick local storage. The RAM disk itself will survive power cycles, but the contents will not. Given that USB storage is so cheap, to avoid losing your files and to keep your sanity I would advise against using the RAM Disk!

As indicated above RISC OS also provides some device filing systems which allow the keyboard, screen and printer to be treated as filing systems. This mechanism makes input/output more consistent across all of the standard peripherals. We shall examine these peripheral devices in more detail later in this chapter.

The rest of this chapter deals with the fundamentals of the filing system and in particular how files are organised and referenced, how the information is kept with files and what software tools are available to make file access quicker and more seamless. This information will provide you with the ability to access and work on a file located on or across any filing system.

Naming Conventions

Most filing systems consider data as an arbitrary collection of bytes referred to by name; this is the computer definition of a file. Every file has a name — the filename, — which uniquely identifies it within the current area of work. Filing systems do not themselves make any distinction between the types of data stored in a file; it is up to the Operating System, the user and the application to determine whether the data in a given file is in a suitable format.

The naming of files must obey certain rules in order to allow filing systems to operate in a consistent way. In particular, filenames should ideally be composed exclusively of letters, digits or underline symbols. Filenames should not contain any punctuation symbols because most of these are reserved and have special meaning under RISC OS.

Earlier versions of RISC OS only supported filenames with a length of up to ten characters. However, this restriction has now been removed, although the storage medium used must support long filenames for this to work. FileSwitch makes no distinction between upper and lower case filenames, so a file named 'Letter' is the same as 'letter' or 'LETTER'.

The usual limiting factor for filenames is the 256 byte length of a Wimp message (typically when displayed in a message box in a window on the Desktop). When the message headers are allowed for, it leaves 236 bytes for the complete path. The actual filename length limit will then depend upon how deep it is buried in the directory structure.

The punctuation symbols shown below have special meanings that prevent them from being used in filenames; if you use them by mistake you can expect error messages to result:

```
- * # @ $ & \ ^ %
```

Each file and directory also has a number of attributes that determine what can and cannot be done with the file or directory. For example, whether it can be deleted or locked from deletion. These attributes can be set by the user and changed as and when required using the *ACCESS command. This and other FileSwitch commands are detailed in the next chapter.

Directories

Most filing systems provide a means of grouping files together in groups known as directories (sometimes called folders). It is entirely up to the user how directories are used, but it is common to group related files in the same directory to make them easier to find. An important restriction is that all the filenames within a given directory must be unique otherwise it would be impossible to be sure which file was being referred to. However, directories may contain other directories, called sub-directories, which in turn may contain sub-sub-directories (and so on), leading to a hierarchical arrangement of nested directories.

Perhaps perversely (from an arborist's point of view) the top of a directory hierarchy is known as the root and is represented in RISC OS filing systems by the dollar symbol $. Each disc device, whether it is floppy or hard, has a root whose real directory name is the name of the disc. Thus the disc name (preceded by a colon :) can usually be used interchangeably with the dollar symbol to refer to the root directory.

At any given time in file operations one of the directories in the hierarchy will be in use; this is known as the Currently Selected Directory (CSD) and is represented by the ampersand symbol @. If you execute:

```
*CAT
```

then you will produce a catalogue of the directories and files in the CSD.

Files within the CSD may be referred to by their name alone; files in other directories must be referred to by a name sequence which uniquely identifies them and is known as their pathname.

The pathname is formed by stringing together the appropriate sequence of directory names connected by full stops. Thus, a file called 'Prog10' in directory 'Programs', which is itself located in the directory called 'Book' which is in turn a sub-directory of the root has the full pathname:

```
$.Book.Programs.Prog10
```

The more dots in a filename, the deeper in the directory structure you are going. The rightmost item in the list is always the filename.

The other reserved punctuation symbols noted earlier have special meanings when used in pathnames. These are listed in Figure 10a.

Symbol	Function
. (dot)	A dot joins directory/file names in a pathname, eg: Programs.Prog10
: (colon)	Precedes a disc name (equivalent to $), eg: :MyDisc.Book (Note that the colon is also used to follow a filing system name; see later.)
$	Root directory of the disc, eg, $.Books
&	User Root Directory (URD)
@	Currently Selected Directory (CSD)
A	Parent directory
%	Currently Selected Library (CSL)
\	Previously Selected Directory (PSD)

Figure 10a. Punctuation and its meaning, reserved for use in pathnames.

The URD and CSL have not been mentioned before, but are discussed later in this chapter. The parent directory is defined as the directory which contains the directory so far specified in a pathname. The use of the caret symbol ^ is intended to convey movement up the hierarchy tree, with the root imagined as being at the top.

Files on Other Filing Systems

A useful and practical extension to pathnames allows them to specify that a file is to be found on a particular filing system — this can be other filing systems to the currently selected one. Thus pathname strings can be composed for any file on any filing system, but without the burden of needing to change filing systems back and forth manually.

A filing system name is introduced by following it with a colon, for example:

```
SDFS:$.Programs.Prog10
```

This refers to the file 'Prog10' in the directory 'Programs', which is a sub-directory of the root of the currently-selected network fileserver. Similarly:

```
FAT32FS:USB1.Book.Programs.Prog07
```

This refers to the file 'Prog07' which is in the sub-directory 'Book.Programs'. on the disc entitled 'USB1' which is mounted on the FAT32 Filing System. Note that here two colons are required, one to follow the filing system name and the other to precede the disc name.

Device Filing Systems

Another very useful aspect of filing system naming is that the keyboard, display and printer may be treated as filing systems in themselves for the purpose of byte-oriented operations. But obviously it is not sensible to try to load or save programs to the device filing systems!

Six different device filing systems are currently supported (seven if we include null:). They are listed in Figure 10b below along with a brief note on their functionality:

Device Name	Functions Available
kbd:	Input only, returned by OS_ReadLine
rawkbd:	Input only, returned by OS_ReadC
vdu:	Output only, processed by GS_Read then sent to OS_WriteC
rawvdu:	Output only, issued through OS_WriteC
printer:	Output only, issued direct to current printer
null:	None
Input/Output:	Input returns End Of File, Output is discarded

Figure 10b. Device filing systems.

The raw forms of the keyboard and VDU devices deal with characters exactly as they are encountered, whilst the refined forms apply the specified pre-processing (mainly to cater for <ESCAPE> sequences using the vertical bar |) before passing the data on. Note that the way to generate an End Of File (EOF) condition on the keyboard is to type <CTRL-D> and press <RETURN>. It is also possible to access these options in many cases using a filing system style command line:

```
Devices:$.FastParallel
```

Load and Execute Addresses

As well as having a name, every file has two 32-bit fields associated with it which supply RISC OS additional information about the file. These are set when the file is first created, and can convey two possible sets of information:

- Load and Execution Addresses
- Filetype and Date Stamps

If the file is a machine code program then its load and execution address are encoded in the fields. These are where the file should be loaded into the RISC OS memory map and the address where execution of the file should begin from, which may be different from the load address.

If you use the *LOAD command to load a file into memory, the load address associated with the file is used by default. It is possible to override this by supplying a different load address as part of the *LOAD command, though clearly this requires the file to be relocatable if it is a piece of machine-code.

The *RUN<filename> command (and its synonyms *<filename> and /<filename>) allow machine code programs to be loaded and executed in one operation — in this case the file is loaded at its load address and then executed starting from its execute address.

A small caveat here: load and execution addresses should not be relied upon when using more modern filing systems such as FAT32 as they are rarely used by them and are often corrupted.

Date Stamping

If the top twelve bits (ie first three digits) of the load address are set, e.g. to &FFF, the file is treated in a special way. Such an address is outside the addressing range for filing systems so RISC OS uses this as a flag for storing filetype information, allowing a number of useful automatic features to be provided including a date and time stamp, initially indicating precisely when the file was created. Clearly it is very useful to have this information because it allows us to keep track of the age of files and programs. Furthermore, specifying the file's type allows us to let RISC OS decide how to deal with a file when we issue non-specific commands such as *<filename>.

The format of the file type, date and time information stored in the load and execute address fields is as follows:

```
Load Address field:      FFFtttdd
Execute Address field:   dddddddd
```

Here, the filetype information is represented by the three hexadecimal digits shown as 'ttt', and the date and time by the ten hexadecimal digits 'dddddddddd'. When a file is created or has its date stamp updated, the absolute time is stamped onto the file in the form of the number of centiseconds (hundredths of a second) since 00:00:00 on the 1st January 1900. This is usually a fairly large number! Whilst such accuracy is not generally required, it is readily available by accessing a real-time clock (normally the Web in case of the Raspberry Pi) and internal counters.

The command *STAMP may be used to update the date and time stamp on a given file, and this is discussed later in this chapter.

Command Files

A command file is a file whose contents are a sequence of commands to be executed as if they had been typed at the keyboard. You can use a variety of methods to create a command file. Using Edit is probably the easiest, especially if the Edit application is already loaded and can be activated from the desktop. See the RISC OS Applications Guide for details on using Edit.

Another way of creating a command file is to use the *BUILD command. If you type

```
*BUILD keyfile
```

everything subsequently typed from the keyboard is sent directly to the file called 'keyfile'. If there is a file named 'keyfile' already, it is deleted when the *BUILD command is given. Press Return at the end of each line. When you finish entering the commands, press <ESCAPE> to end keyboard input to keyfile.

Executing a command file

There are two main ways of executing a command file. If the file contains a sequence of commands to a language, such as BASIC, then you should *EXEC it, with:

```
*EXEC <filename>
```

This causes the contents of the named file to be taken as input, exactly as if it had been typed in. You can make the command even shorter by setting the filetype of install to COMMAND using the command:

```
*SETTYPE <filename> COMMAND
```

This converts the file into an executable file. Once you have done this, you can *EXEC the file just by giving its name as a command, for example:

```
*<filename>
```

or by double-clicking on it.

The other way in which a command file can be executed is to *OBEY it. If you do this, each line in the file is executed as a * command. It is then passed to the operating system command line interpreter only; and not to BASIC. In this case you do not see the lines that are being executed on the screen, and *OBEY allows parameter substitution, whereas *EXEC does not.

File Types

RISC OS uses a file's filetype to decide what action to take when it is requested to *RUN a file. Since a command of the form *<filename> is a synonym for *RUN, we can be lazy and type only the name of a file to save time. It then looks up the filetype and decides what to do.

RISC OS aliases may be defined for each possible filetype — they allow the two cases of *LOADing and *RUNning the file to be determined separately. Each filetype may have two such aliases:

```
Run$Type_ttt    for *RUN, (and other synonyms)
Load$Type_ttt   for *LOAD
```

Whenever either of these actions is applied to a file, RISC OS checks for a defined alias and uses it if possible. For example, the aliases for files whose type is 'BASIC program' (type &FFB) are:

```
Load$Type_FFB BASIC -Load %*0
Run$Type_FFB BASIC -Quit %*0
```

These file types cause the BASIC interpreter to kick in and to be entered with the appropriate options set and the remainder of the command line passed on with %*0.

The filetype aliases may be set using the *SET command as is usual for RISC OS variables, so where we have files for our own software (filetype &XYZ) we can establish them with:

```
*SET Load$Type_XYZ MyProgram %0
*SET Run$Type_XYZ MyProgram %0
```

You can use *SHOW to display the current settings for file types. Figure 10c below shows the original range of filetype allocation sets denoted by Acorn.

Type Range	Allocated for:
&000-&0FF	Personal usage (non-distributed)
&100-&3FF	Non-commercial distributed software
&400-&9FF	Commercial Software
&A00-&AFF	Acornsoft and other commercial software
&B00-&DFF	Commercial software
&E00-&FFF	Acorn {RISC OS]

Figure 10c. File Type allocation ranges.

The minimum requirement for a valid allocation is that double-clicking the file loads an application specified by the assigned RunType and does something meaningful with it. Use existing file formats (not just within the Acorn world), and make data interchange as painless as possible. If you plan to write software for general distribution you should get an allocated filetype via RISC OS Open so as to avoid clashes. The !Typeinfo website keeps an unofficial database of file types and it is worth having a look at it to see what is available. You may be surprised!

Libraries and Search Paths

When a command is passed to the CLI, RISC OS first establishes whether the command is supported by any of the modules installed. If not, and it is not defined via an alias, it looks to find a file of the same name in the CSD and attempts to execute it. Clearly, if all our extensions to the Operating System had to be provided in one directory, the hierarchical directory system would be wasted. In order that we may enter * commands to run files which are not in the CSD, we need to be able to indicate where else the filing system should search. This is achieved through the use of libraries. A second directory, known as the Currently Selected Library (or CSL), may be nominated as the place for the filing system to search when it encounters an unrecognised command.

The CSL is represented by the percent character % in pathnames, and may be set using the *LIB command, which is followed by the pathname of the chosen library directory. Thus, one or more directories (though only one at a time) can be used to keep a library of command files. To allow us to override this, whenever a directory name is included explicitly in the command then other searches do not take place.

RISC OS takes this idea a stage further and provides system variables which allow multiple search paths to be defined. Two different classes of search path are available; one for commands, analogous to the library system described above, and one for other read functions such as loading or opening files for input. The two system variables and their functions to establish these search paths are:

```
Run$Path  for execute operations
File$Path for read operations
```

These may be set using *SET in the usual way. Each may contain a sequence of directory pathnames, separated by commas and terminated by a full stop. The default settings for these variables are:

Run$Path ,%.

File$Path

This indicates that command files for execution are searched for first in the CSD, then in the CSL and that files to be read are only searched for in the CSD. What makes this facility particularly useful is that since pathnames may contain filing system names, the path strings can specify libraries on one or several different filing systems. Obviously, the amount of time spent dealing with the command increases as the number of items in the path strings increases, particularly where multiple filing systems are in use, but usually the impact of this is scarcely noticeable to the user. Neat!

Filing system names can be added to the search path of either variable by using the *Set command. An example of two different paths to search on the network, when loading a file is provided below.

**   *Set File$Path ,%.,Net:Software.,Net:Modules.,Net:Lib*.**

This would result in the FileSwitch module looking in the following paths for a given file:

**   @.file, %.file, Net:Software.file and Net:Modules.file and Net:Lib*.file**

Other system variables can be used by an application to set up a list of paths to search. In addition, some SWIs can also allow for alternative path strings to be used to search for a file, or to perform the action without any form of look up. To assign an alternative path variable, use the *Set command:

**   *Set Programs$Path SDFS:$.Programs.,net:$.Programs.**

The pseudo filing system could then be accessed as Programs:

11: FileSwitch Commands

The FileSwitch is a RISC OS module which makes *commands and SWIs available for general filing system control. By separating out those filing system functions which are common to all filing systems, the FileSwitch ensures the consistency of the user interface and makes the implementation of new filing systems easier by reducing the number of functions that need to be supported.

All FileSwitch commands are non-filing system specific, and they include commands for file and directory creation, deletion, cataloguing, examination, copying and so forth. Most of the FileSwitch OS_CLI commands have one or more equivalent SWIs which are used to call the selected filing system as appropriate.

The following pages cover each of the FileSwitch commands in some detail. *HELP will provide an on-line summary. In describing the syntax of these commands the word 'object' is used to mean either a file or a directory.

*Access

Syntax: *ACCESS <object name> {L}{R}{W}{/R}{/W}{/RW}

The *ACCESS command allows the user to control the access attributes of a file. It takes the name of a file (optionally including wildcards) — and a string of attribute symbols. These attributes are applied to the object, replacing those that were previously present.

The attributes available are:

L   This attribute locks the object, preventing it from being deleted, written to or overwritten except by specifically overriding the lock. This is primarily to prevent accidental damage to files. Of course, the locked bit doesn't prevent the contents of directories being altered — only the deletion of the directory itself.

W   This attribute allows the file to be written to. A file cannot be assigned a W and L attribute at the same time. This attribute has no relevance for directories.

R   Denotes that the file may be read. This attribute has no relevance for directories.

The /R, /W and /RW options are for use on public filing systems such as NetFS.

Example:

*ACCESS MyProgram L

This locks and prevents reading and writing to 'MyProgram'. To unlock and make the file available for reading and writing:

*ACCESS MyProgram WR

To get information about a file's attributes use *FILEINFO.

*Back

Syntax: *BACK

This command swaps the user back to any previously selected directory. If it is used again it restores the original directory. Thus *BACK is an easy way of toggling between two directories. However, unfortunately the command does not work on all filing systems.

*Build

Syntax: *BUILD <filename>

*BUILD creates the named file (or, if it already exists and its attributes permit, overwrites it.). It writes to the file all text entered from the keyboard. Its most common use is for the creation of *EXEC files (see below). *BUILD is terminated by an <ESCAPE> condition (that is usually, but not necessarily, by pressing the <ESCAPE> key). The default filetype used by *BUILD is &FFD (Data), which must be changed to &FFE using *SETTYPE (see later) if the file is to be *EXECed automatically.

Example:

*BUILD !BootFile

Creates and allows text to be entered into !BootFile.

*Cat

Syntax: *CAT {<directory>}

The *CAT command catalogues (lists the contents of) the specified directory. If no directory pathname is given, the CSD is catalogued.

Examples:

*CAT

```
*CAT $.Programs
*CAT -FAT32FS-
```

These catalogue the CSD, the directory $.Programs and the root directory of a connected device using the FAT32FS.

*Cdir

Syntax: *CDIR <directory> {<maximum size>}

Creates a new empty directory with the specified pathname and sets its attributes to the default of 'DL'. The NetFS accepts the optional maximum size parameter and ensures that the directory will be able to contain the specified number of objects. SDFS takes no notice of this parameter.

Example:

```
*CDIR NewDir
```

This creates a new directory 'NewDir' in the CSD.

*Copy

Syntax: *COPY <source> <destination> {<options>}

This is a general-purpose file duplication command. It requires at least two parameters: a source specification and a destination specification (both of which may contain wildcards) and then copies all the specified objects from the source to the destination. Directory names may be used in both source and destination specifications, but are interpreted differently. When a wildcard is used in a source directory name, only the first match is used; when used in filenames a wildcard must appear in both source and destination, in which case the wildcard field is preserved. For example:

```
*COPY $.Book.* FAT32FS: Backup.Book.*
```

Here all the files in $.Book on the current filing system are copied into the Fat32FS Backup.Book, preserving the names of the files as the process takes place. However, the following:

```
*COPY *.Program12  NewProg
```

will only copy the file called 'Program12' from the first sub-directory of the CSD to the file 'NewProg'.

Sym	Function	Meaning
A	Access	Force destination access to same source.
C	Confirm	The user is asked to confirm that each file is to be copied.
D	Delete	Files are deleted after they have been copied.
F	Force	Destination files are overwritten if they already exist.
L	Look	Destination is examined before the source file is loaded.
N	New	Copy only if the source file is more recent than the destination file.
P	Prompt	The user is prompted for disc changes when copying between discs. (This is for use with single disc drives.)
Q	Quick	Allows application memory to be used during copying, thus speeding up lengthy copies considerably. However, programs in the application space will be destroyed, and the user will be returned to the OS Supervisor on completion of the command
R	Recurse	Causes sub-directories to be copied as well, saving time when an entire directory structure needs copying.
S	Stamp	Restamp the destination file(s) after copying
T	sTructure	Copy only the directory structure and not the files within.
V	Verbose	Displays information about each file copied.

Figure 11a. *COPY options and their meaning.

A range of options may be appended to the *COPY command, or if omitted the settings of the RISC OS System variable <Copy$Options> contains the default settings of these options. The options available are listed in Figure 11a.

By default the <Copy$Options> settings are as follows:

```
A C ~D ~F ~L ~N ~P ~Q ~R ~S ~T V
```

151

The ~ (tilde) character signifies that the option is off and it may be used in the command line as part of the definitions:

```
*COPY Here There ~RV
```

Any attribute not specified after the command assumes the state specified in the default Copy$Options variable. Specifying an option causes the corresponding action to be selected. Specifying an option prefixed by 'a' causes the option to be de-selected and the corresponding action is not taken.

In the above example, we specify that a recursive copy (R) is not to take place but that we want to force verbose mode (V) to be selected. The other options revert to their default settings.

*Count

Syntax: *COUNT <file> {<options>}

*COUNT totals the size of the file(s) that match the specification (which may contain wildcards) and displays the results rounded to the nearest 1 kB. It also responds to the C, R and V options in the same way as *COPY, allowing multiple directories to be sized and the files involved to be displayed.

Example:

```
*COUNT $
```

This finds the total size of all files in the CSD, whereas:

```
*COUNT $ R
```

finds the total size of all files on a disc, and:

```
*COUNT $ RC
```

This will prompt you at each sub-directory to confirm that you want it included in the count.

*Create

Syntax: *CREATE <filename> {<size> {<execute addr>
{<load addr>}}}

This command reserves space for a file without actually writing any data into it. The optional size parameter sets the number of bytes reserved, zero being used by default (a file of zero length). The execute and load addresses may be set, the load address defaulting to zero if not supplied. Where both addresses are omitted, the filetype is set to &FFD (Data). Example:

```
* CREATE BigFile 20000
```

Here, a new file 'BigFile' 128k long is created.

*Delete

Syntax: *DELETE <objectname>

The *DELETE command deletes the named object from the catalogue so that the space it occupies may be re-used. An error message will be generated if the object does not exist or is locked or, in the case of directories, if the directory is not empty. Wildcards may be used in all fields of the pathname except the last. Therefore to delete several files at once *WIPE should be used instead (see below).

Example:

    *DELETE BigFile

This deletes the file called 'BigFile'

*Dir

Syntax: *DIR {<directory>}

This command changes the Currently Selected Directory (CSD) to the named directory. If no directory name is supplied the current directory is set to the user root directory (URD). If the command was processed successfully, the directory which was the CSD when the command was issued becomes the previously selected directory (PSD) and is accessible with *BACK. The CSD is represented by the symbol '@' and the PSD by the symbol '\'.

Examples:

    *DIR
    *DIR $ .Book.Programs

Here, we re-select the URD as the CSD, and set the CSD as '$.Book.Programs'.

*Dump

Syntax: *DUMP <filename> {<offset> {<start>}}

*DUMP opens the specified file and displays its contents in hexadecimal and ASCII as text lines in the following format:

    Address :   00 01 02 03 04 05 06 07 {etc}   : ASCII data
                 42 43 44 45 46 47 48 49   : BCDEFGHI

Each line shows the address, hexadecimal value and ASCII value of each byte, with unprintable ASCII codes represented by full stops. The width of the displayed lines varies according to the display mode selected.

The address field usually shows how far through the file each byte appears, starting at the file's load address for code files or at zero for time stamped files.

The optional offset parameter allows dumping to begin part way through the file — useful for skipping past the beginning of files. The optional start parameter enables you to substitute the load address of the file for a different address, making the displayed address of each byte the start address plus the offset within the file.

*Enumdir

Syntax: *ENUMDIR <directory> <file> {<search pattern>}

This is rather like a file-orientated version of *CAT. It lists the objects found in the specified directory into the named file as a series of text lines delimited by line feeds (ASCII 10). By means of a wildcard search, the optional search pattern may be used to restrict the objects listed out.

Example:

```
*ENUMDIR @ CatFile
```

This lists the contents of the CSD in the file 'CatFile'. The file is saved as a data file.

*Ex

Syntax: *EX {<directory>}

The *EX command examines the contents of the specified directory (or the CSD if none is specified) and displays a line of information about each, as shown in Figure 11a.

Figure 11a. Typical output when using *EX, regarding file information in specified directory.

The command lists the following for every entry it finds: Filename, attributes, file type, time, date, and length. On ADFS it may also provide the address of the file on the disc.

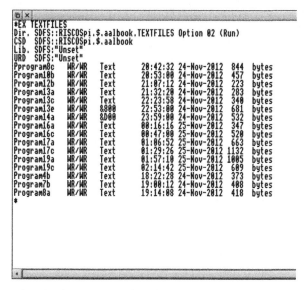

```
[o][x]
*EX TEXTFILES
Dir.  SDFS::RISCOSpi.$.aalbook.TEXTFILES Option 02 (Run)
CSD  SDFS::RISCOSpi.$.aalbook
Lib.  SDFS:"Unset"
URD  SDFS:"Unset"
Pprogram8c    WR/WR    Text      20:42:32 24-Nov-2012   844  bytes
Program10b    WR/WR    Text      20:53:00 24-Nov-2012   457  bytes
Program12b    WR/WR    Text      21:07:12 24-Nov-2012   223  bytes
Program13a    WR/WR    Text      21:32:20 24-Nov-2012   283  bytes
Program13c    WR/WR    Text      22:23:58 24-Nov-2012   340  bytes
Program13e    WR/WR    &800      22:53:00 24-Nov-2012   681  bytes
Program14a    WR/WR    &D00      23:59:00 24-Nov-2012   532  bytes
Program16a    WR/WR    Text      00:16:16 25-Nov-2012   347  bytes
Program16c    WR/WR    Text      00:47:00 25-Nov-2012   520  bytes
Program17a    WR/WR    Text      01:06:52 25-Nov-2012   663  bytes
Program17c    WR/WR    Text      01:29:26 25-Nov-2012  1132  bytes
Program19a    WR/WR    Text      01:57:10 25-Nov-2012  1005  bytes
Program19c    WR/WR    Text      02:14:42 25-Nov-2012   609  bytes
Program4b     WR/WR    Text      18:22:28 24-Nov-2012   373  bytes
Program7b     WR/WR    Text      19:00:12 24-Nov-2012   408  bytes
Program8a     WR/WR    Text      19:14:08 24-Nov-2012   418  bytes
*
```

Figure 11b. Typical output by *EX regarding file information in specified directory.

*Exec

Syntax: *EXEC {<filename>}

*EXEC reads the contents of the named file as though they had been entered at the keyboard. The file is opened for input and characters are read from it until the end of the file is reached, when it is closed automatically and input is restored to the keyboard.

The *EXEC function may be terminated early by the inclusion of *EXEC without a filename. Alternatively, including another *EXEC <filename> command will close the current file, open the new one, and start accepting input from the new file instead.

Example:

*EXEC !BootFile

This switches character input to the file '!BootFile'.

If you have a BBC BASIC file saved as a text file then you can load it into the BASIC interpreter by using *EXEC. Each line, provided it is terminated by <RETURN> character, is entered as though it has been typed at the keyboard. (You can save a BBC BASIC program as a text file using the TEXTSAVE command.)

*Fileinfo

Syntax *FILEINFO <object_spec>

*FILEINFO provides full file information about the specified object, which may be wildcarded files or directories. The information provided consists of the filetype and date stamp or the load and execution addresses (in hexadecimal).Also displays the length of the file in hexadecimal.

Example:

*FILEINFO ThisFile
ThisFile WR/ Text 15:54:37.40 04-Jan-1989 000007F

*Info

*Syntax: *INFO <objectname>

The *INFO command behaves in much the same way as the *EX command but deals with an object name (optionally including wildcards) rather than a directory name. Thus *INFO * is equivalent to *EX.

Example:

*INFO SomeFile

This displays detailed information about 'Somefile'.

*Lcat

Syntax: *LCAT {<sub-directory>}

*LCAT displays a catalogue of the currently selected library, or one of its sub-directories if a parameter is supplied.

*Lex

Syntax: *LEX {<sub-directory>}

*LEX displays file information for the currently selected library, or one of its sub-directories, in the same way as *EX. On its own *LEX is equivalent to

*EX %

*Lib

Syntax: *LIB {<directory>}

*LIB sets the currently selected library (CSL) to the named directory, so that it will be searched when a file to be *RUN is not found in the CSD. The CSL is represented by the symbol % and it is necessary to set the OS variable Run$Path to include % so that the library is searched.

*List

Syntax: *LIST <filename>

The *LIST command displays the contents of the specified file in the format specified by *CONFIGURE DumpFormat. Each line is displayed with a line number in a format specified by the OS_GSRead configuration.

*Load

Syntax: *LOAD <filename> {<address>}

The *LOAD command loads the specified file into memory. If no load address is provided, the file's existing load address is used; otherwise the file is loaded at the address supplied. If the file is date stamped, then the action of the load command changes. RISC OS looks for a system variable of the type Alias$@LoadType_ttt, where 'ttt' is the type of the file being loaded. If the variable exists then the OS executes the string assigned to the variable by sending it to OS_CLI.

For example, by default, the variable:

```
Alias$@LoadType_FFB BASIC -Load %0
```

is set up by the OS. All BASIC programs are saved in files which are stamped with the filetype FFB. Thus if we *LOAD a BASIC program, RISC OS actually performs:

```
*BASIC -load <filename>
```

This automatically starts up BASIC with the specified BASIC program resident in memory.

Several known file types are aliased in this way so that appropriate action is taken if a date stamped file of the corresponding type is *LOADed. A similar scheme is used to deal with attempts to *RUN a date stamped file.

You can use *SHOW to display the current filetype settings.

*Nodir

Syntax: *NODIR

*NODIR unsets the current directory.

*Nolib

Syntax : *NOLIB

*NOLIB unsets the library directory.

*Nourd

Syntax: *NOURD

*NOURD unsets the User Root Directory (URD). This is shown as an '&' in pathnames.

*Opt

Syntax: *OPT <option> {<value>}

The *OPT command is used to set various filing system options for the current filing system. These are as follows:

*OPT 0   Resets the *OPT options to their defaults
*OPT 1, < x >   Affects whether *INFO-style file information is displayed
                when files are loaded or saved. The value of <x> is
                interpreted as follows:
                        0—No information displayed.
                        1—The filename is displayed.
                        2—The filename and its load address, execution
                            address and length are displayed.
                        3—Either the above, or filetype and date-stamp
                            information are displayed, depending on the file type.
*OPT 4,<x>   Sets the auto-boot option as follows:
                        0—No auto-boot
                        1—*LOAD the boot file
                        2—*RUN the boot file
                        3—*EXEC the boot file
This command should not be confused with the OPT setting used with the BBC BASIC Assembler.

*Print

Syntax: `*PRINT <filename>`

The *PRINT command opens the named file for input and sends the contents of the file to the VDU drivers. This means that ASCII control codes will have their VDU effect, rather than being displayed as split-bar | sequences.

*Rename

Syntax: `*RENAME <currentname> <newname>`

The *RENAME command changes the pathname by which the specified object is known. Therefore, it is able not only to change the name of an object, but also to move it within the directory hierarchy. The object must already exist and its new name must not exist in the target directory. This command will not move objects between filing systems or between discs using the same filing systems. To do this use *COPY with the D(elete) option.

Examples:

```
*RENAME File01 Prog01
```

This changes the name of file 'File01' to 'Prog01'.

```
*RENAME &.Book.Research $.OldFiles.UsedInfo
```

This moves the file 'Research' from the sub-directory 'Book' of the CSD into

```
$.OldFiles and renames it 'UsedInfo'
```

*Remove

Syntax: `*REMOVE <objectname>`

This command operates as for *DELETE except that no error is generated if the specified object does not exist. Note that wildcards are not permitted — you should use *WIPE instead.

Example:

```
*REMOVE NoSuchFile
```

This appears to delete the file 'NoSuchFile' even if the file does not exist.

*Run

Syntax: *RUN <filename> {<parameters>}

The command *RUN both loads and then executes the specified file, using the load and execute addresses associated with the file. Parameters may optionally be added which are accessible to the program when it begins execution.

The given filename is searched for in the directories listed in the system variable Run$Path. If a matching object is a directory then it is ignored, unless it contains a !Run file.

The first file, or directory !Run file that matches is used:

- If the file has no file type, it is loaded at its own load address, and execution commences at its execution address.

- If the file has type &FF8 (Absolute code) it is loaded and run at &8000

- Otherwise the corresponding Alias$@RunType variable is looked up to determine how the file is to be run. A BASIC file has a filetype of &FFB, so the variable Alias$@RunType_FFB is looked up, and so on. You are unlikely to need to change the default values of these variables. If the corresponding Alias$@RunType variable does not exist then a suitable error is generated.

By default, Run$Path is set to "%.". This means that the current directory is searched first, followed by the library. This default order is also used if Run$Path is not set.

Example:

    *RUN 4YourLife

This loads and executes the file '4YourLife'.

    *RUN 4YourLife datastats

This loads and executes the file '4YourLife'and 'datastats' is passed as a parameter to '4YourLife' which the program can access. If this is required then the decoding process can expect the following information to be passed in the registers, which will be done in User Mode with interrupts enabled:

R0 = pointer to command line
R1 = pointer to command tail
R12 = pointer to workspace
R13 = pointer to workspace end (stack)
R14 = return address

The workspace is 1024 bytes long, in the location given by R12 and R13 on entry.

Note that R0 points to the first character of the command name, and R1 points to the first character of the command tail (with spaces skipped). This would be a control character if there were no parameters.

*Save

```
Syntax: *SAVE <filename> <startaddr> <endaddr>
{<execaddr>{ <reload addr> }}
```

```
Syntax: *SAVE <filename> <start addr> + <length>
{<exec addr>{ <reload addr> }}
```

*SAVE copies the specified area of memory to a named file. The memory area and the file's associated load and execute addresses may be specified in one of the two forms shown above. In the first case the start address and the address of the byte after the last byte to be saved are supplied; in the second case the start address and the length in bytes are supplied.

A reload address may optionally be supplied, causing the file thereafter to be loaded at a different address from where it is saved. Where execute and reload addresses are not supplied, defaults of the start address for saving are assumed.

Example:

```
*SAVE TheWorld 8000 +40000
```

This saves 256k of memory starting at &8000 into a file called 'TheWorld'.

```
*SAVE TheMoon 8000 9000 9400 9400
```

This saves memory from &8000 to &9000 as a file called 'TheMoon' and sets its load and execution address as &9400.

*Settype

```
Syntax: *SETTYPE <filename> <type>
```

*SETTYPE allows the filetype set by RISC OS for the file to be changed. The 12-bit 'type' is applied to the named file, normally entered as three hexadecimal digits.

Example:

```
*SETTYPE Alphabet ABC
```

Here, we set the filetype of file 'Alphabet' to the hex value &ABC.

*Shut

Syntax: *SHUT

This command has the same effect as *CLOSE (ie, it closes all open files) but it affects all filing systems rather than just the currently selected one. Like *CLOSE it should be used with care as it wil also break any other programs running.

*Shutdown

Syntax: *SHUTDOWN

This command has an even broader effect than *SHUT. It performs all the functions of *SHUT and also logs the user off any network file servers in use and dismounts any discs, so leaving the computer in a disconnected state.

*Stamp

Syntax: *STAMP <filename>

*STAMP overwrites the old date and time-stamp for the specified file with the current date and time. The filetype is set to &FFD if the file was not already stamped.

Example:

    *STAMP PennyBlack

This stamps the file 'PennyBlack' with the current date and time.

*Spool

Syntax: *SPOOL {<filename>}

The *SPOOL command opens the named file (this is called the spool file) and sends all subsequent VDU output to it. In many ways *SPOOL is the inverse operation of *EXEC. If the file already exists then its contents are overwritten. If an error occurs the file is closed.

*Spoolon

Syntax: *SPOOLON {<filename>}

*SPOOLON has the same effect as *SPOOL, except that VDU output is appended to the file if it exists, rather than overwriting it. If the file does not already exist, *SPOOLON is exactly equivalent to *SPOOL.

Either *SPOOL or *SPOOLON without a parameter will close the spool file (effectively a *SPOOLOFF).

If an error occurs the file is closed.

*Type

Syntax: *TYPE <filename>

The *TYPE command has a similar effect to the *LIST command, in that it displays the contents of the file in the way defined by the configuration DumpFormat. However, it differs in that it does not commence each line with a line number.

Example:

*TYPE programnotes

This displays the contents of file 'programnotes' on the screen.

*Up

Syntax: *UP {<how_far>}

The *UP command moves a specified number of levels up through the directory hierarchy of the currently selected filing system, equivalent to *DIR followed by a sequence of caret symbols ^.

Example:

*UP 2

This performs a *DIR ^^ to move two levels up the directory structure.

*Urd

Syntax *URD [directory]

*URD sets the User Root Directory (URD). This is shown as an ampersand '&' in pathnames. If no directory is specified, the URD is set to the root directory.

*Wipe

Syntax: *WIPE <object> {<options>}

The *WIPE command deletes the specified object(s), and wildcards are permitted. This allows several files or the contents of directories to be deleted in one pass. A number of options may also be included:

C   Confirm.   Prompts you for confirmation before each deletion.

F   Force   Deletes objects even if they are locked.

R   Recurse   Deletes sub-directories and their contents as well.

V   Verbose   Displays file information prior to deletion.

The RISC OS System variable Wipe$Options contains the default settings for these options. They may be overridden when issuing *WIPE by specifying the desired attribute set after the command. Again use a tilde to de-select a particular feature, for example:

*WIPE this_file ~C

No confirmation is required.

The default settings for Wipe$Options are:

C ~F ~R ~V

12: Filing System Control

Many of the * commands we looked at in the previous chapter are performed using OS_FSControl (SWI &29) as part of the FileSwitch module and thus we have the ability to use the SWI from within our own applications. The SWI is called with a reason code in R0 which defines the action required; other registers are used to pass further parameters as required. Figure 12a below lists the more common of these operations which are also described in the following pages.

A large number of the calls not listed here are provided to deal with situations arising in circumstances where you are considering writing your own filing system. So if that is your aim, investigate OS_FSControl in the PRMs 2-80 and 5a-168.

Directory Actions

With the exception of one, the calls listed in this section all deal with directories and the options we can apply to them. This includes the SWI equivalents of *DIR, *LIB, *RUN, *CAT, *EX and *LEX.

&00 — Set Current Directory

This call is used to change the currently selected directory (CSD) for the filing system. It is equivalent in its effect to the Operating System command:

```
*DIR <dirname>
```

On entry to the routine, R1 must point to a zero-terminated string which contains the name of the directory to be selected. If the directory name is null, then the current directory reverts to the root directory by default.

&01 — Set Library Directory

This call is similar to the above, but is used to change the currently selected library directory (CSL). It is equivalent in function to the RISC OS command:

```
*LIB <dirname>
```

On entry to the routine, R1 must point to a terminated string which contains the name of the directory to be selected as the library. If the directory name is null, then the library directory reverts to the default, typically $.Library for SDFS (if this is present).

&04 — Run File

This call will *RUN the named file. The name of the file to be loaded and executed must be contained in a terminated string which is pointed to by register R1. The file is searched for in the directories specified in the system variable Run$Path. By default, this is set up to be the current directory and then the library directory.

If the file being *RUN is date stamped then a suitable RUN alias is looked for which corresponds to the file type. See the section on *LOAD for a description of the action taken.

&05 — Catalogue a Directory

This routine performs an equivalent function to the command:

```
*CAT <dirname>
```

The name of the directory to be catalogued is contained in a terminated string which is pointed to by register R1. If this name is null, for example:

```
SYS "OS_FSControl", 5,""
```

then the currently selected directory is catalogued.

&06- Examine Current Directory

This call prints out full catalogue information on each file in the specified directory. It is therefore equivalent to the command:

```
*EX <dirname>
```

The name of the directory to be examined is contained in the null-terminated string pointed to by register R1.

&07 — Catalogue Library Directory

This performs a similar function to the call with R0=&05, except that it displays a catalogue of the currently selected library directory like *LEX.

Again R1 points to a terminated directory name. If this is null then the current library directory itself is catalogued. Otherwise the name is taken to be that of a sub-directory within the library directory, which is catalogued instead.

&08 — Examine Library Directory

This call is similar to that using R0=&06 except that information on files in the current library directory is displayed. If R1 points to a null string, then the files in the library directory itself are examined. Otherwise R1 is assumed to point to the name of a sub-directory within the library. The catalogue details of the files in this sub-directory will then be printed instead.

Object Actions

This section contains details of the calls that deal with objects and files. This includes calls &09 through to &15 inclusive.

&09 — Examine Specified Objects

This call allows a possibly ambiguous filename and a path to be specified. It then prints out information on any file which matches this specification. On entry, R1 points to the file name/path to be used. For example, if R1 pointed to the string:

```
A*
```

then information would be printed on all files beginning with an 'A' in the current directory. Similarly:

```
$.Results.A*
```

would examine every file beginning with an 'A' in the sub-directory 'Results'.

&0A — Set Filing System Options

This call is equivalent to the command:

```
*OPT n,m
```

where 'n' is the option number to be set and 'm' is the value. On entry, R1 contains the option number (n) and R2 the parameter value (m). For example, if:

```
R1=4
```

and:

```
R2=3
```

then the call would perform:

```
*OPT 4,3
```

and select a *EXEC boot option. If R1=0, then the settings of all of the filing system options are reset to their default state. For example:

```
MOV R0,#&0A \ Set * OPT 4,3
MOV R1,#4
MOV R2,#3
SWI "OS_FSControl"
```

&0B — Set Filing System from Named Prefix

This call sets the currently selected filing system to be that specified in the string pointed to by R1. This becomes the temporary filing system. If this string does not contain a valid filing system name then no action is taken. As an example, consider the following program:

```
MOV R0,#&0B
ADR R1, string
SWI "OS_FSControl"
:
.string
EQUS "SDFS.Results"
EQUB 0
```

The file manager will recognise the filing system name within the string and select the SDFS system.

On Exit:

R1 = An address set to immediately after the filing system's name if one was present in the string.

R2 = 1 if no filing system name specification was found.

R3 = Points to a special field if one was present.

Note that 'name:' is the preferred way of specifying a filing system name within a command. However, the older alternative '-name-' can be used instead.

&12 — Translate File Type Number to Name

This call allows a filetype number to be converted into the corresponding filetype name. On entry R2 contains the filetype number. On exit, registers R2 and R3 contain eight bytes which are the ASCII representation of the filetype name. As an example, if R2 = &FFB on entry then R2, R3 would contain the following bytes on exit:

```
&49534142 20202043
( I S A B      C)
```

These bytes are the ASCII representation for the characters 'BASIC' — the name of the file type. The &20 bytes are spaces for padding:

Program 12a below prompts for a filetype number and attempts to convert it to a filetype name. The name is then printed out.

R0	Function	*Command
&00	Set Current Directory	*DIR <dirname>
&01	Set Library Directory	*LIB <dirname>
&04	RUN file	*RUN <filename>
&05	Catalogue a Directory	*CAT <dirname>
&06	Examine Current Directory	*EX <dirname>
&07	Catalogue Library Directory	*LEX
&08	Examine Library Directory	
&09	Examine Specified Object	
&0A	Set File System Options	*OPT
&0B	Set File System from Named Prefix	*<filesystem>
&12	Translate File Type Number to Name	
&15	Return File System Handle	
&16	Shut	*SHUT
&17	Shut down	*SHUTDOWN
&18	Set File Attributes from String	*ACCESS
&19	Rename Objects	*RENAME
&1A	Copy Objects	*COPY
&1C	Count Objects	*COUNT
&1D	Wipe Objects	*WIPE

Figure 12a. The more common OS_FSControl operations

Program 12a. Use of OS_FSControl to convert a filetype number to name.

```
10 REM >Prog12a
20 REM OS_FSControl to convert a filetype number
30 REM RPi RISC OS Programming
70 :
80 DIM work 8
110 REPEAT
120 PRINT'
```

169

```
130 INPUT "Please Enter File type number : &" type$
140 PRINT
150 :
160 type=EVAL("&"+type$)
170 SYS "OS_FSControl",&12,,type TO ,, byte1,byte2
180 :
190 !work=byte1
200 work?4=13
210 PRINT $work;
220 :
230 !work=byte2
240 work?4 = 13
250 PRINT $work
260 UNTIL FALSE
```

&15 — Return Filing System Handle

When dealing with files, we usually identify them using a unique file handle provided by the file manager. This call translates this file manager's file handle into the corresponding one actually used by the selected filing system.

On Entry:
R1=file manager's file handle

On Exit:
R1 = the corresponding handle as used by the filing system

Block Actions

This final set of calls provides either block options on files or closes the filing system down emulating the *SHUT and *SHUTDOWN commands.

&16 — Shut

This call provides an equivalent function to the *SHUT command. It closes all files on the filing system.

&17 — ShutDown

This call provides an equivalent function to the *SHUTDOWN command. It closes all files on the filing system. In addition it logs off all file servers and dismounts any discs that may require doing so.

&18 – Set File Attributes from String

This call provides an equivalent function to the *ACCESS command. It allows the attributes for any named files to be set. On entry, R1 points to a string specifying the files to be affected. This may include a wildcard in order to affect several files at the same time. R2 points to a string which contains the new attributes to be set. This is illustrated in the snippet below, which would cause all files that start with the filename 'VitalData' in the current directory to be locked. Thus files named, VitalData001, VitalData002, VitalData003 and so like would all be locked.

```
MOV R0, #&18
ADR R1, filename
ADR R2, lockAttribute
SWI "OS_FSControl"
:
MOV PC, LR
:
.filename
EQUS "VitalData*"
EQUB 0
ALIGN
.lockAttribute
EQUS "L"
EQUB 0
```

&19 – Rename Objects

The call performs a *RENAME. On entry, R1 points to the first file/path name and R2 points to the second. The call then renames the first specified file as the second file specification.

&1A – Copy Object

The call is the equivalent of *COPY. All files matching the first file/path specification are copied to the second file/path specification.

On Entry:
R1=Pointer to first file/path name
R2=Pointer to second file/path name
R3=Action mask
R4=Optional start date
R6=Optional start date
R7=Optional end date
R8=Optional end date

Various options for the copy can be specified in the flags contained in R3 — the action mask. The flags in the low byte are as shown in Figure 12b:

Bit	Function
8	Set to select printing of information during copy
7	Set if the original file is to be deleted after the copy
6	Set if user is to be prompted to change disc as required
5	Set if copy is allowed to use application space to speed up copy
4	Set to select verbose mode during copy
3	Set if user is to be prompted to confirm each copy
2	If set, only files between the given time/date stamps are to be copied
1	If set, locked files are unlocked and overwritten by the copy
0	Set to allow recursive copying of file through sub-directories

Figure 12b. Action mask bit profiles for copy objects.

&1B — Wipe Objects

This routine provides an equivalent operation to the *WIPE command and can have devastating results if used incorrectly! On entry the registers must be set up as follows:

R1 = Pointer to file/path name to delete
R3 = Action mask
R4 = Optional start date
R6 = Optional start date
R7 = Optional end date
R8 = Optional end date

Various options for the wipe can be specified in the flags contained in R3 — the action mask. The flags in the low byte are as shown in Figure 12c below:

Bit	Function
8	Set to select printing of information during copy
7	0
6	Set if user is to be prompted to change disc as required
5	Set if wipe is allowed to use application space to speed up copy
4	Set to select verbose mode during wipe
3	Set if user is to be prompted to confirm each wipe
2	If set, only files between the given time/date stamps are to be copied
1	If set, locked files are unlocked and overwritten by the wipe
0	Set to allow recursive wiping of file through sub-directories

Figure 12c. Action mask bit profiles for wipe objects.

&1C — Count Objects

This routine provides an equivalent operation to the *COUNT command. On entry the registers must be set up as follows:

R1 = Pointer to file/path name to count
R3 = Action mask
R4 = Optional start date
R6 = Optional start date
R7 = Optional end date
R8 = Optional end date

The option flags in R3 are the same as those used in the *COPY routine. On exit from the routine, R2 contains the total number of bytes counted in all matching files. R3 contains the number of matching files counted.

13: OS_File SWIs

OS_File (SWI &08) forms another significant part of the FileSwitch Module. OS_File operations act on entire files and in the main deal with loading, saving and modifying their attributes. Register R0 contains a function code indicating what action is to be taken. Other successive registers contain the required parameters. When required the defaults are:

R1=pointer to filename string
R2=load address of file
R3=execution address of file
R4=start address of data in memory
R5=end address of data in memory

Figure 13a below summarises the calls discussed below. For further details on OS_File consult the PRMs at 2-32.

&00- Save Memory to File

The first OS_File commands allow sections of memory to be saved to a file. When R0=0, R1 contains a pointer to the filename to be utilised, with R2 and R3 seeded with the load and execution address to be given to the file. R4 and R5 hold the start and end address of the block of data to be saved to the file.

As an example, the program given below will save some text held in strings to the CSD with the filename "SavedText".

Program 13a. Save a file with OS_File.

```
10 REM >Prog13a
20 REM Example of OS File to save
30 REM RPi RISC OS Programming
70 :
80 DIM string% 256
90 A$="Raspberry Pi "
100 B$ "RISC OS Programming"
110 endstring%=string%
120 string%=LEN(A$)+LEN(B$)+1
```

```
130 PRINT "Saving textfile"
140 SYS "OS_File", 0,"SavedText",0, 0,string%, endstring%
150 *INFO SavedText
```

RUN this program and the 'SavedText' file will be created. The *INFO will return:

```
SavedText WR/        00000000  00000000  36 kbytes
```

R0	Function
&00	Save memory to file
&01	Write Catalogue Information
&02	Write Load Address Only
&03	Write Execution Address Only
&04	Write Attributes Only
&05	Read Catalogue Information
&06	Delete an Object
&07	Create an Empty File
&08	Create a Directory
&09	Write Date/Time Stamp
&0A	Save Memory to Date/Time Stamped File
&0B	Create a Date/Time Stamped File
&0C	Load File with Path String
&0D	Read Catalogue Information with Path String
&0E	Load File with Path Variable
&0F	Read Catalogue Information with Path Variable
&10	Load File Using No Path
&11	Read Catalogue Information Using No Path
&12	Set File Type Only
&FF	Load File Into Memory

Figure 13a. OS_File calls detailed.

&01 – Write Catalogue Information

This call makes it possible to change the catalogue information for a specified file. The new catalogue information is held in the same registers as in the previous command. However, this time R5 contains a series of flags which specify the access type to the file. The format of these attribute flags is given in Figure 13b.

Bit	Function id Set (=1)
7	Not used
6	Not used
5	File has write access for others
4	File has read access for others
3	File is locked
2	Not used
1	File has write access for you
0	File has read access for you

Figure 13b. Write Catalogue Information attribute flags.

The concept of you and others is only relevant in the NFS system. In SDFS bit 0 and 4 should be the same, as should bits 1 and 5.

Using the example created earlier as Prog13a which created a text files called 'SavedText' we could change the attributes of the file like this:

```
SYS "OS_File",1,"SavedText",&FFFFFE12,&3456789A, , 8
```

The '8' value at the end of the line denotes the file is to be to locked by setting b3 as detailed above.

```
*INFO SavedText
```

This would reveal the new details.

&02 – Write Load Address Only

The load address is supplied in R2, with the pointer to filename string in R1.

```
SYS "OS_File",2,"SavedText",0
```

Using the previous example, this would set the load address to &00000000.

&03 – Write Execution Address Only

The execution address is supplied in R3 with the pointer to filename string in R1.

```
SYS "OS_File",3,"SavedText",0,, &3456789A
```

Using the previous example, this would set the load address to &3456789A.

&04 — Write Attributes Only

Attribute flags in R5 as shown above with R1=pointer to the filename string.

&05 — Read Catalogue Information

This call will read the catalogue information about a file and return it for use as required. On entry to the call R1 points to the filename string. On return from the call the attribute information is passed back via registers as follows.

On Exit:
R0 = object type (0=not found, 1=file, 2=directory)
R1 = (the same) pointer to filename string
R2 = load address
R3 = execution address
R4 = length
R5 = access attributes (bottom byte)

Program 13b will prompt for a filename, read its catalogue details and then display them.

Program 13b. Use of OS_File to read file information.

```
 10 REM >Prog13b
 20 REM Use OS_File to get file details
 30 REM RPi RICOS Programming
 40 REPEAT
 50 INPUT filename$
 60 SYS "OS_File",5,filename$ TO type,, load, execution,
length,attributes
 70 :
 80 IF type =0 THEN PRINT "Could not find the specified
object"
 90 IF type =2 THEN PRINT "Object is a Directory"
100 IF type =1 THEN
110 PRINT "Object is a File"
120 PRINT "Load address is : "~load
130 PRINT "Execution address is : "~execution
140 PRINT "Length of file is : "length
150 IF attributes AND 1 PRINT " File has read access"
160 IF attributes AND 2 PRINT " File has write access"
170 IF attributes AND 8 PRINT " File is locked"
180 ENDIF
```

&06 – Delete an Object

Returns catalogue information as above, after deleting the specified object.

&07 – Create an Empty File

As for the first call R0=&00 (Save Memory to File), but the start and end addresses in R4, R5 are used only to determine the size — no data is written.

&08 – Create a Directory

This call has the same effect as *CDIR: it takes a zero-terminated name string pointed to by R1 and the minimum number of entries that the directory should contain in R4 (zero is the default).

The minimum number of directory entries is not relevant to SDFS and is ignored. However, it is of use with the NFS system. As an example, the following code fragment will create a sub-directory called 'Results' in the root directory ($):

```
ADR R1, filename
MOV R4,#0
MOV R0,#8
SWI "OS_File"
:
MOV PC, LR
:
.filename
EQUS "$.Results"
EQUB 0
```

&09 – Write Date/Time Stamp

This call acts in exactly the same way as *STAMP; it takes a filename string pointed to by R1 and applies the current date/time to the file. On return the file has a filetype of &FFD.

&0A – Save Memory to Date/Time Stamped File

This is just the same as the R0=&00 case, but since the load and execution addresses are not required, only the filetype is needed. R1 points to the filename string and R2 holds the file type. R4 and R5 hold the start and end addresses of data in memory respectively.

&0B – Create a Date/Time Stamped File

This is the same as the R0=&07 case, but again the parameter in R2 is the filetype since the load and execute addresses are not required.

&0C — Load File with Path String

Files are usually searched for using the path sequence set by the RISC OS System variable File$Path. This call allows File$Path to be overridden by providing a path string pointed to by R4. Any filename pointer held in R1 that is passed into this call is ignored.

On Entry:

R1=pointer to filename string
R2=load address (if R3 lsb=0)
R3=file/override flag
R4=pointer to control-character terminated comma-separated path string

On Exit:

R0 contains the object type:

>   0 — Not found
>   1 — File found
>   2 — Directory found
>   3 — Image file found (ie both file and directory)

If the object name contains any wildcards, only the first object matching the wildcard specification is read. The others are ignored.

&0D — Read Catalogue Information with Path String

This is the catalogue form of OS_FILE &0C above, so it is equivalent to R0=&05 except that R4 holds a pointer to the chosen path string which overrides File$Path. The results are returned just as they are for R0=&05.

&0E — Load File with Path Variable

This is the same as R0=&0C except that it requires the path string to be held in an RISC OS variable, so R4 points to this variable instead of an immediate string.

&0F — Read Catalogue Information with Path

This is the same as R0=&0D except that the path string must be in an RISC OS variable pointed to by R4.

&10 — Load File Using No Path

The minimal version: the filename is taken as supplied, with no path being used to prefix it. Otherwise, this is the same as R0=&0C, with the same parameters.

&11 — Read Catalogue Information Using No Path

The same as R0=&0D except that no path string prefixes the filename.

&12 – Set File Type Only

In much the same way as for R0=&02, &03 and &04, this call allows just the filetype to be set.

&FF – Load File Into Memory

This call is the general-purpose file loading SWI. It reads a file's catalogue information and then loads it at one of two addresses: either the one supplied by the file's information, or an overriding address in R2. Which of the two addresses is used is determined by the bottom byte of R3: if zero, the override in R2 is used, otherwise the file's own load address is used.

On Entry:
R1=pointer to filename string
R2=load address (if R3 lsb=0)
R3=file/override flag (see above)

On Exit:
R0=1 (object type is file)
R1=(the same) pointer to filename string
R2=load address
R3=execute address
R4=length
R5=access attributes

14: Open, Close, Read, Write

This is the third and final chapter covering the SWIs associated with the FileSwitch module, and it concentrates on the opening and closing of files and the writing of bytes and blocks of bytes to them.

File Open and Close

The OS_Find SWI (&0D) is used by the programmer to inform the filing system that a file needs to be made available for byte or block access. This is known as opening a file. The converse closing operation must be performed when the file operation is completed. Opening a file causes the filing system to translate a filename string into an integer handle — a number representing the file which is used extensively by other file operations. To close a file, this handle must be supplied to uniquely identify the file for closing. The only purpose of OS_Find is to open and close a file. A somewhat important purpose!

Currently, the file manager allows 24 files to be open at any one time. A given file can be opened for read access up to 24 different times, allowing multiple read access to the same file. However, a file can only be opened once for write access. If a file has been opened for write access then it cannot be opened for read access. Similarly if a file is already open for read access then it cannot be opened for write access.

For these calls R0 again defines the type of action and R1 points to the filename or contains the handle (depending on the operation) of the file. R2 points to a path string, in cases where the option to use it is chosen.

In the examples below the 'x' is used to indicate a path prefix, a pointer to it is placed in R2 and the appropriate value from the table below added to the base R0 function number:

0 — Use File$Path to prefix the specified filename
1 — Use the string pointed to by R2 as a path
2 — Use OS string variable pointed to by R2 as a path
4 — Use no path at all

Thus an OS-Find call with R0=&41 would open an already existing file for input using the string whose address is held in R2 as the path to that file.

In addition, error handling can be catered for by further adding a value to the 'x'. There are two types of error that can be generated by OS_Find. The first allows an error to be raised if an attempt is made to open a directory, the normal action being to permit it but disallow any operations on that handle.

The second allows an error to be raised if the specified file does not already exist, the normal action being simply to return a handle of zero. Where a path prefix or error handling extension is desired, values from the table below should be added to the base R0 function number as appropriate:

4 — Generate an error if a directory is opened.
8 — Generate an error if the file doesn't already exist.

&00 — Close all Files

If R1=0 then all currently open files are closed. If R0<>0 then the value in R1 is taken to be the handle of the file to be closed. The file or files are always closed if an error occurs. You can get the handle of a file by using the appropriate OS_File call.

&4x — Open File for Input

R1 is a pointer to the filename, and the resultant handle is placed in R0 on exit. The file must already exist, otherwise a handle of zero is returned.

&8x — Create and Open File For Output

R1 is a pointer to the filename and the handle is returned in R0. If the named file exists, it is opened for output and the file pointer and length are reset to zero. If the file doesn't exist, it is created and opened.

&Cx — Open File for Input/Output

This is the same as R0=&4x except that it allows output to the file as well as input. A handle of zero is returned if the file does not already exist. (See the discussion of paths later in this chapter.)

```
SYS "OS_Find", &C0, "SavedText" TO fh%
```

This would return the file handle allocated by RISC OS to the file 'SavedText' into the variable fh%.

```
PRINT fh%
```

This would return the file handle value .

You will need to use *SHUT to close the file.

Get & Put with Files (OS_GBPB)

Whereas OS_Find will open and close files for the reading and writing of bytes, OS_GBPB (SWI &0C) supplies the calls that allow multiple bytes to be read from or written to the files.

The first four calls provided by OS_GBPB are for reading from or writing to an open file using either the file's current pointer or a new pointer which is supplied. The pointer is an index of the number of bytes it is into the file, with the file being defined by its handle. The remaining OS_GBPB function codes perform a variety of miscellaneous filing system functions. The general form of entry to the call throughout is as given below.

On Entry:
R0=function code
R1=file handle
R2=memory address (for reading from or writing to)
R3=number of bytes to be transferred
R4=new pointer (where relevant)

Both R2 and R4 are updated during the call to reflect the final memory address and pointer value. For read operations, R3 returns the number of bytes not transferred (usually zero) and sets the Carry flag in the CPSR if any bytes were not transferred.

Figure 14a below lists the calls listed in this section. More details about OS_GBPB can be found in the PRMs at 2-66.

R0	Action
&01	Write Bytes to File at New Pointer Psn
&02	Write Bytes to File at Current Pointer Psn
&03	Read Bytes from File at New Pointer Psn
&04	Read Bytes from File at Current Pointer Psn
&05	Read Title and *OPT 4 Boot Setting
&06	Read CSD Name and Privilege Byte
&07	Read CSL Name and Privilege Byte
&08	Read Entries from CSD
&09	Read Entries from Specified Directory
&0A	Read Entries and Information from Specified Directory

Figure 14a. OS_GBPB calls detailed here.

&01 — Write Bytes to File at New Pointer Position

This call requires a valid new pointer in R4 (see above).

&02 — Write Bytes to File at Current Pointer

R4 is ignored for this call.

&03 — Read Bytes from File at New Pointer

This call requires a valid new pointer in R4 (see above).

&04 — Read Bytes from File at Current Pointer

The contents of R4 are ignored for this call.

&05 — Read Title and *OPT 4 Boot Setting

This call should be made with R2 pointing to a block of memory where the results are returned as follows:

- The length of the name string

- The name string itself

- The boot option (one byte)

&06 — Read CSD Name and Privilege Byte

Here, R2 should point to a block of memory on entry. The information is returned at this point in the following format:

- A zero byte

- The length of the CSD name

- The CSD name itself

- The privilege byte

The privilege byte is used by the NetFS to indicate a status of 'owner' (byte=&00) or 'public' (byte=&FF). For SDFS, this byte is always zero. (NetFS is rather ancient now, and rarely used so there is probably not much need to worry about this!)

&07 — Read CSL Name and Privilege Byte

This call is the same as R0=6 but returns details of the currently selected library (CSD).

&08 — Read Entries from CSD

This call returns a block of directory information comprising the names of successive objects in the CSD. Data is returned in memory at the address supplied in R2. The number of entries to be read is supplied in R3, and R4 should contain the first object number. If R4 contains zero, the first name to be returned will be the first alphabetically. The resulting data in memory is of the form:

- Length of name

- Name (null-terminated)

This is repeated for the number of objects specified.

If all the names could not be supplied, the Carry flag in the CPSR is set (C=1) and R3 is left containing the number of those names that are outstanding. Otherwise R3 contains zero and the Carry flag is clear (C=0).

&09 — Read Entries from Specified Directory

This call is an extended form of the previous one and therefore is much more versatile. As well as the parameters shown above, the call also allows the directory that you wish to read to be specified (by supplying a pathname pointed to by R1). The size of the memory buffer is held in R5 (so that it doesn't overflow) and a wildcard string is pointed to by R6 (to select which entries are to be returned).

Names that match the wildcard are returned in the buffer as a series of null-terminated strings, their number being returned in R3. R4 is updated to allow more entries to be read. If there are no more entries R4 contains -1.

&0A — Read Entries and Information from Specified...

This call performs the SWI version of *EX. Its parameters are the same as above, but it returns a block of information for each entry rather than just the name. This block is word aligned and formatted as shown in Figure 14b.

Offset	Information
&00	Load address
&04	Execute address
&08	Length
&0C	Access attributes
&10	Object type
&14	Object name (null-terminated)

Figure 14b. Format of block for SWI version of *EX.

Get Byte from File

OS_BGet (SWI &0A) reads the next sequential byte from an open file whose handle is specified and then increments the file pointer by one to move to the next byte to be read. On entry, R1 should contain the file handle and on return, R0 will contain the byte read. The Carry flag of the CPSR is clear (C=0) if the byte was read correctly and the flag is set (C=1) if a problem arose (most likely through an end-of-file condition or an invalid handle).

Program 14a below uses OS_BGet to sequentially read each byte in a file which it assumes to contain text. In doing so it counts the number of spaces (ASCII 32) that it encounters to give — albeit approximately, an indication of the number of words in the file.

Program14a. Using OS_BGet to count spaces and words.

```
 10 REM >Prog14a
 20 REM Word count using OS_ BGet
 30 REM RPi RISC OS Programming
 40 :
 50 DIM WordCount 256
 60 FOR pass = 0 TO 3 STEP 3
 70 P%= WordCount
 80 [
 90 OPT pass
100 .start
110 SWI "OS_WriteS"
120 EQUS "Please Enter Filename: "
130 EQUB 0
140 ALIGN
150 :
160 ADR R0, filename
170 MOV R1, #16
180 MOV R2, #32
190 MOV R3, #128
200 SWI "OS_ReadLine"
210 :
220 MOV R10,#0        \ space count
230 ADR R1, filename  \ Points to file name
240 MOV R0,#64        \ Open for read access only
250 MOV R2,#0
260 SWI "OS_Find"     \ Returns file handle in R0
```

```
270 :
280 MOV R8,R0
290 .countloop
300 MOV R1,R8
310 SWI "OS_BGet"     \ Get byte from file
320 BCS quitloop      \ If EOF quit loop
330 CMP R0,#32        \ Is it a space ?
340 ADDEQ R10,R10,#1 \ If so, increment the count
350 B countloop       \ If not end of file then loop
360 :
370 .quitloop
380 MOV R1,R8
390 MOV R0,#0
400 SWI "OS_Find" \ Close file
410 :
420 MOV R0,R10 \ Make word count available to USR
430 MOV PC,LR
440:
450 .filename
460 EQUS "--------------------"
470 ]
480 NEXT
490 :
500 words = USR(WordCount)
510 :
520 PRINT "Number of words counted is : " word
```

Put Byte To File

A byte can be written to a file using OS_BPut (SWI &0B). The call writes the byte passed in R0 to the file whose handle is supplied in R1. The byte is written to the position pointed to by the current file pointer. The call then increments the file pointer by one to allow further OS_BPut calls to work correctly.

Read/Write Open File Information

The SWI OS_Args(SWI &09) is what could be regarded as another general-purpose SWI and is used to perform read and write open file information. The format of the call is that on entry, R0 contains a function code, R1 contains a file handle and R2 contains data to be written (for write operations). Usually all registers are preserved, except where information is being read, in which case the read information is returned in R2.

Figure 14c below lists the OS_Args discussed here. As ever, further details can be found in the PRMs.

R0	Action
&00	Read Sequential File Pointer/Filing System Number
&01	Write Sequential File Pointer
&02	Read File Extent
&03	Write File Extent
&04	Read Allocated Size
&05	Read End-of-file Status
&06	Write Allocated Size
&FF	Ensure File Buffers

Figure 14c. OS_Args calls discussed here

&00 — Read Sequential File Pointer/Filing System.

As a complication, this function code has two meanings, making it a special case. When entered with R1=0 (instead of a valid file handle) it returns the number of the current filing system in R0. If R1 holds a valid file handle (ie, a non-zero value) this call returns the current value of the sequential pointer of that file in R2.

&01 — Write Sequential File Pointer

The reverse of the above call, this allows the sequential file pointer to be written (set). It should be entered with a valid file handle in R1 and the new file pointer value in R2. If the new pointer value is beyond the current extent of the file then its size is increased accordingly and the new area is filled with zeros.

&02 — Read File Extent

This call allows the current file length to be read into R2 for the file whose handle is supplied in R1.

&03 — Write File Extent

This call allows the extent of the file whose handle is supplied in R1 to be set to the value supplied in R2. If this value is larger than the existing extent, the file is extended accordingly and the new area is filled with zeros.

&04 — Read Allocated Size

This call allows the amount of space actually allocated to the file to be read, enabling you to determine how much space is left before new space need be allocated. It returns in R2 the allocated space for the file whose handle is supplied in R1.

&05 — Read End-of-file Status

This is one of two ways of sensing the end-of-file condition (the alternative being OS_Byte call &7F). When supplied with a file handle in R1, this call returns a non-zero result in R2 if the file pointer is equal to the file's extent; otherwise it returns zero.

&06 — Write Allocated Size

This is the reverse of the call that uses R0=&04 (above) — allowing you to advise the Operating System that the amount of space in R2 should be reserved for the file whose handle is supplied in R1. On return, R2 contains the amount of space actually allocated.

&FF — Ensure File Buffers

This call is equivalent to part of the closing process for files (under OS_Find). It ensures that all filing system buffers are written out to their corresponding files, thus allowing them to be closed. On entry, R1 must contain either zero (in which case all files are ensured) or a valid file handle (in which case just the chosen file's buffers are ensured).

15: FileCore

As its name suggests, FileCore provides all the core services required by all filing system. The FileCore module is device independent — it does not access hardware directly. It takes the normal calls that FileSwitch sends to a filing system module and converts them to a simpler set of calls to other secondary modules that actually access the hardware.

File systems such as SDFS and FAT32FS are implemented via their own modules created from FileCore. The original ADFS and RAMFS were created entirely from FileCore. FileCore translates FileSwitch file-level API requests into file block-level actions that clients such as SDFS, SCSI and ADFS can perform. The on-disc format provided by FileCore for these clients is unique to the Acorn-orientated RISC OS world. FAT32FS is a FileSwitch FS that uses its own version of FileCore for block access due to the different on-disc format of the filing system (FAT32).

A programmer looking to create a new filing system module can create it in most cases by linking to FileCore SWIs and providing their own specific information — FileCore acts as a template. However, unlike FileSwitch, it creates a new instance of itself for each module it supports.

So from the programmer's point of view, a FileCore-based filing system utilises all the SWIs provided by FileCore and the following are provided by the programmer for the new filing system:

- low-level routines to access the hardware.
- a * Command that can be used to select the filing system.
- additional * Commands that may be necessary.
- a SWI interface.

In reality there shouldn't be any need for you to add any additional * commands — those provided by FileCore and FileSwitch should be more than enough. But the option is yours, and as with FAT32FS there is an actual need to (see later). Additional SWI calls may be required, and you may need an interface to handle this. A typical FileCore-based filing system will have SWIs that functionally are a subset of those that FileCore provides. So unless you need to provide a lot of extra SWIs, you need do little more than provide the low-level routines that control the hardware.

Filing System modules use the SWI FileCore_Create to register themselves with FileCore as part of the filing system. This SWI is passed a pointer to a table giving information about the hardware, and entry points to low-level routines in the module. FileCore communicates with the module using these entry points.

When a module is registered with FileCore it creates a fresh instance of itself, and returns a pointer to its workspace. The new module then uses the pointer to identify itself on future calls to FileCore.

New versions of FileCore are occasionally released. These can be installed and used if you so wish, and are included in new releases of the distro. Specific versions of FileCore are also supplied with RISC OS Pi to handle the different interfaces.

The PRMs (starting at PRM 2-529: Chapter 19 Writing a Filing System) cover FileCore and the writing of Filing Systems in some detail. The remainder of this chapter documents the * commands supplied by FileCore as they have good general programming applications, although many of them are limited to use on filing systems such as SDFS and ADFS and are not relevant to USB drives. If your current filing system returns a 'File xxxx not found' error, where 'xxxx' is the command you were looking to use, then the filing system does not support that command.

SDFS

One of the key requirements of porting RISC OS to the Raspberry Pi was the need for a general-purpose MMC/SD filing system. SDFS is almost entirely supported by FileCore and FileSwitch and all commands within these, where relevant, are supported. At the time of writing the SDFS module supplies just two * commands as required by FileCore:

    *SDFS

This selects the SD Filing System

    *CONFIGURE SDFSdrive <drive>

This sets the value the default drive is initialised to for SDFS. <drive> is a number and is 0 by default.

The main card types supported by SDFS are: MMC, MMCplus, RS-MMC, MMCmobile, SD, SDHC, SDXC, MiniSD, MicroSD and MicroSDHC, of capacities up to 256 GB.

RISC OS has never included partition support in its implementation.

RAM FS

There are those of us who can remember having to use cassette players to save and load our programs and files from cassette tape at 300 baud. The screeching of data being transferred into sound through the player's speaker was a common sound emanating from many a home. Even when the first hard drives came along, they were so expensive as to put them out of the reach of most. A quick and efficient way of saving data came in the form of a RAM Disc, which to all of us at the time was a godsend solution.

Allocating an area of RAM to be used for file storage was a wonderful idea — now all one had to do was copy the files there, and they would stay until deleted or the power was switched off. You just had to remember to copy what you wanted to save from the Ram Disc to cassette tape or floppy before you turned the computer off.

Now that media is so inexpensive, is available in large quantities and is quick to use the concept of a RAM Disk and a RAMFS has waned, but you can still install one on RISC OS Pi.

To do this:

- Access the task manager by clicking on the Raspberry Pi logo to display it.

- Scroll down to the System memory allocation area.

- Locate RAM disc and click to the right of the 0k, dragging out the desired area of memory to allocate to the RAMFS. You will see a red bar appearing in this space.

- A memory chip icon should have appeared with your drives labelled RAM.

To select the RAMFS you use the command:

    *RAM

*CONFIGURE RamFsSize sets the configured amount of memory reserved for the RAM Filing System to use (when the RAMFS module is present) after the next hard reset. The default value is 0, which disables the RAM filing system.

Example:

    *CONFIGURE RamFsSize 128k

This will set a RAM Disc to 128k on the next reboot — note the use of the unit size here with the use of 'k'.

Note that using *RAMFS will not work to select the RAM filing system — *RAM must be used. I normally create an alias to get around this.

ADFS

The Advanced Disc Filing System (ADFS) can be thought of as the original RISC OS filing system. It was created using FileSwitch and FileCore, and as its name suggests, it provides a disc-based (floppies and motherboard hard drive connections) filing system based around the FileSwitch interface. The ADFS module provides two commands:

*ADFS

This selects it, and:

*FORMAT

This is a command to format ADFS discs.

FileCore Commands

Both SDFS and RAMFS are created directly from FileCore and specifically support all the FileCore * commands where they are relevant. They are detailed below.

*Backup

Syntax: *BACKUP <source> <destination> [<Q>]

This command can be used to create an exact copy of one disc to another. Only data is transferred and no free space is written. <source> and <drive> may be values in the range 0-3. If the same number is supplied you will be prompted to swap the disc as necessary. Q speeds up the operation by using the application work area as a buffer if extra room is needed to perform the backup so that fewer disc accesses are done. Works with SDFS and ADFS but the command is not recognised by FAT32FS.

Example:

*BACKUP 0 1

*COPY provides additional options and can be used to copy across drives that do not incorporate discs and may also be across different filing systems.

*Bye

Syntax: *BYE

In ADFS and other floppy-based filing systems *BYE ends a filing system session by closing all files, unsetting all directories and libraries, forgetting all disc names and parking the heads of hard discs. By including the filing system name you can limit the effects of *BYE to that format thus:

*ADFS:BYE

*CheckMap

Syntax: *CHECKMAP [disc_spec]

*CHECKMAP checks that the map of a floppy or hard disk has the correct checksums and is consistent with the directory tree. If only one copy of the map is good, it allows you to rewrite the bad one with the information in the good one. In doing so, it closes all files on the disc.

Example:

    *CHECKMAP:DataDisc

*Compact

Syntax: *COMPACT [disc_spec]

*COMPACT collects together free space on a floppy or hard disc by moving files so that they are not fragmented across storage space. If no argument is given, the *COMPACT command is carried out on the current disc. *COMPACT works on either hard or floppy discs. This command is still useful, as it will attempt to gather together any fragmented files, and will generally tidy up the disc.

Example:

    *COMPACT :0

*Defect

Syntax: *DEFECT <disc_spec> <disc_addr>

This reports what object contains a defect, or (if none) marks the defective part of the disc so it will no longer be used. The command requires two parameters:

<disc_spec>: This the name of the disc or number of the disc drive

<disc_addr>: This is the hexadecimal disc address where the defect exists, which must be a multiple of &100 – that is, it must end in '00'

If the defect is in an unallocated part of the disc, *DEFECT will render that part of the disc inaccessible by altering the map of the disc. If the defect is in an allocated part of the disc, *DEFECT tells you what object contains the defect, and the offset of the defect within the object. This may enable you to retrieve most of the information held within the object, using suitable software. You must then delete the object from the defective disc.

*DEFECT is typically used after a disc error has been reported, and the *VERIFY command has confirmed that the disc has a physical defect, and given its disc address.

    *VERIFY VitalData
    Disc error 08 at :0/00010400

```
*DEFECT VitalData 10400
$.Datadir must be moved
.Datafile1 has defect at offset 800
.Datafile2 must be moved
```

*Dismount

Syntax: *DISMOUNT [<disc_spec>]

*DISMOUNT closes all files, and forgets any current libraries and the disc name on specified disc. If no disc is specified, the current disc is used as the default. *DISMOUNT is useful before removing a particular floppy disc, and it is essential if the disc is to be taken away and modified on another computer. However, the *SHUTDOWN command is usually to be preferred, especially when switching off the computer.

*Drive

Syntax: *DRIVE <drive>

*DRIVE sets the current drive if NoDir is set. Otherwise, *DRIVE has no meaning. The command is provided for compatibility with early versions of ADFS. Example:

```
*DRIVE 3
```

*Free

*FREE [disc_spec]

Works on most filing systems. The command calculates and displays the total free space remaining on a disc. If no disc is specified, the total free space on the current disc is displayed. For example:

```
*FREE 0
Bytes free &5FCF2C00 = 1,607,412,736
Bytes used &1570D400 =  359, 715,840
```

*Map

Syntax: *MAP [disc_spec]

*MAP displays a disc's free space map. If no disc is specified, the map of the current disc is displayed. This command does not work with FAT32FS but works on *SDFS and *ADFS and associated filing systems. Example:

```
*MAP :Mydisc
```

*Mount

Syntax *MOUNT [disc_spec]

*MOUNT prepares a disc for general use by setting the current directory to its root directory, setting the library directory (if it is currently unset) to $.Library, and un-setting the User Root Directory (URD). The default drive is used. This command is implemented on most filing systems. Example:

```
*MOUNT:mydisc
```

*NameDisc / *NameDisk

Syntax: *NAMEDISC <disc_spec> <new_name>

*NAMEDISC (or *NAMEDISK) changes a disc's name and is the same as rename. Examples:

```
*NAMEDISC:0 DataDisc
*NAMEDISK OldDisk NewDisk
```

*Verify

Syntax *VERIFY [disc_spec]

*VERIFY checks that the whole disc is readable, except for sectors that are already known to be defective. The default disc examined is the current disc.

Use *VERIFY to check discs which give errors during writing or reading operations or to ensure integrity for your own satisfaction. Beware of using this on SD discs as it can take a while to respond.

Note that *VERIFY does not work with FAT32FS.

Example:

```
*VERIFY 0
*VERIFY :Mydisc
```

Fat32FS

FAT32FS is a filing system for USB mass storage devices, and has been written and kept updated for RISC OS by Jeff Doggett. FAT32 format is utilised by PC-based systems running operating systems such as Linux and Windows and thus is the ideal medium through which to transfer files to and from RISC OS. Up to eight may be connected at the same time.

While FAT32FS is implemented using FileCore and whilst FileSwitch * commands are fully supported, it introduces several new commands and SWIs relevant to deal with its own on-disc operations. It can be used with discs larger than 2GB — smaller USB drives may not be recognised. The filing system also supports the FAT12 and FAT16 interfaces.

USB devices attached to the Raspberry Pi are by default numbered from 0, and added drives are attached to the icon bar from the left with drives incrementing in number — 1, 2, 3 etc. If a USB drive has previously been named, then the name will be displayed once the drive has been opened. This is most commonly done by clicking on the icon.

It is an efficient filing system using space effectively and is generally faster than other filing systems, with the exception of RAMFS.

But beware when using FAT32FS and a write-protected SDFS together. Write behind caching is used for file transfer. That means that the library won't discover that an SD card is read-only until after the fact, so the write will appear to work but the file won't actually be there! So it is always good to confirm that SD cards are set to WR before using them in conjunction with FAT32FS.

The maximum filename length is 190 characters, with a maximum path length of 1024 characters. Unicode is used for the long filenames.

Fat Command Line

The Fat32FS module provides a number of * commands which are detailed here. Many of the * commands are for debugging purposes. Some of them accept options which are listed below in Figure 15a.

Option	Use
-px	Use partition x
-v	Be extra verbose
-s	Be silent

Figure 15a. Options accepted by some Fat32FS commands.

When you need to use more than one option then combine them together as a string with no spaces in between each option:

```
-sp1
```

When you need to enter a drive number then you can use :1 or :NAME if the drive is already known to FAT32FS. Up to four partitions are available under FAT32FS and these are numbered 1-4 When you click on a USB drive it opens the default partition — usually 1. If you hold down a key representing the number of the partition when you click on the drive icon then that partition will be opened instead. This can also be done from the command line thus:

```
*FAT32FS::MOUNT -p3 :2
```

This will mount the third partition of drive 2. option. Note that only one partition can be active at once. If the drive is already mounted then the partition selection will be ignored.

If you want the silent or extra verbose option as well then it must not have a space:

```
MOUNT -sp3
```

or:

```
*MOUNT -vp4
```

or:

```
*MOUNT -p2v
```

The command line:

```
*SHOWFREE -FS Fat32Fs 0
```

will show the free space on drive 0 as a bar graphic.

The FAT32FS does not implement any SWI calls for use, but the following * commands are available.

*Dismount

Syntax: *DISMOUNT [<disc spec.>]

Flush the write-cache and release the disc buffers, closing all files. *DISMOUNT is useful before removing a particular USB drive, and is essential if the disc is to be taken away and modified on another computer. However, the *SHUTDOWN command is usually to be preferred, especially when switching off the computer.

*Fat32FS

Syntax: *FAT32FS

This command selects FAT32FS as the current filing system.

*Fat32Map

Syntax: *FAT32MAP {<MSDOS extension> {<RISC OS filetype>}}

*FAT32MAP specifies an MSDOS extension to RISC OS filetype mapping which overrides the one held in the central Mime Map. The RISC OS filetype can be given as either a 12bit hex ASCII number or its text identifier (see Chapter 10 for further details). If no RISC OS filetype is provided, the existing MSDOS extension (if present) will be removed. If no parameters are given, then the current mappings are displayed.

*Fat32MapLoad
Syntax: *FAT32MAP <Filename>

*FAT32MAP loads a mapping file which must conform to the format specified by the Fat32Map command.

*Fat32MapClear
Syntax: *FAT32MAPCLEAR r

*FAT32MAPCLEAR will clear the mime mappings.

*FatInfo
Syntax: *FATINFO [<disc spec.>]

This gives details about the drive specified, returning all of information you would require. Figure 15abelow shows a typical output by the command.

*FatFileInfo
Syntax: *FATFILEINFO <File>

Gives details about file and allows you to see how fragmented it is — if it is fragmented at all.

*FatFileDeFrag
Syntax: *FATFILEDEFRAG <File>

This will attempt to defragment the named file. If the file does not need defragmenting you are informed of the fact.

*FatDirCompress
Syntax: *FATDIRCOMPRESS <Dir>

This command attempts to compress the names directory by removing entries for deleted files.

*FatReadSize
Syntax: *FATREADSIZE <n>

FAT32FS is not the most effective filing system at reading ahead and caching file or directory information, and this can lead to inconsistent results especially with larger discs. *FATREADSIZE allows you to specify the number of clusters that it reads ahead into its cache, where <n> is the number of clusters.

Example:

```
*FATREADSIZE 9
```

*FatBufQty

Syntax: *FATBUFQTY <n>

Information like directories and the file allocation table are read into buffers. These buffers are 512 bytes long. You can specify the number of buffers used for this purpose in <n>, and thereby improve performance.

    *FATBUFQTY 1024

*FatDumpSector

Syntax: *FATDUMPSECTOR <drive spec> <n>

This command reads a sector from a specified drive and displays its contents on the screen. The sector is taken from the drive and sector number specified. The dump is provided in a hexadecimal block of digits 16 wide and 16 deep. ASCII values for the hex numbers are also displayed. Also the physical and logical sector number.

Example:

    *FATDUMPSECTOR 0 1024

This reads sector &40, logical &3C0 on drive 0.

*FatDumpCluster

Syntax: *FATDUMPCLUSTER <drive spec> <n>

This command reads a cluster from a specified drive and displays its contents on the screen. The cluster is taken from the drive specified and starts at the cluster number. The dump is provided in a hexadecimal block of digits, and ASCII values for the hex numbers are also displayed. The physical and logical sector numbers for each sector are also displayed.

Example:

    *FATDUMPSECTOR 0 10

*FatNextCluster

Syntax: *FATNEXTCLUSTER <drive spec> <cluster>

This displays the next cluster number in the free space search.

Examples:

    *FATNEXTCLUSTER 1 0

This will show the next cluster that FAT32FS will start searching from.

    *FATNEXTCLUSTER 1 1

This will search for the next free cluster after the last one found.

    *FATNEXTCLUSTER 1 10

And this starts the free search from cluster 10.

*Free

Syntax: *FREE [<disc spec.>]

*FREE displays the total free space on a disc, as bytes free and bytes used. The disk may be specified, otherwise the currently mounted disk details will be returned.

*Mount

Syntax *MOUNT [disc_spec]

*MOUNT prepares a FAT32FS disc for general use by setting the current directory to its root directory. The default drive is used. See earlier for parameters that may be used with this command.

Example:

```
*MOUNT :mydisc -sp3
```

*NameDisc

Syntax: *NAMEDISC <disc spec.> <disc name>

*NAMEDISC changes the disc's name to the new one.

*WriteProtOn

*WRITEPROTON [<disc spec.>]

Prevent any write actions to the drive specified, where [<disc spec.>] may be the drive number or drive name. This does not prevent files being copied using the Desktop filer, but it will produce an error message you to decide what to do!

*WriteProtOff

*WRITEPROTOFF [<disc spec.>]

Allow writes to the drive specified, where [<disc spec.>] may be the drive number or drive name.

The Filer

The term Filer is used a lot, so it is probably worth saying a word or two about it here. The Filer is responsible for providing a graphical representation of the filing system structure. It uses standard filing system calls to do its work, and so will work with any filing system. When you double-click to open a window on a directory - this is the Filer in action.

Each filing system has its own desktop filer, such as SDFSFiler and this provides the iconbar icon for each drive provided by that filing system.

16: Window Manager

When you boot into RISC OS Pi you arrive at the Desktop. The individual components of the Desktop are delivered by the Windows Manager which provides a Wimp interface that creates a windowing system supported by context-sensitive menus and drag-and-drop functionality. And it is all configurable. (WIMP has now becomes a generic term in its own right — it was originally an acronym that stood for Windows, Icons, Menus, Pointer.)

The purpose of the Window Manager is to provide all the functionality required to develop applications that work within the RISC OS Desktop window environment. It also contains the necessary mechanisms that allow the two to communicate, and the Window Manager will also inform applications when it needs to do some associated housekeeping.

The consistent thing about all this is the look and feel of everything — and this is defined by the RISC OS Style Guide and controlled by use of the Window Manager.

The Window Manager provides a rich set of facilities and co-ordinates the user interface aspects namely: windows, icons, mice and pull-down menus. This ensures that applications look and work consistently and should benefit from being compatible with future releases of RISC OS Pi.

An Involved Process

Programming the Wimp using SWIs is an involved process — there are no specific RISC OS based * commands for this reason. It requires the implementation of a great deal of infrastructure definitions and setting-up. Whether you are using assembler, BASIC or C you have to do a lot of groundwork before you can even start setting about what you actually want to do. And you must do all of it before you can even test whether what you have done works — you cannot test a window application stage-by-stage, since there is too much interaction between the components for this to be feasible.

The overriding issue is that you can't run a multi-tasking program from a task window in the same way you can outside a task window as it is pre-emptive rather than explicit (this is detailed shortly once we've looked at the SWI calls involved). If you try you will simply get an error message stating 'Window manager is currently in use'. So the advice at this stage is to avoid trying to program the Wimp until such stage as you have gained the proficiency required and you understand fully why it is so difficult to do.

Because of the complexity of programming the Wimp, Acorn developed the Toolbox module to provide SWIs to deal with specific aspects on the interface. This aided the process but at the same time confirmed how involved the process was — not least because of the sheer volume of information required and the need to cover all bases to account for every eventuality. However, a number of excellent applications were developed around the Toolbox. These provided graphical design environments and function libraries for BASIC and programming veneers for C which have made creating Desktop components a fairly straightforwardl task. Beyond this, some language implementations under RISC OS such as RiscLua make programming the WIMP almost too simple!

That doesn't mean to say that you cannot create your own desktop Wimp applications relatively easily, as a number of excellent packages have been developed over the years that can assist in this process. We'll look at these packages and options in more detail in the next chapter. In the remainder of this chapter we'll take a general look at how the Wimp is implemented and what is actually involved in setting up a multi-tasking environment and the calls needed. This will go a long way to helping you understand the size and complexity of what is required, as well as understanding the processes taking place when using the aforementioned utilities.

Window Anatomy

Let's start off by taking a look at the anatomy of a typical window which is displayed on the desktop. There are two main areas, namely the work area and the system area. The work area contains all the application-specific output whilst the system area contains all the control mechanisms for the window. Figure 16a (over) shows a typical window and you will be able to recognise these areas for yourself.

The main component of a window is the Visible Work Area (VWA) sometimes also known as the Physical Work Area (PWA), which is bounded by a number of controls for the window. In the centre of the top of the window is a title bar which contains the textual name attached to the window. A window may be dragged around the display by holding down the select button while the pointer is within the title bar, and then moving the pointer elsewhere, releasing the button when the desired destination is reached.

At the top left corner of most windows are two buttons: go to back, which moves the window behind any other windows on the screen; and close which removes the window completely. At the top right corner is the toggle button which causes the window to expand to its full size and move to the front (if it is not already there).

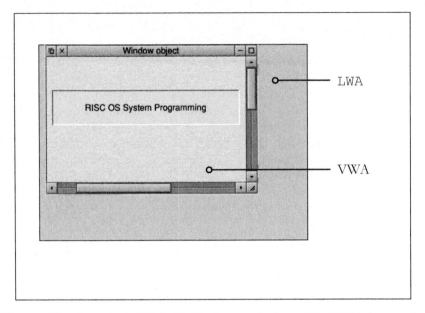

Figure 16a. A typical RISC OS Desktop window. The VWA may only
be a small only a portion of the bigger LWA.

In the bottom right-hand corner of most windows is a stretch button. Dragging
it allows the overall size of the window to be increased and decreased within
limits set by the programmer. The maximum possible size is the same as that
achieved by clicking on the full size button.

Along the right-hand side and/or the bottom edge of many windows are scroll
bars, which only appear if the whole window cannot be seen on the screen.
When the window is not as large as the maximum working area it is possible
to scroll the VWA over the whole extent of the work — known as the Logical
Work Area or LWA — in order to make any portion visible. At each extreme
of the scroll bars are arrow buttons which scroll the VWA in the appropriate
direction by a small amount, unless you click on them and hold, in which case
the visible area moves until you release. Within the scroll bars are shaded boxes
whose size indicates how much of the LWA is visible within the VWA. Their
position indicates which part (rather than how much) is visible. You can drag
these boxes within the scroll bars to make large changes to the visible portion;
repeated clicking on the arrows gets a little tedious.

The Co-ordinate System

The main part of any window is its Visible Work Area (VWA). This is bounded
by two co-ordinate pairs which define its position on the display — the bottom
left-hand corner (minimum values of X and Y) and top right-hand corner
(maximum values of X and Y). These are known as:

```
VWA_min_X, VWA_min_Y
```

and:

```
VWA_max_X, VWA_max_Y.
```

In addition, an offset co-ordinate is required to define which part of the Logical Work Area (LWA) is being displayed by the window. This co-ordinate is relative to the LWA origin, and it is known as (Scroll_X_offset, Scroll_Y_offset). It can be seen that by adjusting the values of these offsets it is possible to control which part of the LWA is visible within the VWA.

Note: confusingly, the Scroll_X_offset is the offset of the left edge of the VWA from the left edge of the LWA, but the Scroll_Y_offset is the offset of the top edge of the VWA from the bottom edge of the LWA. The reason for this appears to be that graphics origins are usually at the bottom left corner of the display, whereas text origins are usually at the top left.

Finally, the LWA origin may be displaced from the graphics origin of the display, thus adding another level of complexity to co-ordinate calculations! The co-ordinate of the LWA origin (and bottom left-hand corner) is defined by (LWA_min_X, LWA_min_Y) and its other extreme by the co-ordinate (LWA_max_X, LWA_max_Y).

These systems of co-ordinates allow applications and the Window Manager to decide where on the display to plot text and graphics. All plotting is achieved relative to the LWA origin, so co-ordinates must be calculated in these terms before plotting. Furthermore, the Window Manager provides the moveable parts of the scroll bars automatically, so it needs to be able to divine what amount of the LWA is visible in each direction.

SWIs — The Stages

Writing applications which take advantage of the Window Manager requires an approach which programmers whose experience is limited to BASIC may find a little unusual. Window applications respond passively to advice from the Window Manager about what to do next, rather than actively testing for the occurrence of particular conditions. This approach, known as event-driven programming allows the Window Manager to pass information to each window application selectively. This is done by using a system of reason codes. Such selectivity allows the Window Manager to time-slice the computer's processing power. This Wimp polling process is discussed later in the chapter.

A look at the PRMs will indicate just how many SWIs there are in relation to managing a Wimp interface and the majority of these will need to be catered for at some point in order to implement and run a fully defined system. However, for the purpose of discussion there are five calls that are essential to display a window and maintain its presence on the screen. These are:

Wimp_Initialise	SWI &400C0
Wimp_CreateWindow	SWI &400C1
Wimp_GetWindowState	SWI &400CB
Wimp_OpenWindow	SWI &400C5
Wimp_Poll	SWI &400C7

We'll look at function and requirements for each of these in turn below.

One of the key requirements that is fundamental to all these calls (and the many others associated with the Window Manager) is the requirement for a dedicated block of 256 bytes in memory — the window data block (WDB). In virtually all the calls R1 points to the location of this data block and information may be passed to and from the SWI being called. (There are other calls involved and I have taken a bit of creative licence here — but these calls in themselves provide a useful insight as to the process. Studying the Apps outlined in the next chapter will allow you to dig deeper.)

Wimp_Initialise (SWI &400C0)

In order to start a window application, the first thing to be done is to make a call to the Window Manager's initialisation process — SWI "Wimp_Initialise". The call should only be used once and requires and returns the following information:

On Entry:
R0 = Window Manager Version x 100
R1 = "TASK" (&4B534154)
R2 = Pointer to description to display in Task Manager
R3 = Pointer to list of acceptable User Messages

On Exit:
R0 = preserved
R1 = Task handle

On calling, R0 holds the version of the Window Manager (not the OS) whose API is being used. This is passed without the a decimal point — thus version 5.19 would be 519..The ASCII word value for "TASK" is passed in R1 and covers a compatibility issue with previous incarnations of the WIMP. R2 holds a pointer to an ASCII string that has the name to be displayed in the windows title bar. R3 stores the list of user message numbers that are acceptable. A value of 0 in R3 means that no messages are classified as important except for the Quit message. (The subject of messages is not discussed here in any detail and for the most part in the learning stage a value of 0 would be placed in R3). On exit the value in R1 is a task handle number for the process.

In BASIC we might be tempted to use the following code:

```
SYS "Wimp_Initialise", 519, &4B534154, A$, 0
```

Where A$ holds the title string. Although the structure of this SYS call is apparently fine it will generate an error for the reasons given at the start of this chapter and for reasons outlined in Chapter 6.

Wimp_CreateWindow (SWI &400C1)

The next step is to define the window required by setting up the window data block (WDB) which contains information in a specific format that will be utilised by Wimp_OpenWindow. On entry to the call, R1 has the address of where the data starts. The call will return the handle to the window so that it can then be displayed. This handle is used to identify the window from now on and it sits in the first word of the WDB itself. (Because this WDB is specific to the window and provided memory does not get corrupted, it should remain in this location.) It's worth bearing in mind that icons can also be created at the same time as the window itself. Several of the data items denote multiple options; for example, each of the 32 bits at +28 (Window Flags) denotes whether a particular condition is set or not. Figure 16b shows the WDB layout.

Note that this call does not actually cause the window to appear; it merely copies the block parameters into the Window Manager's workspace and returns a handle for the Window in R0. We use this handle to display the window.

Offset	Function
+00	Visible area minimum x (inclusive)
+04	Visible area minimum y (inclusive)
+08	Visible area maximum x (exclusive)
+12	Visible area maximum y (exclusive)
+16	Scroll x offset
+20	Scroll y offset
+24	Window Locations: -1=Top of the window stack -2=Bottom of the window stack -3=iconized (not visible) x=Behind the window with handle 'x'
+28	Window Flags *
+32	Title foreground and window frame colour 1
+33	Title background colour
+34	Work area foreground colour
+35	Work area background colour2
+36	Scroll bar outer colour
+37	Scroll bar Slider colour
+38	Title background colour (input focus)
+39	Extra Window Flags*
+40	Work area minimum x
+44	Work area minimum y
+48	Work area maximum x
+52	Work area maximum y
+56	Title Bar Icon Flags *
+60	Window Button Types *
+64	Sprite area control block pointer (+1 for Wimp sprite area)
+68	Minimum width of window (2 bytes)
+70	Minimum height of window (2 bytes)
+72	Title data (Icon Data)
+84	No. icons in initial definition (0 or more)
+88	0 or more Icon Block (32 bytes each)

Figure 16b. The Window Data Block layout. *Multiple options in each of these cases so check PRMs for what you need

Wimp_GetWindowState (SWI &400CB)

This call returns information about the window defined above into the defined workspace. At first nothing will change as the window has not been created, but this may not be the case when we wish to update the window. The entry and exit conditions are:

On Entry:
R1=Pointer to block
        Block+0 Window handle
R2="TASK" (&4B534154)
R3=Window handle, or
        -1 for top level window
R4= Nested Window Flag

On Exit:
R1 = Pointer to block
    Block

+0	Window handle
+4	Visible area minimum x
+8	Visible area minimum y
+12	Visible area maximum x
+16	Visible area maximum y
+20	Scroll offset x
+24	Scroll offset y
+28	Window Locations
+32	Window Flags if bit 0 of nested flags is set, or

        0 to flush all pending window opens to the screen

The Window handle is passed at the start of the data block and on exit from the call. The block will have been seeded with the relevant information to allow the window to be opened. A number of flag bits are included at offset !32 in the block: Figure 16c lists these and their effects if set on entry.

To make the window appear we ensure that the window's handle is at the start of a block (the remaining space in the block is reserved for parameters to be returned) and we call the SWI "Wimp_OpenWindow".

Wimp_OpenWindow (SWI &4000C5)

With the WDB set correctly from the Wimp_CreateWindow call, calling this SWI will open the window on the screen.

Bit	Function when set (=1)
0	Title bar present
1	Window may be moved
2	Vertical scroll bar present
3	Horizontal scroll bar present
4	Window only contains icons
5	Window is a sub-window of another
6	Window may be moved off display
7	Window has no 'back' or 'close' buttons
16 *	The window is open
17 *	The window is un-obscured
18 *	The window is full size
	* These bits are flags set by the Window Manager to return status information and have no effect if set by the application.

Figure 16c Window Flags and their effect.

Wimp_DeleteWindow SWI(&400C3)

The final step in the process is to call the Wimp_DeleteWindow(&400C3) which takes the window handle pointed to by R1 and removes the window from the display.

Wimp_Poll (SWI &400C7)

Because window applications are event-driven, the main focus of any application is the polling loop in which the application repeatedly asks the Window Manager what to do next. Remember, the Windows Manager controls everything that is going on the Desktop. Each window has to co-operate with it to ensure the smooth running of the Wimp environment, and it does this by responding to codes the Windows Manager supplies to it.

The Window Manager provides the SWI Wimp_Poll (&400C7) to achieve this; it takes a function mask in R0 (see below) and a pointer to a block (for results returned) in R1. The call returns a reason code in R0 and a pointer to the result block in R1.

On Entry:
R0   Poll Mask
R1   Pointer to 256 byte block

R3   Pointer to poll word in RMA (if R0 bit22 is set)

On Exit:

R0   Reason Code

R1   Pointer to block of data

R2   Sender's task handle

The reason code returned indicates the action to be taken by the application from the list give in Figure 16d.

No	Meaning	Reason to Call
0	No activity required	Null_Reason
1	Window needs re-drawing	Redraw_Window_Request
2	Window needs to be (re)opened *	Open_Window_Request
3	Window needs to be closed *	Close_Window_Request
4	Pointer leaving window	Pointer_Leaving_Window
5	Pointer entering window	Pointer_Entering_Window
6	Mouse buttons changed	Mouse_Click
7	User dragging window *	User_Drag_Box
8	User pressed a key	Key_Pressed
9	User selected a menu	Menu_Selection
10	User 'scrolling' window *	Scroll_Request
11	Lose_Caret	
12	Gain_Caret	
13	PollWord_NonZero	
14	Reserved	
15	Reserved	
16	Reserved	
17	User_Message	
18	User_Message_Recorded	
19	User_Message_ Acknowledge	

Figure 16d. Wimp_Poll Reason Codes.

When calling "Wimp_Poll" the bits in the function mask word supplied in R0 can be used to disable many of the reason codes listed above. For a given reason code number, the bit with the same number should be set to disable it (those marked with '*' may not be disabled). The normal requirement is for all events to be enabled, in which case a mask of zero is used, or alternative a mask of 1 if you mask out null polls so your app doesn't waste time looking at things not to do!. Refer to the PRMs for more detail on the mask bits outside of this situation. Also be aware that your application should not consume too much time between polling, otherwise other tasks may be prevented from running.

Reason Codes

For an application to work correctly it needs to respond to many of these reason codes by taking appropriate action, frequently by calling other Window Manager routines. The window's unique window handle is used as the identifier in all these calls that also require the parameter block to be active. A brief description for each reason code follows. A list of these and a brief note on what they do is provided in Figure 16e.

Co-operatively Done

RISC OS is a *co-operatively multi-tasked* OS. If you're used to programming other systems, you might discover it behaves a little differently in the ways programs co-exist together.

Co-operative multitasking means that, once a program is running, it has full use of the CPU. With the exception of interrupts and other background operations, once your program is running all other programs are paused. This isn't very helpful if we want to run more than one program at once, so it's up to each program to yield the CPU on a regular basis so that other programs can run. Programs do this by calling SWI Wimp_Poll. Control will only return from Wimp_Poll to your program if there's some action to be handled (like a mouse button clicked on one of the programs windows). Alternatively you can elect for your program to receive *null polls*, which means the OS will return control to your program once all the other programs are done handling their own Wimp_Poll events.

Wimp programs are therefore *event-driven*, something happens, a message is issued through Wimp_Poll and the event must handled, the event type being signified by a reason code. Once done, Wimp_Poll again and wait until the next event happens. If you're program is trying to do some work (like copying some files or converting an image) it has to be split into small pieces that can happen between calls to Wimp_Poll. Take too long and the desktop starts slowing down because other programs don't have enough CPU time to get their own work done. The important point here is that you have to write your code so that it remembers what you were last doing before the CPU is whisked away by Wimp_Poll so that it can jump straight back at the point where it left off.

No.	Function	Description
0	No Activity	User has not taken any actions which affect the application. Issued each time the mouse pointer is moved out of the VWA.
1	Window Needs Re-drawing	Indicates start of the sequence to update a window.
2	Window Needs to be (Re) Opened	Issued whenever a window is brought to the front, re-sized, or scrolled.
3	Window Needs to be Closed	Indicates user has clicked on the 'close' box of the window.
4	Pointer Leaving Window	Issued each time the mouse pointer is moved out of the VWA.
5	Pointer Entering Window	Generated each time the pointer enters the VWA part of the window.
6	Mouse Buttons have Changed	Issued each time the mouse buttons change state.
7	User Dragging Window	Sent at the end of a drag sequence whose effect is application-specific.
8	User Pressed a Key	Issued if the user presses a key when the pointer is within one of the application's windows.
9	User Selected a Menu	Returned when the user has made a selection from an active menu (which has been set up using SWI "Wimp_CreateMenu").

Figure 16e. Reason codes issued by the Window Manager and their meaning

This can be awkward for some programs, so there's a way of doing *pre-emptive multitasking*. This is a way that your program just gets on with its work and the OS decides when to pause us and hand over control to other programs. Other operating systems like Windows and Linux use this method. On RISC OS it's achieved by the TaskWindow module, which is a way to run single-tasking command-line programs in the multitasking desktop. A TaskWindow task consists of the program running as a separate task, plus handlers for input and output. The most common handlers for I/O are text editors such as !Edit, and StrongED.

If you're writing lower-level code, Wimp programs and TaskWindow clients may not be sufficient. For example, if you're writing some code to play an MP3 music file. You need to make sure that you get enough CPU time every few milliseconds, otherwise the music would stop. You want the music to continue to play, even if the computer is busy doing something else. You can do this if you're writing a module by using timers. If you call SWI OS_CallEvery, you can register a routine that will be called repeatedly after a given number of centiseconds. If you use OS_CallAfter you'll be called only once after the delay. Another way is to claim one of the timer events, which happen every centisecond or every video frame (only use the latter if you want to synchronise with the display, as it changes if you change screen mode).

Transient Callback

One problem with these timers is that they run in Interrupt Mode, or Supervisor Mode with interrupts disabled. This means other parts of the system will be paused, for example, it may skip keypresses if you take too long. And many SWIs aren't available, if you try to print any characters to the screen or read from disc you may crash the machine. (The reason for this is *re-entrancy*, which you might see noted in SWI descriptions in the PRM. If interrupts are turned on, one routine could get interrupted by another, which eventually calls the first routine. Many modules can't cope with running one concurrent operation inside another, and this will cause a crash.) A way around this is *transient callbacks*.

A transient callback is set using OS_AddCallBack. You supply this with a pointer to a routine that will be called when the CPU is next idle and in User Mode. This means it can access all the usual SWIs. If your routine takes too long the desktop will still slow down as no other programs will get a chance to run, but all the usual housekeeping can still carry on.

So the MP3 player could do this: Register a routine to be called every three centiseconds with OS_CallEvery. This routine, which is running in supervisor mode with interrupts disabled, does nothing but register a callback routine with OS_AddCallBack. The callback routine is now running in User Mode, so can grab an MP3 frame from disc, decode it, and schedule it to be played. When you return from this routine you'll return to the user program—only to receive some CPU time again in 3 centiseconds time.

Callbacks and event routines sit in a middle ground —more precise timing and more guaranteed CPU than Wimp programs or TaskWindows, but are limited in how much CPU they can use in each slice without affecting the machine. If you need more accurate timing you have two options: either use the RTSupport module (which is not mentioned in the PRM but is described on the RISC OS Open wiki), or you can claim the hardware timer interrupts yourself. Handling the timer interrupts is one way to get more accurate timing than a centisecond if you need that.

Putting it all together: TaskWindow starts a program as a normal co-operative Wimp program. The program doesn't call Wimp_Poll itself, so ordinarily the rest of the desktop would hang until the program completed. So TaskWindow claims the timer event that happens every centisecond. On this timer, it registers a callback (actually a *callback handler*, a slightly different type from the transient callback mentioned above). The callback happens next time the CPU is in user mode. Inside the callback routine TaskWindow calls Wimp_Poll on behalf of the application, and deals with incoming messages. So the program runs as a normal single-tasking program, but in the background timers go off frequently calling Wimp_Poll so the rest of the Desktop is given a chance to run. As far as the program is concerned it's doesn't even know the Desktop exists, yet there can be dozens of TaskWindow programs running like this concurrently. And it makes full use of all the methods described in this section!

Menu Support

Besides providing overall control of windows, the Window Manager also contains a number of SWIs which offload the more mundane aspects of dealing with user selections from menus. The idea behind menus is to minimise the scope for user error by predefining the valid selections available. The Window Manager supports multi-level or hierarchical menus, which allow complex sequences of selections to be made from almost any number of menu levels.

The user opens a menu by clicking on the middle mouse button: the application determines which window the pointer is over at the time, and the Window Manager displays the appropriate menu and allows the user to make a selection. By taking advantage of the Window Manager support for menus, application programmers may be relieved of the burden of dealing with menu selections and simply concern themselves with the nature of these selections. The results of selections are returned in a control block provided by Wimp_Poll reason code nine.

The Structure of Menus

A menu is described by the application to the Window Manager in a similar way to that used for windows. In fact, menus are really just windows whose contents are predefined — this predefinition allowing the Window Manager to do most of the work in dealing with user selections.

A menu consists of a list of entries displayed as a column of lines of text within a window. The window has none of the control buttons and scroll bars associated with normal windows, but instead each of the menu entries may have three graphical effects associated with it:

- It may be dimmed, a shading effect which indicates that it is not valid to select the entry.

- There may be a tick or check mark which indicates that the entry is already selected or is a default value.

- There may be an arrow facing off the right-hand side of an entry which indicates the presence of a sub-menu or window. Moving the mouse to the right over one of these arrows causes the sub-menu to appear to the right of the first menu, and this process may continue through more levels of sub-menu.

The Window Manager attempts to be intelligent about the positioning of menus, so if the sub-menu is selected from a menu which is already near the right-hand edge of the screen it will be displaced left to ensure it is completely visible.

Programming Menus

To prepare the Window Manager for the handling of menus it is necessary to call the SWI Wimp_CreateMenu for each menu in the application. This call takes a pointer to the menu's control block and a co-ordinate pair which specifies where it should initially appear on the display. The program should then return to the main polling loop to await the issue of reason code nine which indicates that a selection has actually been made.

SWI Wimp_CreateMenu (SWI &400D4)

This call advises the Window Manager that a menu structure should be installed in its tables. On entry, R0 must either contain -1 (in which case all menus are closed) or a pointer to the menu definition block for the new menu. In the latter case (R2 and R3) give the co-ordinates of the top left-hand corner of the menu when it is displayed.

The menu control block consists of a series of entries, each of which is in the same format. The first entry defines the top level menu and its entries, with pointers leading the way to the sub-menu definitions and so on. The structure of the menu control block is given in Figure 16f.

Offset	Description	Default
+0	Menu title (if null, then the menu is untitled)	
+12	Title foreground and frame colour	7
+13	Title background colour	2
+14	Work area foreground colour	7
+15	Work area background colour	0
+16	Width of menu items (in pixels)	
+20	Height of menu items (in pixels)	44
+24	Vertical gap between items (in pixels)	0
+28	Menu Items (24 bytes each)	

Figure 16f. Structure of a Menu control block.

To enable menu windows to open on the other alternate side of the menu window, the menu title should be prefixed with '\'. This also reverses the sides on which ticks and sub-menu arrows appear, and reverses the text alignment settings.

The menu entries consist of 24-byte blocks which contain the names and flags for each entry. Their format is as shown in Figure 16g.

Offset	Contents
+0	Flags: Bit 0 - Set means 'tick' the entry Bit 1 - Set means follow this entry with a dotted divider Bit 2 - Set means this entry may be overwritten by user Bit 7 - Set means this is the last item in the menu
+4	Pointer to sub-menu or handle of sub-window or -1 (for neither)
+8	Icon flag
+12	Text of entry terminated by zero (11 characters maximum)

Figure 16g. Menu Item format.

Where an entry has a sub-menu, the presence of a valid pointer or window handle at offset +4 causes the arrow to appear automatically. For sub-menus, the offset of the sub-menu in the menu control block should be inserted here; for sub-windows, the window handle of the appropriate window should be inserted.

The structure of sub-menu entries is just the same as that for the first menu, with all the information indicated above repeated as necessary.

Desktop Components

Although the Wimp is the dominant aspect of the Desktop there are a few other components that you should be aware of.

Pinboard

The Pinboard allows files, applications and directories to be pinned as icons to the Desktop and thus outside the Filer. Several * commands are provided by the module and are listed in Figure 16h.

Command	Action
*AddTinyDir	Add the icon of a file to the iconbar
*Backdrop	Display a sprite on the desktop background
*Pin	Add a file, application or directory to the desktop pinboard
*PinBoard	Initialise the pinboard, removing any existing pinned icons and backdrop.
*RemoveTinyDir	Remove the icon of a file added to the iconbar

Figure 16h. * Commands provided by the Pinboard Module.

With the exception of *PIN all these commands require additional information to be supplied, and this can be located in the PRMs (3-291 to 3-296, 5a-487).

TaskWindow

One of the functions of the TaskWindow Module is to provide the pre-emptive multitasking ability. When a task is created from the use of the *TaskWindow command, the resultant output is called the child task. The parent task is the process that displays the output of the child. Thus the parent task is controlling the child task and any screen output produced by the child is intercepted and sent in Wimp messages to the parent. Note that a task does not necessarily need to open a window other than to get input and display output.

You can think of task windows having two parts: a task that makes a command line multitask by pre-empting it, and a means to pass the text input and output of that program to another task for display. The display program could be a terminal program like Nettle, but more often is an editor like !Edit, Zap or StrongED.

ColourTrans

The ColourTrans Module is another used by the Desktop (and Font Manager); it handles the representation of colour on screen and also when printing. It provides the functionality of the palette in determining the most appropriate colour available, given input values of Red, Green and Blue, and the colour depth of the screen mode.

ColourTrans provides three * commands but are reserved fr system use . A number of SWI calls are also provided and the majority of these deal with colour calibration and conversion of values.

ColourTrans also provides an intelligent way to handle colour with sprites.

A Reminder

The Window Manager is not an overly complex mechanism to use but it is a long winded one simply because of the amount of information that has to be processed. The data block and its management should be considered a serious task and even a byte of information out of place at any point can create havoc (as I have proved on previous occasions!). Because of this be careful with your programming. In BASIC managing these data blocks can be quite messy and require lots of CASE statements. If you have the option then you may find it easier to deal with to use C and to set up a series of typedef'd structs, placed inside a master structure. Libraries like OSLib make this easier. Using Assembler you can at least make use of labels to each of the data offset points.

To reiterate the point made at the start of this chapter — this has been an overview of how the Window Manager works and an introduction to the essential calls that must be implemented and managed in order to get started. These in themselves will not allow you to write your own Wimp and you will need to reference the PRMs and other tutorial sources.

A far better solution is to utilise a third party application to create and manage the Wimp. This is discussed in the next chapter.

17: WIMP Utilities

The Toolbox ultimately provides an easier but not necessarily simpler way of programming the Wimp. A lot of the code that needed to be written in the past is now provided automatically by the Toolbox libraries.. While effective, the process was still time consuming and clunky and required a much understanding of what you were trying to do.

Toolbox was originally designed with the C programmer in mind, but gradually a number of programs came to the fore that allowed the BBC BASIC programmer to developer their own Wimp applications using graphical interfaces and user libraries. These tools have all proven to be effective in their own way and I would strongly recommend anyone considering creating their own Wimp application to look at these as good tools-for-the-job. Most of them are also free. They all have relatively small learning curves, the time for which is well worth investing in. The end of this chapter also looks at a small utility called !MultiTask, which all RISC OS System programmers should know about.

Links to all the programs and applications mentioned in this chapter can be found on the Book Resource Pages on my website.

Toolbox

A Toolbox application uses a Resources file to define templates from which it can create a large number of user-interface objects including windows, menus and icons. !ResEd is the tool used to do this and is also used by several applications mentioned here (It may already be included as part of your distro; if not you can download it through PackMan and have a look.). At run-time, the application manipulates its objects by using methods, which are driven through Toolbox SWIs. The Toolbox will dispatch these methods to the appropriate module which implements the class of object (This defines what it does; for example, a button is pressed) and to which object the method is being applied.

At a SWI level, an object is created using Toolbox_CreateObject. The calling application will supply either the name of a template for the object, or the address of a block of memory containing such a template (does this sound familiar?). If its creation was successful, an object handle will be passed back to the calling application. Given the object's id, it is possible to find out the name of the template used to create it using Toolbox_GetTemplateName. An object is shown on the screen using Toolbox_ShowObject and can be deleted using the Toolbox_DeleteObject. As you can see, the names in use are all reasonably self-explanatory. Where, when and how the object is displayed on the screen is defined by flag bits at the appropriate point of the definition.

An important part of managing the Toolbox user interface is the Toolbox event. This is a Wimp event which is delivered to the calling application with Wimp_ToolboxEvent. Each Toolbox event has its own specific event code, which is a 32-bit integer defined in a similar manner to Wimp message numbers.

Toolbox events are similar in principle to Wimp events and are captured by polling. They are there to flag application operations and also used to warn the client application that a particular action has been taken by the Toolbox. For example, if an application creates and shows a Print Dialogue Box when the user clicks on the Print button, a Toolbox event will be delivered to the application indicating that a Print operation has been requested, and giving the number of pages to be printed, the scale factor to use during printing etc. Information is supplied in a format not dissimilar to the Wimp_Poll block. A Toolbox event is raised using the SWI Toolbox_RaiseToolboxEvent.

As mentioned earlier Toolbox was initially aimed at the C programmer — and so provides veneers including Toolbox classes and libraries for use in C programs.. However, applications and extensions using BBC BASIC have been developed that make using Toolbox almost transparent and a couple of these, AppBasic and Dr Wimp, are discussed below.

The Toolbox is extensive and I would refer readers to the User Interface Toolbox Manual which is 525 pages long. This can be found on-line and a link to this can be found on the Book Resources Page of my website.

!AppBasic

AppBasic is really interesting in that it creates an interface between BBC BASIC and the Toolbox that acts as a framework on which you can visually build Wimp applications. It uses a combination of GUI and BASIC programs to do this in what is a remarkably easy manner, and takes advantage of other existing applications.

The Manual that is supplied with AppBasic includes a few worked examples that show you how you can go about achieving similar outcomes in different ways. When you create a new application in AppBasic it creates all the necessary infrastructure and files required. Indeed, it is possible to create applications without having to write a single line of code.

Before you get started you will need a copy of AppBasic downloaded from its website (a direct link can be found on Book Support Pages), and a copy of !ResEd (as mentioned above) You may also find that some of the keyboard-mouse combinations detailed in the manual to get at certain features do not work, in which case you simply need to experiment a little. For example, I found that a required ALT-Double Click was replaced by a simple single click (no ALT necessary).

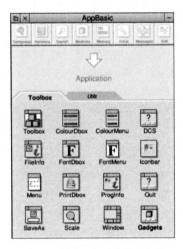

Figure 17a. The AppBasic main window.

The simple example window shown in Figure 17b took just a handful of actions to complete.

Applications are built by using templates and copying gadgets into them, editing their details as you go — the latter being a matter of simple form filling and box ticking. The final programs can be compiled and the size is significantly smaller than that which can be achieved using the Toolbox on its own.

The installation comes with a set of examples which are well worth investigating — the help files with them allow you to click and step through them nd see what routines and events are being captured and used. An hour or so spent with these will give you some detailed insight into how versatile AppBasic is. All the completed programs include checks to ensure that all the relevant Toolbox modules are in place before the applications are run.

Programming AppBasic consists of placing files in the !RunImage directory (at any level). These files are BBC BASIC libraries containing lists of procedure and function definitions, as such files consist of sequences of DEF PROC and DEF FN blocks. There are a few rules here but these are mainly to do with avoiding name clashes. The Utils library has a small collection of procedures and functions and these can be used to perform some of the routine tasks which arise when coding an application. The only code as such that the programmer has to provide is that needed to deal with Desktop events such as selecting a menu entry, clicking an action button or pressing a key. Everything is handled by AppBasic — not just windows, but menus, icons, sprites and more.— anything you need.

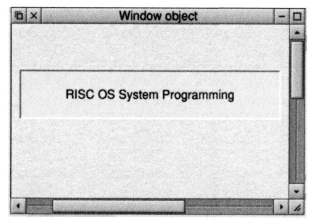

Figure 17b. A simple example window completed quickly.

Working through the manual examples and then looking at the completed application examples, should provide you with enough knowledge to start writing your own Wimp applications knowing that the Toolbox and BBC BASIC is underpinning them all to achieve what should be consistent and bug-free results.

Dr Wimp

Dr Wimp can be downloaded and installed through PackMan. It consists of a set of utilities and a function library designed to make multi-tasking Desktop Wimp programming easy for anyone reasonably familiar with BBC BASIC. It comes with an extensive manual that documents just about everything and also guides you through some worked examples.

For many requirements, the skeleton application provided (!MyApp) will do most of what you want, and using a copy of this as a starting point is a good idea. !MyApp contains a number of files but the two key components are DrWimp and !RunImage. DrWimp is a library that contains BASIC function definitions for every Wimp occasion. The !RunImage file contains user-defined DEFs which you edit with the information that is required to create the Wimp that you want. !RunImage contains files with default settings to produce what might be termed a standard Wimp, but once you have edited it to contain your own requirements you are ready to fly.

As with AppBasic, with Dr Wimp you never have to worry about window data blocks and the various flag settings required. In just a few lines of BBC BASIC,

223

you can create a window that is opened by clicking on a dedicated icon on the icon bar. To develop an application, you expand the information and add relevant BASIC code to one or more of the user-function definitions in the !RunImage until you have what you want. And because you have the structure and outline in place for a complete Wimp at the start of adding your own modification, you can actually test it as you go.

Whilst a lot of the drudgery is removed you still have to take responsibility for the parameters you require for your Wimp. You must seed these into the template and ensure that the default values provided by DrWimp are updated correctly by any returned details. But this is a requirement of your design regardless of what method you use to get there.

Post-production utilities are also include that will automatically allow you to strip away sections of the DrWimp library that you are not using, thereby reducing application space and increasing execution speed. Another utility — !Fabricate — also exists; with this you can create a customised starter application for your own needs.

The great benefit of a library implementation such as the one Dr Wimp provides is that you don't need to bog yourself down with complications. Want to push text into an icon? Forget memory blocks, dealing with indirected icons and the like, just call the SetIconText function. There is a learning curve with Dr Wimp, and once you have a full understanding of all the functions provided in the library it is quick and easy to create Wimp applications that really work.

Dr Wimp C

Dr WimpC is the C incarnation of the original Dr Wimp application outlined above. It provides a full conversion of the DrWimp library into C, along with a front end project management tool for creation and maintenance of source code and application resources.

The native RISC OS application structure is used so that applications can also be compiled and edited independently of Dr WimpC. Any template editor can be used to design window definitions for use in an application.

The DrWimpC library can operate in the same way as the original and it implements an equivalent library function and user function for each FN and PROC defined in the BASIC DrWimp Library. Only the events used by an application are included into the final !RunImage file. It can also operate using template code functions whereby C functions can be linked directly to an icon by name. This makes the final code much more compact as only the functions used by the file are compiled. This methodology makes it easy to build up your own libraries of template code files which you can reuse as the need arises.

GGC and ROOL C are the two main compilers supported by !DrWimpC.

Basalt

Basalt is a BASic ALTernative module that adds new commands and additional functionality to existing commands in all versions of BBC BASIC V. Basalt provides extensive support to the Toolbox with a range of new keywords to utilise its features. Programs using Basalt can be written, using StrongEd for example, developed and tested as if was a BASIC program. The only real requirement is to make sure the Basalt module is loaded and that the command:

```
*BASALTINIT
```

is the first effective line of a program. This ensures that the relevant vectors are claimed to ensure Basalt is integrated with the BASIC module.

Basalt is free so it is well worth downloading and having a look at it. If you are a regular BASIC programmer (it is not compatible with BASIC VI at the time of writing) then you will find the improvements that it brings useful. The short snippet below is taken from a bigger Basalt program and is included to show you how a procedure can be defined to display a window. The procedure requires a little data passed into it, but from what you will have learned in the previous chapter, you should be able to see what is happening here, even if you know nothing more about Basalt!

```
DEFPROCdisplay(x%,y%,c%,w%,f%,i%,g%,h%,n%,o%,p%)
  `MainW#@Xcoord.Value=STR$x%
  `MainW#@Ycoord.Value=STR$y%
  `MainW#@Colour.Value="&"+NUM$(c%,1,3)
  `MainW#@Wimphd.Value="&"+NUM$(w%,1)
  `MainW#@Wimpfg.Value="&"+NUM$(f%,1)
  `MainW#@Iconhd.Value=STR$i%
 IF g%=0 THEN `MainW#@Taskhd.Value=" " ELSE
`MainW#@Taskhd.Value="&"+NUM$(g%,1)
  `MainW#@Iconfg.Value="&"+NUM$(h%,1)
 IF w%<=0 THEN `MainW#@Tasknm.Value="Iconbar" ELSE
`MainW#@Tasknm.Value=RETURN$(n%)
 IF o% THEN
   `MainW#@Object.Value="&"+NUM$(o%,1)
   `MainW#@Compnt.Value=STR$p%:REM"&"+NUM$(p%,1) :
 ELSE
   `MainW#@Object.Value=""
   `MainW#@Compnt.Value=""
 ENDIF
ENDPROC
```

Other Options

WimpWorks is a paid-for application that interfaces with BBC BASIC to produce multi-tasking applications. It is based around a system of editors and plug-in components that you can configure using fill-in boxes.

For the C programmer who wants better access to the Toolbox, DeskLib provides a general-purpose C library. It provides support for window and icon manipulation, menu creation, graphics routines, message handling, filing operations, font handling and string manipulation. High level event management functions are provided in order to build coherent and powerful code. As we saw in Chapter 6, OSlib is also another library that provides a great set of veneers to the Toolbox.

!MultiTask

!MultiTask is a multi-tasking desktop utility which allows you to examine the contents of files and to load, run and edit BASIC programs from the desktop. It is available from !Store and clicking on the icon installs it on the icon bar. Dragging and dropping a BASIC file onto this will load the program into its own window from where you can type RUN to fire it up as though it was a multi-tasking program. The upshot of this is that it takes away the need to leave the Desktop to run a graphics program.

The standard way of doing this would be to press F12 to display the CLI prompt at the bottom of the screen and then typing BASIC to enter the BASIC interpreter. A CLS will remove the Desktop, thus giving you a whole screen to work with as you wish. Any graphics you set up now should work as expected. Typing *QUIT and then hitting the RETURN key a second time would restore you back to the Desktop.

The other advantage in using !MultiTask in this way is that it automatically sets the CSD (currently selected directory or @) to the last opened directory window or last opened BASIC program, thus allowing 'LIBRARY "file_in_same_csd"' to work. Also, just entering SAVE "name" works, for those too lazy to use a full pathname! There are plenty of other bonuses when using !MultiTask and these are detailed in the readme file supplied with the utility.

In addition, the program is RUN in such a way (using *WimpTask) that when it is terminated it is retained in memory so that the variables are available for inspection. During the debugging process the error procedure of the program concerned may be amended to offer the option of termination after an error or sequence of errors.

Normally most programs are *run from a Task Window (CTRL-F12). This allows single-tasking non-Wimp programs to be run in the multi-tasking desktop alongside other programs. It handles pre-emption of the program and all its input and output. However, it does not actually present the program to the user, which is done through another desktop program, the host. The host is normally a text editor like StrongEd which display text but not graphics and are thus ignored. (Simplified version.)

Chapter 18 — The Font Manager contains a BBC BASIC program that demonstrates the use of fonts. Try running this program from a Task Window (running BASIC) and then by dropping it onto !MultiTask. This is a really good demonstration of the difference between the two and what !MultiTask does!

The action of pressing F12 can be simulated with the following command:

```
*FX 138,0,204
```

Alternatively place this in an Obey file which you can leave on your Desktop and click on it when you need the full-screen CLI.

18: Font Manager

Whatever you do in a programming sense, being able to display and tabulate information is important and RISC OS supplies the facilities for you to do this given almost any situation. Not only can you vary the size of your text, but you can define its colour, its orientation, its background and very much more.

The Font Manager and the Font Painter allow characters to be displayed in a number of fonts, anti-aliased, scaled to any size, proportionally spaced and with optional position justification. When RISC OS was first launched fonts were still only just stepping outside the bounds of character matrices and anti-aliased character sets were all the rage, so this was cutting edge stuff at the time. Now a wide variety and range of fonts are available — from TrueType to Unicode — along with some excellent utilities for editing your own Font sets.

The Font Manager module supplies an extensive range of SWIs and we'll be looking at some of these in due course. The Font Manager also supplies a number of * commands. These have limited practical use in a programming sense in that they are mainly for interrogating what is installed and what is available. In this sense they are utilised in immediate mode rather than in programs.

Figure 18a overleaf lists these * commands and provides a brief description of their function.

Font Manager

The Font Manager deals with the business of reading font definitions into memory (a process known as caching) scaling the fonts to the required size as it does so. An area of memory may be set aside for the Font Manager's cache using the configuration option FontSize, and this limits the number of fonts which may be cached at any moment. If insufficient space is available in memory, the Font Manager will delete some of the existing fonts to make room for fresh ones. Thus the application does not have to deal with memory management issues.

The Font Painter takes the cached font definitions and paints the fonts onto the display either by means of SWI calls or through the normal VDU channel for printing text. This latter technique is achieved by intercepting the VDU extension vector VDUXV.

Command	Description
*FontCat	Lists the fonts in <Font$Path>
*FontInstall	Installs a font directory for use by the Font Manager, and also ensures that the directory is re-scanned.
*FontLibrary	Temporarily installs a font directory for use by the Font Manager. There is normally only one such directory at a time.
*FontList	Lists fonts currently cached.
*FontMax	Max point height of rescaled bitmaps (use outlines if bigger).
*FontRemove	Removes a font directory from the Font Manager's list.
*LoadFontCache	Load font cache from a file (only allowed if no fonts are claimed).
*SaveFontCache	Save font cache to a named file.

Figure 18a. The *commands provided by the Font Manager.

So that the Font Manager and the Font Painter can communicate with each other effectively there is a fixed relationship between the scales each use. The Font Manager works in 1/1000s of a point, a typographer's measure which is itself 1/72nd of an inch. Thus the Font Manager's basic units are 1/72000ths of an inch. The Font Painter, on the other hand, works with screen units (pixels) which it assumes to be 1/180th of an inch.

Font Management

The Font Manager handles the movement and scaling of font files which are stored on the selected filing system. The RISC OS variable Font$Prefix specifies where the font files are to be found. Font files are stored in sub-directories of a directory whose name is the name of the font, so a full pathname is derived by using the contents of Font$Prefix followed by the name of the font.

```
*SET Font$Prefix $.Welcome.Fonts
```

This indicates that all the files for the font named Trinity should henceforth be found in:

`$.Welcome.Fonts.Trinity`

To allow the Font Manager to perform caching and de-caching automatically it is necessary to follow this procedure:

- Request the font using SWI "Font_FindFont" by name, specifying its point size and screen resolution. A font handle is returned by the Font Manager; use this handle in any subsequent requests to the Font Manager.

- Advise the Font Manager that the font is no longer needed by calling SWI "Font_LoseFont" with the handle.

When an application requests a font, the Font Manager first checks the cache to see if the font is already available in the specified size. If so, the handle of the font is returned immediately; otherwise, the Font Manager loads the font information from the filing system (evicting other fonts from the cache if necessary) and returns a new handle to the application.

Display & Performance

The Font Manager has a number of techniques available to it to optimise font quality for both on-screen and printed fonts. A couple have already been mentioned so let's look at them in more detail. They are:

- Anti-aliasing

- Hinting

- Font caching of bitmap fonts

Anti-aliasing

If the outline of a character passes partially through a pixel on the screen, then the non-anti-aliased font will appear to have a jagged pyramid-type edge. To counter this, anti-aliasing relies on an optical trick and smoothing out the edges by painting intermediate pixels in intermediate colours.

You can see how this is done by typing some text in an Edit window using a 12 point font and then select Display/Font/Trinity/Medium to display the text in an anti-aliased font. Then use the !CloseUp utility to zoom in on the font edges!

Hinting

With this technique the outline of the character being displayed (or printed) is changed to suit the resolution of the image being created. It is used automatically by the Font Manager when anti-aliasing is disabled. The technique is especially effective where fonts are scaled, and when half-tones are not available (as on most printers).

Bitmap font caching

RISC OS keeps as many bitmap fonts as it can in an area of memory called the font cache.

Displaying fonts can be a processor intensive task. Too slow and writing information to the screen can become visibly slow. The Font Manager tries to balance this and provide a reasonable blend of screen quality and performance. This is not always satisfactory so RISC OS provides you with two ways of adjusting it:

- Change the way anti-aliasing is done (or switch it off altogether)

- Change the size of the font cache

Where possible, it is better to use fonts of a larger size as they do not require anti-aliasing. This is because their edges cover more pixels and are therefore naturally smoother. So, for screen use at least, it is better to use the Fonts Configuration window in !Boot to place an upper limit on the size of anti-aliased fonts

If the font cache is not large enough to hold all the fonts that you require then excluded fonts will need to be loaded on-the-fly as required. This can cause delays which can reflect on screen performance and the speed of painting the font on the screen. If you see an hourglass on the screen as the desktop is redrawn you may need to increase the font cache size. Increasing the minimum size of the cache means that the text is drawn more quickly. A computer with 4MB of memory can benefit from a cache of 256kB and ideally you'll have enough memory to utilise a cache of at least 1Mb for optimum performance

The Font cache size set in the Memory allocation screen is overridden by the value given in your Desktop boot file. If you change the Font cache size you must also save your Desktop boot file again so that your change can take effect.

One extra type of font painting is sub-pixel anti-aliasing which creates four sets of a font in memory to help render on screen more quickly. The proviso here is that you should adjust your memory cache to account for this extra requirement. But this is not really a major concern on the Raspberry Pi!

An Example

Program 18a uses the Font Manager to display both text and colour palettes on the screen using a number of SWI calls. The program demonstrates co-ordinate conversion and a number of other useful techniques.

Program 18a Displaying text and colour palettes on the screen using SWI calls.

```
 10 REM >Prog18a
 20 REM Font Demonstration
 30 REM RPi RISC OS Programming
 40 :
 50 REM Font$Prefix should be set to font directory
 60 :
 70 *SET Font$Prefix $.Welcome.Fonts
 80 :
 90 SYS "Font_CacheAddr" TO version%,cacheused%,cachesize%
100 vers$="Font Manager vers. "+STR$(version%/100)
110 SYS "Font_FindFont",,"Trinity.Medium",48*16,48*16 TO
Trinity%
120 SYS "Font_FindFont",,"Corpus.Medium",32*16,32*16 TO
Corpus%
130 SYS "Font_FindFont",,"Trinity.Medium",24*16,18*16 TO
SmallTrinity%
140 :
150 REM Set up the palette and show them as stripes.
160 SYS "Font_SetPalette", ,0,1, 6, &00000000, &F0F0F000
170 SYS "Font_SetPalette", , 7, 8, 7, &F0F0F000, &00600000
180 :
190 FOR s%=0 TO 1279 STEP 80
200 GCOL s%/80
210 RECTANGLE FILL s%,0,79,1023-32
220 NEXT
230 :
240 REM Choose the colours and the Trinity font.
250 SYS "Font_SetFontColours",Trinity%,7,8,7
260 SYS "Font_SetFont",Trinity%
270 :
280 REM Define rub out box and print a message.
290 MOVE 50,800
300 MOVE 1230,940
310 SYS "Font_Paint",,vers$,%10010,50,840
320 :
330 REM Position cursor after justification.
340 MOVE 100,516:MOVE 1180,572
350 MOVE 1180,532
360 :
370 REM Select the font and display a message.
```

```
380 SYS "Font_SetFont", SmallTrinity%
390 SYS "Font_Paint",,"This is 24pt justified Trinity",
%10011,100,532
400 :
410 REM Select some new colours and the Corpus font.
420 SYS "Font_SetFontColours",Corpus%,0,1, 6
430 SYS "Font_SetFont",Corpus%
440 :
450 REM Define a rub out box
460 MOVE 0,160
470 MOVE 1280, 300
480 :
490 REM Find point size of rub out box and string size
500 text$="This is on the right"
510 SYS "Font_Converttopoints",,1280,140 TO
,BoxXinPts%,BoxYinPts%
520 SYS "Font_StringWidth",, text$,BoxXinPts%,BoxYinPts%,
32, LEN(text$) TO ,,XoffPts%,YoffPts%
530 :
540 REM Convert size back to OS units and print right-
justified
550 SYS "Font_ConverttoOS",,XoffPts%,YoffPts% TO
,Xoff%,Yoff%
560 SYS "Font_Paint", ,text$, %10010, 1280-Xoff%, 208
570 END
```

The program starts by ensuring that the Font$Prefix variable is pointing to the fonts which we are going to use (line 70). It then uses SWI "Font_CacheAddr" to determine which version of the Font Manager is being used, and to return the total size of the font cache and the amount already used. This call is made with R0 containing zero and returns with the version number*100 in R0, the amount of cache used in R1 and the total cache size in R2.

Next (lines 110 to 130), three different combinations of font and size are requested from the Font Manager using the SWI "Font_FindFont". This takes a pointer to the font name in R1, the width in points*16 in R2, the height in points*16 in R3, and optionally the X and Y resolutions of the display in pixels per inch in R4 and R5 (if zero is supplied then the default is used). The Font Manager returns a handle to the font in R0. The following line of BASIC places the handle in Trinity% for a 48 point square version of the supplied font "Trinity Medium":

```
SYS "Font_FindFont", , "Trinity .Medium", 48*16, 48*16 TO
Trinity%
```

The palette needs to be set up to anti-alias the fonts correctly. Fonts are inherently anti-aliased using 16 colours, so in modes where this number of colours is not sparc, the number of anti-aliasing levels must be reduced. This is achieved (line 160 and 170) by issuing SWI "Font_SetPalette" which takes as parameters the background logical colour in R1, the foreground logical colour in R2, the foreground colour offset (see below) in R3, the physical background colour in R4 and the last physical foreground colour in R5.

Consider the following line:

```
SYS "Font_SetPalette" , ,0,1,6, &00000000, &F0F0F000
```

The last two figures indicate the start and end physical colours. These are in the form &BBGGRR00 where BB, GG and RR are the blue, green and red intensities respectively.

Having identified to the Font Manager those fonts which will need caching, and having set up the palette for anti-aliasing, we may now proceed to actually display text.

The first stage is to identify the colours in which we wish to display the chosen font using SWI "Font_SetFontColours". This SWI takes a font handle in R0 (or 0 for the current or most recently used font), a back-ground logical colour in R1, a foreground logical colour in R2 and a foreground colour offset in R3 (as above). This call returns no results, but simply establishes the colours that will subsequently be used. The following line is used in the program at line 250:

```
SYS "Font_SetFontColours", Trinity%, 7,8,7
```

The second stage is to ask the Font Manager to be prepared to print in the font we intend to use (line 260). This is achieved using the SWI "Font_SetFont" which takes the font handle in R0 and returns no results:

```
SYS "Font_SetFont",Trinity%
```

Finally, we can actually pass to the Font Painter the text to be displayed, accompanied by a plot type indicating the way in which the text should appear (line 310). The SWI "Font_Paint" achieves this by taking a pointer to the string to be displayed in R1, the plot type in R2 (discussed in more detail below) and the X and Y co-ordinates where the text is to start in R3 and R4 respectively.

It is important to note that the pair of co-ordinates specifying the position where the text will start have their origin (zero reference) in the bottom left-hand corner of the box that one may imagine enclosing the text, rather than the top left-hand corner as is the case when printing text following a VDU 5.

Printing the justified text takes place in lines 230 to 390 and the formatting and positioning of this is discussed below.

```
MOVE 1180,532
```

```
SYS  "Font_Paint",,"This  is  24pt  justified  Trinity",
%10011,100,532
```

The next sections also discussed the formatting of all text including the aligned right segment painted in line 560. The positioning of the text string is calculated using a couple of conversion SWIs first to points and then to graphics co-ordinates using "Font_Converttopoints" and "Font_ConverttoOS" (lines 510 and 550) which are also discussed below.

"Font_StringWidth" (line 520) is one of several string conversion calls available and is discussed shortly.

Plot Options

The plot type parameter contains four flags whose meanings are as follows:

Bit 0: Set-Justify Text

When set, the Font Painter will attempt to fully justify the text string. To do this, you must have supplied the co-ordinates of the right-hand limit to which justification should extend. Only the X-axis part of this co-ordinate is really relevant since the Y-axis value must be the same as that of the text starting position if you want horizontal text! The co-ordinate is supplied by issuing a graphics MOVE command before issuing the SWI, so for example:

```
MOVE 1280,732
SYS "Font_Paint",,"This will be justified",%10001,0,732
```

This will produce the text string "This will be justified" with the lower left-hand corner of the opening 'T' at (0,732) and the lower right-hand corner of the closing 'd' at (1280,732).

Bit 1: Set — Pre-draw Rubout Box

This option tells the Font Painter to rub out a box surrounding the text by filling it with the background colour before the text is painted onto the screen. To do this, two pairs of co-ordinates must have been supplied by issuing MOVE commands: the first to specify the bottom left-hand corner of the box and the second the top right-hand corner. For example:

```
MOVE 0,716:MOVE 1280,772
SYS "Font_Paint", ,"A rub out box",Trinity%,%10010, 0,732
```

If this operation is to be combined with justification, the box co-ordinates must be issued first, followed by the justification limit co-ordinate. For example:

```
MOVE 0,716 :MOVE 1280,772
SYS "Font_Paint",,"This will be justified",%10011,0,732
```

Bit 2: Set — Absolute Co-ordinates Supplied

This bit should allow co-ordinates to be specified relative to the cursor position or absolutely (when set).

Bit 3: Not used

Bit 4: OS Co-ordinates/Font Painter Co-ordinates

This bit allows the co-ordinates of the text display position to be set either in OS units (ie within the theoretical display limits of 1280,1024) or in Font Painter co-ordinates with units of 1/7200ths of an inch. The application of the latter form is limited, so it is suggested that you always set this bit and use OS co-ordinates (as I have).

Co-ordinate Conversions

Two SWIs are provided to convert between Font Painter co-ordinates in 1/72000ths on an inch and RISC OS VDU driver co-ordinates. These SWIs simply take an X,Y co-ordinate pair in R1,R2 and return its converted form in R1,R2.

SWI Font_ConverttoOS (SWI &40088)

This SWI converts a pair of Font Painter co-ordinates in units of 1/72000th inch to OS co-ordinates. On entry, the X,Y pair is supplied in R1,R2 with the converted result being returned in the same registers.

SWI Font_Converttopoints (SWI &40089)

This SWI converts a pair of OS co-ordinates in screen units to Font Painter co-ordinates in 1/72000ths inch units. On entry, the X,Y pair is supplied in R1,R2 with the converted result being returned in the same registers.

Character and String Sizes

The Font Manager provides several SWIs to allow detailed information about the currently selected font to be examined. These are documented below:

SWI Font_ReadDfn (SWI &40083)

This call returns a set of registers containing information about the font whose handle is supplied. On entry R0 should contain a font handle and R1 should point to a buffer large enough to hold the font name (<= 12 bytes).

On Exit:
R1=Still points to the buffer, which now contains the font name
R2=Width of font *16
R3=Height of font *16
R4=Width resolution in pixels per inch
R5=Height resolution in pixels per inch
R6=Number of other users of font
R7=Number of other accesses since this font was last used

SWI Font_ReadInfo (SWI &40084)

This call returns the co-ordinates of a box which is just large enough to accommodate any character in the font, useful for deciding how large a rub out box should be. On entry, R0 must contain the font handle.

On Exit:
R1= X_min (OS co-ordinates, inclusive)
R2 = Y min (OS co-ordinates, inclusive)
R3 = X_max (OS co-ordinates, exclusive)
R4 = Y_max (OS co-ordinates, exclusive)

SWI Font_StringWidth (SWI &40085)

This call performs a number of calculations on a text string in order to determine how much space it will occupy.

On entry R1 must point to the string, R2 and R3 specify the maximum offsets in Font Manager co-ordinates which the string is allowed to occupy (see below), R4 contains the character at which the string may be split if it will not fit entirely and R5 contains the positional index of the last character allowed in the calculation.

The results returned indicate where the cursor would be after the string was printed as (X,Y) in R2 and R3, the number of occurrences of the specified split character in R4 and the positional index of the point at which the calculation terminated (according to the character criteria supplied).

Printing

The printing application !Printers is the user frontend to the printing system. Users can configure different printer types and their connections through it – it can also print some file formats directly.

When an application wants to print, the Printer Manager intercepts graphics rendering vectors such as PlotV and FontV and diverts them to the printer driver. The application draws the document as it would on the screen with the normal SWIs such as Font_Paint, but instead of rendering them on the screen the printer driver draws an image to send to the printer. There are different backend modules which target various output formats like PDriverPS for PostScript. Printer Definition Files (PDFs, not to be confused with the Portable Document Format) are means of installing a particular printer in !Printers and express the individual peculiarities of particular models of printer such as selecting the right paper sizes.

19: Modules

Writing a module is relatively straightforward and you can use them to achieve many programming functions. A module can:

- Implement * commands

- Implement SWI calls

- Intercept and process vector calls

- Run applications

- Store data and libraries

And that is just the beginning. There are restrictions, but these are more a matter of how you implement things rather than what you can actually do. No special software is involved but ultimately the final module code must be ARM machine code. You can achieve that by assembling programs written using the BBC BASIC Assembler or using C. The only consideration is that the start of a module must conform to a pre-determined format. This is called the Relocatable Module Header, if it doesn't conform in this way then RISC OS will reject it and refuse to load it.

This format is important not least because it is RISC OS which does most of the donkey work for you when it comes to identifying a command or SWI provided by your module. Your code does not have to actually do any of this work; RISC OS does it and drops control into your module right at the relevant point, as we shall see.

This chapter describes the format and works through a practical example to provide you with a simple Keyboard Utilities module that you should be able to extend and add to yourself, as well as use as a template for projects of your own choice.

Module Code Format

The first block of data in a module is called its header and this contains a series of vectors, each of which holds a relative offset. It is crucial to remember that these vectors hold relative offsets, not absolute addresses, in order that the module is properly relocatable.

The module header always occupies the first 13 words of the module's memory space and it is divided up as shown in Figure 19a.

Offset	Vector For
&00	Application code
&04	Initialisation code
&08	Finalisation code
&0C	Service Call code
&10	Title string
&14	Module *HELP string
&18	Help and command decoding table
&1C	SWI Base Number for this module
&20	SWI Entry code
&24	SWI Names Table
&28	SWI Name Decode Table
&2C	Messages filename
&30	32-bit Compatibility Flag

Figure 19a. The module header table.

All 13 fields must be present, though they may contain 0 which RISC OS takes to mean that the appropriate function is not supported. The exception is the title message which must point to a text string terminated by zero. The fields which deal with SWIs are optional since not every module will provide SWIs of its own (we will not in this example). Each of the fields is discussed in detail below. Note also that all but the application entry point are entered in SVC Mode.

The segment listing below shows how to implement this in an assembly language program by using EQUB to point to labels which mark where the particular item is identified:

```
.RMhead
EQUD 0              \ Application start entry
EQUD Init
EQUD Die
EQUD 0
EQUD Title
EQUD HelpString
EQUD HelpTable
EQUD 0              \ SWI_base = SWI Chunk number
EQUD 0              \ SWIentry
```

```
EQUD 0            \ SWInames
EQUD 0
EQUD 0            \ Messages filename
EQUD RMFlags
```

Getting the order of these vectors correct is vital. If you do not then your module may fail to load and may even produce a 'This Module is not 32-bit compliant' error. A common error is to insert an EQUB instead of an EQUD in your assembler, so double check this if you get such an error. Once you have a working module header file use it as a template for others!

&00 Application Code

If the module supplies an application this is the offset to where the application code starts. This is normally the result of a *RMRUN command. In addition to being an offset it may also be a one word instruction that will be identified as such by bits in the top byte being set).

Because modules do not have to provide an application it is valid for this offset to contain zero, in which case RISC OS will not attempt to start it up.

On entry through this offset, the CPU will be in User Mode and have interrupts enabled. Registers will not contain any useful information except for R12, which points to the private workspace (detailed later).

The start-up entry is used whenever OS_Module (detailed later) obeys a run or enter reason code. The writing of applications is not covered in this book, but once you have mastered writing relocatable modules you can find information about writing applications in the PRMs.

The BBC BASIC interpreter is a good example of an application module.

&04 Initialisation Code

This is the offset to the module initialisation or start-up code. This is different from the application entry. This code is called when the module is loaded and also after the RMA has been tidied (OS_Module with the Tidy reason code). Naturally the code here can do anything else you need it to do when RISC OS polls modules.

Typical actions are claiming workspace for your own module use (via OS_Module) and storing the workspace pointer. Other actions here may include linking vectors for example. An important point to note is that you must not generate errors in this code. In particular, this means that you must call the X form of SWI, and must not call OS_GenerateError.

All registers should be preserved on entry and restored on exiting the start-up code.

An offset of zero means that the module does not need any initialisation.

&08 Finalisation Code

This is the reverse of the initialisation entry point — it is the last call before the module will be expected to expire. Usually this circumstance is reserved for situations where the module is being explicitly killed as a result of *RMKILL or because the RMA is being tidied up as a result of *RMTIDY. It is possible for a module to refuse to die by causing an error in the usual way; otherwise, an exit should be taken using the link register R14 as normal. In other words, if the module is running, it may not be possible for it to safely shutdown. This is an error.

On entry, R10 contains a flag which indicates whether this finalisation call is because of true death (from *RMKILL) or suspended animation (from *RMTIDY or similar) — 0 is non-fatal and 1 denotes fatal. R10 contains one in the former case and zero in the latter. R12 points to the private word and R13 to the supervisor stack.

It is legitimate for a module to have no finalisation entry, in which case the OS will de-allocate its workspace on the assumption that R12 is a valid pointer to it. All registers should be preserved on entry and restored on exiting the start-up code.

This offset is called whenever OS_Module obeys a reinit, delete, tidy or clear reason code.

&0C Service Call

This entry point is used by service calls and is entered with R1 containing the service call number, which should be preserved. On entry to the service call handling code R1 contains the reason code of the desired service, R12 points to the private word, R13 points to a full descending stack and R14 contains a return address. The module must decode R1 and execute software to deal with it appropriately. It is important to remember that, for much of the time, every module installed in the computer is being offered the same reason codes in sequence and thus it is important to preserve all the incoming information in such a way as to allow other modules to take their own action. In practice, it is legitimate for a module either to ignore a reason code, or to claim it so as to prevent other modules from being offered it.

The processor is normally in either SVC or IRQ mode at this point and therefore any service call processing must happen as quickly as possible so as not to stall any other calls they may occur.

An offset of zero means that the module will not need to recognise any service calls.

&10 Title String

Each module must have a title string, terminated by a 0, to allow it to be identified by name when issuing *RM commands or via OS_Module. This offset points to the start of a zero-terminated string containing the module name, ideally adopting the Acorn standard of capitalising the first letter of each word. Spaces and control characters must be avoided.

```
.Title
EQUS "ModuleName"
EQUB 0
ALIGN
```

&14 Help String

This offset points to the zero-terminated string which will be displayed by *HELP MODULES Spaces and <TAB> characters (which tab to the next eight character column) are allowed, but no other control characters should be included.

It is important to include a help string no matter how trivial the module. And to keep the output of *HELP MODULES tidy it is diplomatic to follow the Acorn standard, viz:

Module name <tab> v.vv (dd mm yyyy)

That is, the module name should be followed by one or more <TAB>s to make it occupy 16 characters, the version number should be three decimal digits in the form v.vv and the date the software was released, if included, should be of the form DD MM YYYY It has also become customary to supply the name of any command supplied by the module. An example is given in the segment below:

```
.HelpString
EQUS      "Keyboard    Utilities"+CHR$9+"0.1    ("+MID$(TIME$,
5,11)+")"
EQUB 13
EQUS "Commands: SLOW , NORM"
EQUB 13
EQUB 0
ALIGN
```

The text string is printed using OS_PrettyPrint, allowing tabs to be freely used within it to ensure tidy formatting on the screen.

&18 Help and Command Decoding Table

The help and command decoding table can be considered as the main stepping off point into the module. It is here that you place details about the * commands which the module provides and this includes their *HELP string and the entry point to the code that the * command performs to complete its function.

It's simple, it's clever and it's very effective. And because it follows a set format it is very easy to add to it, thus enabling you to grow your modules and the functions they provide. We'll look at how this is achieved later in this chapter and see it in action practically in the form of a module which adds a couple of simple commands to the command set.

&1C SWI Base Number

This word actually contains a number rather than an address. The number is the base chunk number for the module. Module creators can apply to RISC OS Open for a chunk of numbers to be allocated specifically to them, and that these are theirs to use uniquely. For example, the Wimp chunk start number is &400C0. A chunk is defined as 64 SWIs in total, so the last number in the Wimp chunk will be &400FF.

RISC OS uses the chunk start number to determine if the module supports the unknown SWI which has been issued. If its number is in the range:

```
base to base+63
```

Where 'base' is the chunk start number, then this should be the module which deals with this SWI, and RISC OS enters the appropriate piece of code through the next offset.

No two modules are allowed to use the same SWI chunk base number unless they are taking over the function of a previous module's routines, or adding extra SWIs within the chunk number.

There are a number of SWI chunk numbers available for general use and this should be restricted to user-specific modules. These are values that have bits 18 and 19 set and therefore with an entry base number of &C0000. However, if you plan to distribute your module you should apply for a specific chunk number.

&20 SWI Entry Code

This vector points to the code that is used to actually locate and execute the SWI in the module. On entry to the code R11 has the SWI number and this will be in the range 0-63. R0-R9 may contain information passed to the SWI by the caller.

The module then checks whether it is one which it recognises and if so, deals with it appropriately. The suggested code for doing this is shown in the segment below:

```
.SWIentry
LDR R12, [R12]            ; get workspace pointer
CMP R11, #(EndOfJumpTable - JumpTable)/4
ADDLO PC, PC, R11, LSL #2 ; dispatch if in range
B UnknownSWIerror         ; unknown SWI
```

```
. JumpTable
B MySWI_0
B MySWI_1
                            ; all SWIs here
B MySWI_n
:
.EndOfJumpTable
.UnknownSWIError
ADR R0, ErrToken
MOV R1, #0
MOV R2, #0
ADR R4, ModuleTitle        ; From module header
SWI "XMessageTrans_ErrorLookup"
ORRS PC, R14, #Overflow_Flag
:
.ErrToken
EQUD &1E6                   ; Same as system message
EQUS "BadSWI"               ; Token to look up
EQUB 0
ALIGN
```

Note that the address calculation on the PC to jump to the appropriate branch instruction relies on there being exactly one instruction between the ADDLO and the B MySWI_0 instruction.

&24 SWI Name Table

This offset points to a table which defines the SWI names implemented by the module. The format of the table is:

```
SWI group prefix as ASCII string, terminated by 0
Name of 0th SWI as ASCII string, terminated by 0
Name of 1st SWI as ASCII string, terminated by 0
Name of nth SWI as ASCII string, terminated by 0
Zero to indicate end of list
```

If a SWI group had the prefix "Key" and contained two SWIs from which the table would be constructed thus:

```
EQUS "Key"   ; Group prefix
EQUB 0
EQUS "Slow"  ; swi +0
EQUB 0
EQUS "Norm"  ; swi +1
EQUB 0
EQUB 0
```

The correct call for both these SWIs would be:

```
SWI "Key_Slow"
SWI "Key_Norm"
```

With RISC OS adding the '_' is the convention. RISC OS will also recognise the 'X' version of each call for you as well. The SWIs are listed in their SWI number order.

The idea of this table is that as many SWIs as possible should have their names included here so that RISC OS can deal with them itself. If RISC OS is trying to deal with a name which does not appear in this table or whose SWI number is greater than that of the last entry in this list, it calls the SWI decode code (as described immediately above).

&28 SWI Name Decode Table

For most instances this word should have 0 in it. The SWI Name Table is used first by RISC OS to discern whether a particular SWI string can be recognised. If it does not appear in the table (ie its SWI number is greater than the last in the table but might still be in your chunk range) it will look to come here to seek it and will expect your assistance.

Therefore in general it is better to use the SWI Name Table fully and put zero here. This keeps the behaviour of RISC OS consistent and reduces the chances of error, although it is a little less flexible.

&2C Messages Filename

This vector gives the offset to a zero terminated string which gives the pathname of a message file used when outputting text from the help and command keyword table. The format of the message file is:

```
<token>:<text><null byte><linefeed>
```

The <text> is output by OS_PrettyPrint

This allows you to translate your help text into different languages.

&30 Compatibility Flag

This vector points to a word which signifies whether the module is 32-bit compatible which is necessary to work on RISC OS 5. This is done by setting the lowest bit of the word, typically just placing 1 at the referenced word address. If this is not present then RISC OS will assume that the Module is not 32-bit compatible and will issue a message to that effect and decline to load the module. This segment of code shows how this should be programmed:

```
EQUD RMFlags    ; RMFlags vector
:
.RMFlags
EQUD 1          ; 32-bit compatible
```

NB: Early versions of RIC OS were 26-bit implementations and this flag ensures they will work on the standard 32-bit version. You can read more about the 26-bit and 32-bit implemntations on the RISC OS Open website.

Workspace Memory

To allow a module to maintain its own status information, and indeed to do its job in the broadest sense, it must have access to an area of memory it can call its own. This workspace must be claimed from the RMA by calling the module manager using the SWI OS_Module with the appropriate reason code. Whenever a module is entered by RISC OS, register R12 is set to point to one word of memory which has been set aside to contain the address of the actual workspace of the module. Such workspace may therefore be addressed by using an instruction like:

```
LDR R12, [R12]
```

This will write the real start address of the workspace into R12. This is normally handled by your initialisation code.

Command Decoding

Let's have a look at how we implement and execute commands in a module. As we have seen, the vector at +&18 points to a block of memory which contains everything a * command provided by the module needs to work and report back on itself. When you type a command name and when you ask for help on that command name, this information comes from within this command block. The segment below (which comes from a full example towards the end of this chapter) shows how the command block for all entries is designed.

```
                            ; Command Block entry
EQUS "Slow"                 ; Command is 'Slow'
EQUB 0                      ; terminate with null
ALIGN                       ; word align
EQUD Slow_Code              ; pointer to start of code to
execute *SLOW
EQUD 0          ; Information word
EQUD Slow_Syntax            ; pointer to *SLOW syntax string
EQUD Slow_Help              ; pointer *HELP SLOW information
```

Additional command entries can be bolted on in a like fashion — there is no need to insert any joining or delimiting bytes between data blocks. The end of the command table is signified by the inclusion of a null word:

```
EQUD 0
```

Each record begins with the ASCII text string of the keyword terminated by a zero. We then align to a word boundary and insert the offset within the module where the code may be found that allows us to interpret the keyword. If the keyword is for help only then we use a zero offset to indicate this. Next comes a word of information about the parameters (described below) and then an offset to a text message indicating that the user has employed an inappropriate syntax for the command. Finally, a word is included which is an offset to the string of help text to be generated when the keyword is used as a parameter to *HELP, e.g.:

*HELP SLOW

Command keywords should only include alphabetic characters in order that they are safe from RISC OS trying to decode them (believing them to be filenames or similar). The decoding process is case-insensitive, but for display purposes it is most elegant to continue the Acorn standard of capitalising the initial letters of each word.

The code offset points to the routine which will be called when the command is entered. If the offset contains zero, the keyword can only be used as a *HELP parameter (and therefore issuing the keyword as a command will result in a 'Bad command' error unless the command is recognised elsewhere). Otherwise, issuing the command *KEYWORD will cause the code to be executed with R0 pointing to the rest of the command line (stripped of leading spaces) and R1 containing the number of parameters discovered by OS_CLI (which uses spaces or double inverted commas as delimiters).

Information Word

The information word is four bytes which provide information about what the command might be bringing with it. Each of the four bytes has a different function as listed in Figure 19b:

Byte	Function
0	Minimum number of parameters allowed (0-255)
1	OS_GSTrans map (see below)
2	Maximum number of parameters allowed (0-255)
3	Flag byte - uses bits b31, b30 and b29 only

Figure 19b. Byte meaning in the information word of a command header.

Byte 0 and 2 is a value that defines the minimum and maximum number of parameters that can be supplied by the code. RISC OS will generate an error if this range is not obeyed. An error message will be followed by the *Help syntax string.

Byte 1 is a bit map used by OS_GSTrans map for each of the first eight parameters which indicates whether RISC OS should pass the parameter through OS_GSTrans before passing it on to the command execution software. For example, this allows the burden of identifying and translating RISC OS variables to be placed on RISC OS. When a bit is set the relevant parameter will be processed by GSTrans before receipt by the routine.

Byte 3 is a flag byte that uses the three most significant bits (b31, b30 and b29) to indicate special cases for commands.

Module Errors

Modules also need to conform to the RISC OS standard for raising errors, so that standard error handlers can deal with them. A module should deal with an error by following these four steps:

An error block (including a valid error number and a text string describing the error) should be made ready.

- R0 should be loaded with the start address of the error block.

- As many registers as necessary should be restored by having their previous contents pulled back from the system stack (via R13). This assumes that the original contents were preserved on the stack when the module was entered in the first place.

The Overflow flag V should be set before returning.

It is important to use an error number which has been allocated specifically to the application in order that upstream error handlers (which the module may not be aware of) can deal with it correctly.

See Chapter 4 and the section titled SWI Error handling for more details.

OS_Module (SWI &1E)

The OS_Module SWI performs the operations provided by the *RM series of RISC OS commands that we looked at in Chapter 7. It also deals with other functions vital to the operation of the module system: for example, the claiming and releasing of RMA space.

OS_Module takes a reason code in R0 to activate each particular function, other parameters being specific to the individual function. Usually RISC OS will prevent you from applying this call to modules which it thinks are currently active — thus you may not kill BASIC by calling that OS_Module function from BASIC itself.

When a filename is required (for example, to load or run a module) the file must have the correct type (&FFA) and respond to initialisation calls when loaded. Where the parameters refer to a module by name, the name is taken to be a string of upper or lower case characters and may include numbers, which is terminated by a character with an ASCII code of less than 33. As ever, the Overflow flag V will be set if an error occurs and R0 will point to an error block in the usual way. The exact cause of such an error is specific to each individual reason code.

For more information on the various OS_Module reason codes and their functions please refer to PRMs 1-230.

Program> KeyUtils

Program 19a below is a basic template file for generating an assembler written module. Some of the code has already been illustrated as segments in the text of this chapter. The program provides a module called 'KeyUtils' which implements two commands — *SLOW and *NORM. These commands are trivial in their actions — they slow down the keyboard auto-repeat rate and then reset it to normal — but the overall functionality of implementing the module is what is important here.

We are using offset assembly to generate position-independent code by setting P%=0 and using O% to assemble the code into dimensioned space above the program (lines 50-110). If you examine the assembled listing you will see that it is assembled at address &00000000. No absolute addresses are generated within the assembled code and all branches are relative to ensure relocatability.

The module header can be seen between lines 120 and 250, followed by the title and help string definitions (lines 300-410). The command decoding blocks for the two keywords can be found in lines 430-590.Again the table for each is largely addresses and the information byte for both commands is set at 0 (lines 480 and 560). Both *SLOW and *NORM are facilitated using an OSByte &11 call with R1 holding the new auto-repeat rate. Note that the 'X' version of this SWI is called. The initialisation (lines 920-950) and the finalisation (lines 970-1000) routines do nothing at present other than saving and restoring all registers on entry and exit — you can see where you can add your own code for anything you require.

The program will assemble and save itself and will also load the newly created module making it available for your use.

Program 19a. A module template that implements two * commands.

```
 10 REM >KeyUtils
 20 REM Keyboard Utilities Module
 30 REM RPi RISC OS System
 40 :
 50 DIM C% 1024
 60 mod$="KeyUtils"
 70 title$="KeyUtils"
 80 :
 90 FOR OPT%=4 TO 7 STEP 3
100 P%=0:O%=C%
110 [OPT OPT%
120 .RMhead
130 EQUD 0            \ Application start entry
140 EQUD Init
150 EQUD Die
160 EQUD 0
170 EQUD Title
180 EQUD HelpString
190 EQUD HelpTable
200 EQUD 0            \ SWI_base = SWI Chunk number
210 EQUD 0            \ SWIentry
220 EQUD 0            \ SWInames
230 EQUD 0
240 EQUD 0            \ Messages filename
250 EQUD RMFlags
260 :
270 .RMFlags
280 EQUD 1            \ 32-bit compatible
290 :
300 .Title
310 EQUS "KeyUtils"
320 EQUB 0
330 ALIGN
340 :
350 .HelpString
360 EQUS  "Keyboard Utilities"+CHR$9+"0.1 ("+MID$(TIME$,
5,11)+")"
370 EQUB 13
380 EQUS "Commands: SLOW , NORM"
390 EQUB 13
```

```
400 EQUB 0
410 ALIGN
420 :
430 .HelpTable
440 EQUS "SLOW"
450 EQUB 0
460 ALIGN
470 EQUD Slow_Code
480 EQUD 0
490 EQUD Slow_Syntax
500 EQUD Slow_Help
510 :
520 EQUS "NORM"
530 EQUB 0
540 ALIGN
550 EQUD Norm_Code
560 EQUD 0
570 EQUD Norm_Syntax
580 EQUD Norm_Help
590 EQUD 0
600 :
610 ; Command Register
620 .Slow_Help
630 EQUS "Use SLOW to reduce the keyboard autorepeat rate"
640 EQUB 0
650 ALIGN
660 .Slow_Syntax
670 EQUS "Syntax: SLOW"
680 EQUB 0
690 .Slow_Code
700 STMFD R13!, {R1-R12,R14}
710 LDR R12, [R12]   ; Get Private workspace addr if needed
720 MOV R0, #11
730 MOV R1, #128
740 SWI &06
750 LDMFD R13!,{R1-R12,PC}    ; Restore and Exit
760 :
770 .Norm_Help
780 EQUS "Use NORM to restore the keyboard auto-repeat
rate"
790 EQUB 0
800 ALIGN
```

```
 810 .Norm_Syntax
 820 EQUS "Syntax: NORM"
 830 EQUB 0
 840 .Norm_Code
 850 STMFD R13!, {R1-R12,R14}
 860 LDR R12, [R12]   ; Get Private workspace addr if needed
 870 MOV R0, #11
 880 MOV R1, #32
 890 SWI &06
 900 LDMFD R13!,{R1-R12,PC}   ; Restore and Exit
 910 :
 920 .Init
 930 STMFD R13!,{R14}
 940     ; put any initialisation code required here
 950 LDMFD R13!,{PC}
 960 :
 970 .Die
 980 STMFD R13!,{R14}
 990     ; put any close code here
1000 LDMFD R13!,{PC}
1010 ] NEXT
1020
1030 OSCLI "SAVE "+mod$+" "+STR$~C%+"+"+STR$~O%
1040 OSCLI "SETT. "+mod$+" FFA"
1050 OSCLI "RMLOAD "+mod$
1060 END
```

Further Details

Writing modules can be either simple or complex, but there is no doubt that if you can master everything that goes into the coding of one that you have truly mastered programming RISC OS at the system level. Once you have grasped the concepts here you can safely add your own routines to the sample module. There is plenty of additional information that you can research and apply. First steps would be adding your own SWIs and decoding parameters passed with your * commands. Then look into the detail of calls provided by OS_Module and processing these, before dealing with responding to Service Calls. The PRMs contain plenty of additional detail in these areas and you should also look at other module source code. There is plenty freely available, but if you are struggling check out the links on the book support pages on the website.

20: Sound

The RISC OS sound interface has undergone some makeovers in recent years. The most fundamental of these has been to rework the way the interface works with attached hardware, providing more familiar mechanisms for control. This has been achieved by the addition of new modules — thus further illustrating how potent these components of RISC OS can be.

The original RISC OS sported an 8-bit system in what was then an 8-bit world. Shortly thereafter a 16-bit mechanism was introduced but this was essentially based on the 8-bit hardware. This has now changed with some clever programming and creativity in creating and re-inventing the sound system whilst maintaining backwards compatibility.

These chapters provide a look at the sound system and some of the commands and SWIs available to interface with it. As with many aspects of RISC OS there is often more than one way to achieve an outcome.

If you are attaching a CD drive to your Raspberry Pi then the CDFS module will be of interest to you, as either a sound input device or maybe to read data as a filing system. There are a range of SWIs available to use and these are documented in the PRMs.

Two Bit Systems

RISC OS has two sound systems: an 8-bit one and a 16-bit one. The 8-bit sound system was first shipped with the original Arthur powered Archimedes and supported by the first releases of RISC OS. In broad terms this could be configured to support between 1 and 8 channels, which would then be mixed together by the hardware and fed via voice generators to produce the two stereo channel output. The sound generators contain samples like on a synthesiser keyboard, and will play them at a specific pitch (like middle C). Sound balance was synthesised by varying the amount of data pushed through the left and right channels to create a stereo position, although this could only be controlled globally and not on an individual channel basis. Playback was controlled by activating the voice (sound) assigned to the designated channel. As a single user system, there was no facility to assign individual channels to particular applications.

However, an innovation of the 8-bit system was its use of logarithmic samples rather than linear ones, which allowed larger dynamic range. All sounds — or waveforms — are created either mathematically or by use of data tables. The sound data is processed entirely by the software which also had to perform any filtering or modulation required. The value of each piece of data can be thought of as an indication of the position of a speaker cone. For example, a constant series of values would not produce any sound at all as the speaker cone would not move. On the other hand a rapidly fluctuating series of values will produce a high frequency tone. The greater the fluctuation of the series, the louder the tone created. Likewise a series which fluctuates only a little would produce a quiet tone.

The sound system generated audible sounds by having the digital data held in its buffer converted into analogue signals. The buffer itself was filled by the voice generators which were implemented as modules and so had access to the sound channels. SoundDMA — DMA standing for Direct Memory Access — was one such module. The *VOICES command was used to control the voice generators. Now any 8-bit sound was converted into two stereo channels in 16-bit linear format and played as such.

A 16-bit sound system arrived with the RiscPC. The provision of a SWI to allow programs to register their own 16-bit sound handlers was the major advance. SWI "Sound_LinearHandler" allowed the filling of both the left and right channels of the sound buffer with data and thereby provided immediate access to high quality stereo sound (assuming suitable hardware was attached). The innovation here was the introduction of the SharedSound module as the standard interface to 16-bit sound in RISC OS, which resolved what had been a major drawback to the 16-bit system, being that only one handler could previously be registered at one time. Now with RISC OS Pi additional modules are provided to control other aspects of hardware settings. We'll look at this shortly.

Playing Sound

The Raspberry Pi has two audio outputs: HDMI — often through an attached HDMI monitor — and 3.5mm analog — perhaps for use with headphones. These both work effectively and you may also have additional hardware attached. If you want to ensure that your sound system is working correctly then you could load one of the sound examples found in $.Documents.Music on the Raspberry Pi SD Card into the Maestro application (in the Apps folder) and try playing it. It may take a few seconds to buffer but once it is playing you are assured you have a working sound system.

Note also that the points made in the Window Manager chapter apply here in respect of the Desktop environment. To play around and experiment with some of the * commands and SWI mentioned here you will need to be outside the

Desktop. To do this press F12 to see the * prompt at the bottom of the screen and type:

```
*BASIC
```

To enter the BBC BASIC interpreter. A command such as:

```
MODE 28
```

will clear the screen and provide a clutter-free backdrop to work on.

You should also ensure that a voice is attached to !Sound in the !Boot directory of the SD Card. Try this if Maestro doesn't seem to be working.

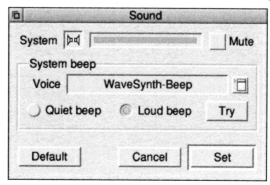

20a. Attach a voice to hear Maestro.

Module Driven

The RISC OS Sound System on the Raspberry Pi is controlled by a number of modules:

- SoundDMA
- SoundControl
- SoundChannels
- SoundScheduler
- ShareSound
- BCMSound

Sound is also configured in a hierarchical setting within the overall RISC OS sound system. The lowest of these is Level 0 which is the SoundDMA, and this in turn activates higher levels which then provide a block of sound data for output — Level 1 and Level 2. Some of the features, commands and SWIs associated with these modules are covered in the next chapters.

Figure 20b illustrates diagrammatically how the modules come together. In the original 8-bit system there was only the 8-Bit Voice Generator and The Sound Channel. The Voice Generator was where the action of *VOLUME was applied. Sound was fed to the SoundDMA and this drove the attached hardware. This function still exists but the attached hardware is now the Raspberry Pi and it passes through the BCMSound module to get to the hardware. On the other side of the figure SharedSound clients are addressed by the SWIs SharedSound_HandlerVolume and SharedSound_DriverVolume. They feed through to SoundDMA. Note that the effects of *SOUNDGAIN are applied at the SoundDMA level.

The sound hardware driver on the Raspberry Pi is provided by the BCMSound module. Rather than talking to the hardware directly, this driver relies on the VCHIQ module to communicate with the audio service running on the GPU. Again, SoundDMA passes these through to the BCMSound module to get to the Raspberry Pi hardware. *MIXVOLUME is applied here on the Raspberry Pi.

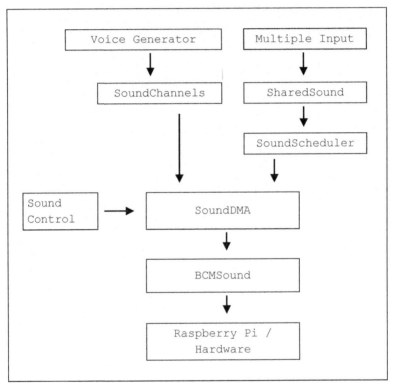

Figure 20b. Overview of sound interaction on RISC OS Pi sound system.

We'll look at these modules – with the exception of BCMSound – in the coming chapters and go through them in the order illustrated in Figure 20a, although it is together that they supply the functionality of the overall sound system.

*Configure

There are a number of configure options which are described below. These can also be changed via the !Boot window. Any changes made are saved and will so will not be affected by any reboots.

*Configure SoundSystem

Syntax: *CONFIGURE SoundSystem 8bit | 16bit
[oversampled] | <n>

This sets the configured value for the type of sound hardware to use, and for whether to use oversampling for 16-bit sound. This has little relevance on the Raspberry Pi at present.

*Configure SoundDefault

Syntax: *CONFIGURE SoundDefault <speaker> <volume>
<voice>

* CONFIGURE SoundDefault sets the configured speaker setting, volume and voice, where:

<speaker> = ON or OFF as per the *Speaker command.
<volume> = 0-7 where 0 is the quietest to 7 is the loudest.
<voice>   = is a number in the range 1 to 16.

This command sets the default sound configuration. As these settings are part of the !Boot configuration they remain in use until the machine is completely reset or until they are changed again. Upon power-up or reset these values are used to initially configure the speaker, master volume control and the default bells' voice's.

The speaker parameter controls whether the internal loudspeaker should be on (1) or off (0). The coarse volume sets the default amplitude of the system sound. This value is equivalent to the *VOLUME setting divided by 16. In other words a coarse volume of 2 is equivalent to a *VOLUME setting of 32. The Voice parameter can be used to set which voice generator channel one, the default system bell channel, will be attached to.

Example of use:

```
*CONFIGURE SoundDefault 1 6 7
```

*Configure Volume

Syntax: *CONFIGURE Volume <n>

This command sets the master volume of the sound system, where <n> is in the range 1 (quietest) to 127 (loudest). The default value is 127.

21: Sound Channels

SoundChannels

The SoundChannels module provides Level 1 control and will produce sound according to the configuration of each channel. This module was implemented in the original 8-bit sound system and is central in the 16-bit system. It provides the means by which pitch and volume are altered. The module will attach channels to voice generators, install and detach voice generators and provide for direct real-time control of musical parameters.

Figure 21a. lists some of the * commands and SWI calls provided by the SoundChannels module.

Command	SWI Name	SWI No.
*VOLUME	Sound_Volume	&40180
	Sound_SoundLog	&40181
	Sound_LogScale	&40182
*VOICES	Sound_InstallVoice	&40183
	Sound_RemoveVoice	&40184
*CHANNELVOICE	Sound_AttachVoice	&40185
	Sound_ControlPacked	&40186
*TUNING	Sound_Tuning	&40187
	Sound_Pitch	&40188
*SOUND	Sound_Control	&40189
*CHANNELVOICE	Sound_AttachNamedVoice	&4018A
	Sound_ReadControlBlock	&4018B
	Sound_WriteControlBlock	&4018C

Figure 21a. The *commands and SWI calls provided by the SoundChannels module.

Before we look at these in more detail, it is worth considering how sound is created using the Voice Generator in the 8-bit system.

The Voice Generator

The Voice Generator is used to fill the DMA buffer on demand. Before it can be used, a generator must first be installed and then channels can be attached to it. The voice generator code contains an eight word entry control block called the Sound Voice Control Block. SVCB entries are used by the Level 1 handler to call the appropriate pieces of code for attaching and detaching the voice (or voices) under supervisor mode, and real-time buffer filling which is entered in IRQ mode. The title is used by the Level 1 handler to identify the voices and should be concise, but informative.

I won't say too much more about 8-bit sound here other than to mention that home grown voice generators should be implemented as relocatable modules. This is necessary because if the machine code moves, or is wiped without the Level 1 handler being informed that the voice is no longer active, subsequent use of sound will probably cause an error requiring a reset of the Raspberry Pi.

A side effect of this is that modules have to be written in such a way that if the RMA is tidied up the voice will be detached before that process, and then reattached afterwards. This is very easily accomplished because of the initialisation and finalisation calls made to a module when such a command is issued (as described in Chapter 19).

The book support pages for this book contain some voice generation code that creates a module which will implement a new voice which can be used in your programs and will be listed with *VOICES. It demonstrates some of the concepts discussed. The listing is also included in the batch of programs from this book that you can download by registering on the website.

*ChannelVoice

Syntax: *CHANNELVOICE <channel><voice no>/<voice name>

This command allows different physical channels to be attached to different Voice Generators, in order for them to play different sounds. It can accept two parameters: <channel> which is in the range 1 to 8 and <voice no> which is in the range 1 to 32.

The voice index is the Voice Generator slot number. This can be determined using the *VOICES command. It can also be specified by name. The <voice name> is the Voice Generator's preferred name, which is registered with the Level 0 handler. Examples:

```
* CHANNELVOICE 1 1
* CHANNELVOICE 1 StringLib-Soft
```

*Sound

Syntax: *SOUND <channel> <amp> <pitch> <duration>

The most direct way to play sound is to simply use the *SOUND command. Providing the selected channel is active and attached, the sound will be produced immediately.

The parameters passed to *SOUND are all unsigned integers. When passing negative numbers all 32 bits should be passed. For example, to pass the value -1 the equivalent hexadecimal number, &FFFFFFFF, should be used. Amplitude and Pitch are described in more detail below.

Amplitude

There are two forms of amplitude — linear and logarithmic. The linear form is expressed as a simple number in the range 0 (silence) to -15 (loud). The logarithmic scale runs from &100 (silence) to &17F (loud), and a change of &10 represents a doubling or halving of the volume. Bit 7 can be used as a toggle to facilitate a smooth change of the sound. For example:

```
*SOUND 1 &17F &4200 &FE
*SOUND 1 &1EF &4000 &20
```

This will cause the first sound to change pitch and amplitude as soon as the second command is issued.

Pitch

There are two ways in which pitch can be specified. The first method allows specification in steps of a quarter of a semitone. The range of values for this method is 0 to 255. The Middle C has a value of 53 with each unit representing a quarter of a semitone.

A finer degree of control can be obtained using a second method in which values are specified in the range &0100 to &7FFF. Each value is constructed from 15 bits. The top three bits (b14, b13 and b12) specify the octave number, while the remaining 12 bits define the fractional part of the octave. Therefore each octave is split up into 4096 different pitch levels. Middle C in this case has a value of &4000.

*Tuning

Syntax: *TUNING <n>

Where <n> is a value in the range -&xFFF to &xFFF

This command overrides the system pitch base. It can be used to raise or lower the pitch of all sounds. The value is a 16-bit number which is split up into two parts.

The top four bits represent the octave number (x) while the remaining bits are the fractional part of the octave (FFF). A value of zero resets the tuning to the default value. The value is relative, so to raise the pitch of all notes by one octave, you would use:

```
*TUNING 41000
```

*Voices

Syntax: *VOICES

This command will list all the currently registered and installed VoiceGenerator's names. Channels that have been attached to these voices are also indicated. The voice number is the voice index which is used in the *CHANNELVOICE command. The numbering of the voices depends on the order in which they were installed, so it may change. Typically the command might return the following listed in Figure 21b.

Voice	Name
1	WaveSynth-Beep
2	StringLib-Soft
3	StringLib-Pluck
4	StringLib-Steel
5	StringLib-Hard
6	Percussion-Soft
7	Percussion-Medium
8	Percussion-Snare
9	Percussion-Noise

Table 21b. Sample output of installed voices.

*Volume

Syntax: *VOLUME <n>

Where <n> is a value in the range 1 to 127 and the default setting is 127.

This command sets the master volume of the sound system. The range is 1 (quietest) to 127 (loudest). This value is used by all voice generators to scale the amplitudes of their sounds. The amplitude of any sound command will be scaled by this value. The legacy of the original 8-bit sound system means that volume is changed logarithmically, and a change of 16 to the value of <n> scales the output by half. For example:

<n>	Factor
127	1.0
111	0.5
95	0.25
79	0.125

Sound SWIs

There are SWI calls for each of the * commands provided by the SoundChannels Module. In addition there are a number of useful calls controlling pitch and converting logarithmic values as well as reading and writing control block data. The SWIs are covered in order of their SWI number as listed earlier in Table 21a. Refer to Chapter 20 for where to find sample code to create Voice Generators.

Sound_Volume (SWI &40180)

This SWI sets the overall volume and is used by the *VOLUME command. Refer to that entry above for more details. The default value is taken from the !boot setting.

On Entry:
R0=Sound volume
          1 (quietest) to 127 (loudest)
          0 will inspect last setting
On Exit:
R0 = Previous volume

Sound_SoundLog (SWI &40181)

This SWI converts 32-bit signed integers to an 8-bit signed logarithmic value using an internal lookup table. It is used to convert sampled data to a logarithmic scaled value for use in Voice Generators.

On Entry:
R0=Signed 32-bit number

On Exit:
R0=8-bit signed scaled logarithm

Sound_LogScale (SWI &40182)

This SWI maps an internal 8-bit signed logarithm to one scaled to the current volume.

On Entry:
    R0=8-bit signed audio logarithm

On Exit:
R0=8-bit scaled logarithm

Sound_Install Voice (SWI &40183)

Use this SWI to install a Voice Generator, at which point any number of physical channels can be attached to it. The installed voice list can be examined by passing zero in R0. On exit R0 will point to the voice name.

On Entry:
R0=Voice Generator Header Code or 0 for don't change
R1=Voice slot specified or 0 for next free slot

On Exit:
R0=String pointer — name of previous voice (or error message)
R1=voice number allocated, but 0 indicates a failure to install

Sound_Remove Voice (SWI &40184)

This SWI is used to remove Voice Generators. It may be called if the Voice Generator is a module and the RMA is tidied, or cleared.

On Entry:
R1=Voice slot to remove

On Exit:
R0=string pointer — name of previous voice (or error message)
R1=voice number removed. 0 indicates a failure to remove a voice

Sound_AttachVoice (SWI&40185)

Sound_AttachVoice allows a particular physical channel to be attached to a voice slot, the number of which can be ascertained from the output information displayed by *VOICES. Voice slot numbers may change so *VOICES should always be used first to obtain the correct number.

When a new voice is attached, the old voice is first shut down and there is no facility to swap voices mid-sound. This call is used by the *CHANNELVOICE command and this level caters for the logical channels.

On Entry:
R0=Physical channel number
R1=Voice slot to attach. 0 to detach voice and mute

On Exit:
R0=Preserved. 0 if illegal channel number
R1=Previous voice number. 0 if not previously attached

Sound_ControlPacked (SWI &40186)

In operation this SWI is similar to Sound_Control, but differs in that its parameters are packed together. For example:

```
SYS "Sound_Control",1, &17F, &4200, 16
```

becomes:

```
SYS "Sound_ControlPacked", &017F0001, &00104200
```

On Entry:
R0=Amplitude and channel (&AAAACCCC)
        High word is amplitude, low word is channel
R1=Duration and pitch (&DDDDPPPP)
        High word is duration, low word is pitch

On Exit:
R0= Preserved
R1= Preserved

Sound_Tuning (SWI &40187)

This SWI sets the tuning parameter, is used to offset the pitch values used throughout the system and is used by the *TUNING command. See the description of the *TUNING command in the next chapter for an explanation of the range of R0.

On Entry:
R0=New tuning value. 0 — don't change

On Exit:
R0=Previous setting

Sound_Pitch (SWI &40188)

This SWI maps a 15-bit pitch to an internal format pitch value. See *TUNING for more details.

On Entry:
R0=15-bit pitch value
        bits 14-12: represent the octave number
        bits 11-0: represent the octave division
On Exit:
R0=32-bit phase accumulator value

Sound_Control (SWI &40189)

This SWI command allows immediate execution of the specified sound channel — the parameters take effect on the next buffer fill entry. The GATE on/off causes a new note to be played resulting in a possible click, whilst the 'smooth' option causes the changing of note parameters without restarting the note. This allows the pitch or volume of a note to be altered while it is playing, and can be effectively used for pitch-bend.

On Entry:
R0=Physical Channel
R1=Amplitude
> Either 0-15 or &100 to &1FF
> of which bit 7 is: 0 for GATE ON/OFF
> 1 for smooth update

R2=Pitch
> Either 0-&FF or &0100 TO &7FFF for enhanced pitch control
> bits 14-12: represent octave number
> bits 11-0: represent fractional part of the octave

R3=duration in 5 centisecond periods except &FF which represents infinity

On Exit:
R0-R3 Preserved

Note: GATE is in effect a switch which allows the sound to be turned off (effectively killing the last note) and then on (to play the next one). The GATE option should not be used if a smooth change from one note to another is required.

Sound_AttachNamed Voice (SWI &4018A)

This call is used by the *CHANNELVOICE command and will attach the physical channel specified in R0 to the named voice. When a channel is attached to a new voice, the previous voice is shut down and the new voice reset. There is no facility to swap voices while a sound is being played. This level will attach the logical channels depending on the number of physical channels.

On Entry:
R0=Physical channel number
R1=Pointer to voice name (zero terminated string)

On Exit:
R0=Preserved
R1=Preserved but 0 if fail

SWI Sound_ReadControlBlock (&4018B)

This SWI will read 32-bit words from the Sound Channel Control Block (SCCB). The values in the SCCB are not standard and they will depend on the particular Voice Generator, as well as the Level 1 handler.

On Entry:
R0=Channel
R1=Offset to read from

On Exit:
R0=Preserved
          0 if fail, invalid read offset
R1=Peserved
R2=32-bit word read if R0 non zero

Word	Function
0	Amplitude, index to voice table, voice instance, control flags
1	Phase accumulator pitch oscillator
2	
3	Number of buffer fills
4-8	Working registers

Figure 21c. SCCB values.

SWI Sound_WriteControlBlock (&4018C)

This SWI allows 32-bit words to be written into the SCCB.

On Entry:
R0=Channel
R1=Offset to write
R2=32-bit value to write

On Exit:
R0=Preserved. 0 if fail, invalid read offset
R1=Preserved
R2=Previous 32-bit word, if R0 non zero

22: Shared Control

This chapter looks at the SharedSound, SoundScheduler and SoundControl modules and what they bring to the RISC OS sound system. The three modules are relatively recent additions to RISC OS and have been included to allow the sound system to provide a more standard user interface in line with what would be expected from current software control, as well as the ability to have multiple sources playing simultaneously.

SharedSound

The SharedSound module allows several sources to be played simultaneously and also provides the ability for separate audio streams to be mixed together and played. SharedSound works in much the same way as other RISC OS operations that can claim a particular action. When a buffer fill request is issued by SoundDMA, SharedSound will pass the data through its list of clients, in order for them to write the data they wish to the buffer, ensuring that existing data is not overwritten.

SharedSound also provides information about the sample rate of the buffer, and allows the volume of each handler — and the type of handle being used — to be changed individually.

The SharedSound module is clever in that it operates by registering its own handler (via the Sound_LinearHandler SWI) and then allows others (clients) to register as many sound handlers as they want via the SharedSound_InstallHandler SWI.

SoundDMA can only accept one stream at a time, and so the tendency now is for programmers to use the SharedSound operators in preference. However, SoundDMA remains the default 16-bit sound handler.

See the book support pages on the website for the link to a program by Jeffrey Lee that demonstrates and describes in great detail the use of SharedSound.

SoundScheduler

The SoundScheduler module provides Level 2 facilities which include the queuing of sounds. In addition it provides the data structures which allow multiple channel music or sound to be synchronised under simple program control — the playing of chords.

Queued sounds are activated as events at the appropriate tempo-dependent time in the future. Unfortunately it is not possible to queue sounds to play in the past, as some sound systems allow. Level 2 also allows changes in tempo and beats per bar to change dynamically whilst maintaining note synchronisation.

Figure 22a lists some of the SWI calls and corresponding * commands associated with the SoundScheduler module.

Command	SWI Name	SWI No.
	QInit	&401C0
*QSOUND	QSchedule	&401C1
*TEMPO	QTempo	&401C5
	QBeat	&401C6

Figure 22a. The * commands and several SWI calls provided by the SoundScheduler module.

*QSound

Syntax: *QSOUND <chan> <amp> <pitch> <dur> <nBeats>

This command differs to the *SOUND command in that it is possible to specify on which beat the note should be played. For full information on the first four parameters see the description for *SOUND in the previous chapter.

The beat is an internal counter which is set to zero at the start of each bar. The beat increment is set by the *TEMPO command. If a value of &FFFFFFFF (-1) is used for nBeats then, instead of being scheduled for a given number of beats, the sound is synchronised with the last scheduled sound. Program 22a below demonstrates this by producing two tones one octave apart to be made 50 beats after the start of the next bar.

Program 22a. QSOUND demonstration.

```
10 REM >Prog22a
20 REM *QSOUND demo
30 REM RPi RISC OS Programming
40 BEATS 200
50 REPEAT
60 UNTIL BEAT =0 :REM Wait for start of next bar
70 *QSOUND 1 &17F &4000 &10 50
80 *QSOUND 2 &17F &5000 &10 &FFFFFFFF
```

*Tempo

Syntax: *TEMPO <n>

where n is a value in the range 0 to &FFFF

This command affects the rate at which scheduled events are played back. The value n sets the rate at which the beat counter is incremented, and is used to queue the scheduled sounds, for instance:

Value	Beat increment	Scheduled sounds
2048	(&0800)	Each beat lasts twice as long (Slowed down)
4096	(&1000)	Default
8192	(&2000)	Each beat is half as long (Speeded up)

The default value is &1000. This corresponds to one microbeat per centisecond.

Each bar is split up into a number of beats. The duration of each beat is affected by the tempo. The beat counter is set to zero at the start of each bar. If sounds or music are scheduled using *QSOUND or the five parameter BASIC SOUND statement, then the execution of notes can be speeded up or slowed down by changing the TEMPO. The durations of the notes are not changed.

SoundScheduler SWI

Four SoundScheduler related SWIs are outlined here, two of which fulfil the *QSOUND and *TEMPO commands.

Sound_QInit (SWI &401C0)

Calling this SWI clears any scheduled sounds queued and resets the tempo and beat variables to their default values. There are no entry conditions, but on exit R0 will contain 0 if the call was successful.

Sound_QSchedule (SWI &401C1)

This SWI is used by the *QSOUND command.

On Entry:

R0 = Schedule period (from start of bar)

&FFFFFFFF (-1) to synchronise with the last schedule event

R1 =0 causes a Sound_ControlPacked call SWI number, of the form &F000000 + SWI number

R2,R3 Are the parameters for R0 and R1 for the SWI

On Exit:

R0=   0 is successfully queued

           <0 for failure, or queue full

This SWI is used by the *QSOUND command. R2 and R3 contain the data which would normally be passed in registers 0 and 1 to the Sound_ControlPacked SWI (discussed in next chapter). R0 holds the nBeats parameter. R1 will normally be zero, in which case the Sound_ControlPacked SWI will be called:

```
SYS "Sound_QSchedule",10, 0, &017F0001, &00204000
```

is equivalent to:

```
SYS "Sound_ControlPacked", &017F0001, &00204000
```

except that it will be played 10 beats after the new bar, when the beat counter is set to zero. This is identical to:

```
*QSOUND 2 &17F &4000 &20 10
```

or alternatively:

```
*SOUND 2,&17F,&4000,&20,10
```

which plays a middle C for &20*5 centiseconds on channel 2 when the beat counter reaches 10.

If R1 is non-zero then other SWIs can be called. For example, if at the start of the third bar in a piece of music you wanted to attach channel 5 to voice 3, instead of having to continually check to see if the piece of music had reached the third bar, you could simply insert in the sound data the following SWI call:

```
SYS "Sound_QSchedule", 0, Sound_AttachVoice, 5, 3
```

where Sound_AttachVoice is the value of the SWI plus &F0000000:

```
Sound_AttachVoice+&F000000
```

Sound_QTempo (SWI &401C5)

This SWI is used by the *TEMPO command, and is used to set the tempo parameter within the Level 2 scheduler.

On Entry:
R0 = New tempo 1 to &FFFF (&1000 default). 0 for don't change

On Exit:
R0=Previous tempo value

Sound_QBeat (&401C6)

This call is used by the BBC BASIC commands BEAT and BEATS. The beat counter is an internal counter which starts at zero and counts up to the beat COUNT value.

On Entry:
R0=0 returns beat counter value

- 1 returns the current beat COUNT value

< 1 resets the beat counter and COUNT to zero

>0 sets the beat COUNT to N, counts 0 to N-1

On Exit:
R0=Current beat counter number is passed

If 0 the previous beat COUNT value is used

SoundControl

The SoundControl module is provided to act directly with the attached hardware and in the case of the Raspberry Pi is applied to the sound driver module BCMSound. It allows the user to alter some of the audio hardware behaviour and in doing so it provides a standard audio interface. The *MIXVOLUME control that it provides is central to this, and in addition it adds three SWIs.

*Mixvolume

Syntax: *MIXVOLUME <system> <category> <index> <mute> [<gain>]

The command *MIXVOLUME is used to adjust the operation of the attached hardware and it simulates the operation of a traditional mixer desk.

<system> is a value that specifies which item of hardware is providing the i/o. A value of 0 would signify the defaults/main hardware and this is the only option available at the time of writing.

<category> is the number representing the device. Options available are:

-1 = speaker

-2 = headphones

-3 = line out

-4 = aux out (a header on the board)

0 = system audio

1 = mic

2 = line in

3 = aux in [index 0 usually CD-ROM]

<index> represents the channel and with a value of 0 meaning both (input and output). It can also provide for multiple CD sources.

<mute> 1=device is muted, 0 = not muted.

[<gain>] sets the nominal volume for the device and is a signed integer of (db*16)

SoundCtrl SWI

There are three SWIs that provide access and feedback from the *MIXVOLUME command.

SWI SoundCtrl_ExamineMixer (&50000)

This call examines all mixer settings and returns their values. It should be called twice: first to determine buffer size required, and then to fill the buffer. This allows the block size to be enlarged at a later point if required. Valid block sizes are four bytes and 16 bytes.

On Entry:
R0 = system
R1 = pointer to a word-aligned buffer
R2 = buffer size (may be 0)

On Exit:
The buffer provided will be filled with a series of 16-byte blocks with the following format:

Bytes	Content	
0-1	flags:	bit 0 set => fixed
		bit 1 = 1 mono, or 0 stereo.
		bit 2 = 1 muted by default
2-3	category	
4-7	minimum gain (dB*16)	
8-11	maximum gain (dB*16)	
12-15	minimum step size/granularity (dB*16)	

R0 = preserved
R1 = preserved
R2= decremented by number of bytes needed for complete description
    (ie if 0 on entry, now holds negative of buffer size required)
R3 = individual block size (bytes) — will be a multiple of four
R4 = number of blocks placed in buffer

SWI SoundCtrl_SetMix (&50001)

The SWI performs the *MIXVOLUME command, which can be used to adjust the operation of the attached hardware where it simulates the operation of a traditional mixer desk. Refer to the entry of *MIXVOLUME for a more detailed description of items passed in registers.

On Entry:

R0 = mixer

R1 = category

R2 = index

R3 = 1=device is muted, 0 = not muted

R4 = gain

SWI SoundCtrl_GetMix (&50002)

This call reads and returns the mixer gain setting.

On Entry:

R0 = system

R1 = category

R2 = channel index

On Exit:

R0 = preserved

R1 = preserved

R2 = preserved

R3 = muted (1 for yes, 0 for no)

R4 = gain (16ths of a dB)

The definitions are as for SoundCtrl_SetMix.

23: SoundDMA

SoundDMA provides the entry level (Level 0) point for sound processing under RISC OS. It is now the default 16-bit sound handler (and emulates 8-bit) for RISC OS Pi. The DMA Buffer Handler is activated whenever a new block of sound data is required, and updates the necessary pointers.

SoundDMA will convert 8-bit data from multiple channels into two stereo channels in a 16-bit linear format. It then calls the linear handler (if any) to fill the DMA buffer with its own sound data. The linear handler can either overwrite the converted 8-bit data already obtained or it can merge it with its own sound data.

If a sound overload occurs, ie if there is simply too much sound data to be processed, Level 0 marks the offending channel as overrun and the real-time buffering is aborted before being restarted. In the past any sound requirements from applications playing audio have been channelled though SoundDMA for processing, but as mentioned earlier SharedSound is now the entry point for many handlers and they in turn now feed audio samples to SoundDMA. Level 0 also caters for any hardware-dependent programming which requires privileged-mode access, such as stereo positioning.

Figure 23a lists the * commands and SWIs provided by this module.

Command	SWI Name	SWI No.
	Sound_Configure	&40140
*AUDIO	Sound_Enable	&40141
*STEREO	Sound_Stereo	&40142
*SPEAKER	Sound_Speaker	&40143
	Sound_Mode	&40144
	Sound_LinearHandler	&40145
	Sound_SampleRate	&40146
	Sound_ReadSysInfo	&40147
*SOUNDGAIN	[No associated SWI]	

Figure 23a. The *commands and SWI calls provided SoundDMA.

*Audio

Syntax: `*AUDIO ON/OFF`

All sound interrupt and DMA activity is stopped when *AUDIO OFF is issued. The DMA buffer is no longer filled so no sound is produced by the DAC. Once audio is turned back on with *AUDIO ON, the DMA and interrupt system are returned to the status they held prior to being turned off, as interrupts are still permitted even if no sound results. This can be advantageous as it allows sounds to be remembered while audio is off, and to be quickly played as soon as AUDIO is turned back on. SWI Sound_Enable can be used to set and return the state of *AUDIO.

*Stereo

Syntax: `*STEREO <channel> <position>`

Here <channel> is in the range 1 to 8 and <position> is in the range -127 to 127.

This command was relevant for the 8-bit sound system and is maintained for compatibility. It will still have an effect, although there are better 16-bit arrangements. It allows the sound position to be set on any of the channels so that sound may be moved through the channel. There are seven stereo image positions. Depending on the number of physical channels, the call can be used to either position the physical or logical channels. Moving the logical channels can be used to produce different stereo positions. Repositioning of the logical channels is not advised.

Program 23a at the end of this chapter provides a demonstration of sound positioning using the SWI version of this call.

*Speaker

Syntax: `*SPEAKER ON/OFF`

This command effectively turns the internal speaker on or off but it has no effect on the external stereo output. It achieves this by muting the monophonic mixed signal to the internal loudspeaker amplifier. All DMA activity continues so sounds will be processed as usual. As there is no internal speaker on the Raspberry Pi this command is of no real relevance.

Calling SWI Sound_Speaker can perform the same task and also read the current state of the speaker.

*Soundgain

Syntax: *SOUNDGAIN <gain>

This command sets the gain for 8-bit to 16-bit sound conversion, where <gain> is 0-7 for 0dB (default) to +21dB, in 3dB steps

Sound SWI

Eight SWIs are detailed below and with the exception of *SOUNDGAIN, there are reciprocal calls for each of the * commands detailed above.

Sound_Configure (SWI &40140)

This SWI configures the sound system and works for both 8-bit and 16-bit sound systems.

On Entry:
R0=Number of channels (n) [rounded up to 1, 2, 4, 8 (n)]. This is ignored by the 16-bit interface.
R1=Samples per buffer
R2=Period in microseconds
R3=Level 1 handler code, [normally 0 to preserve system level 1]
R4=Level 2 handler code, [normally 0 to preserve system level 2]
        Zero for any parameters will not change that setting.
On Exit:
Previous settings.
Default:
R0=1
R1=&D0
R2=48

The Number of Sound Channels (R0)

R0 gives the number of channels for 8-bit sound, as before. It is ignored by the 16-bit system, which always includes the two left and right channel stereo pair. For 8-bit the value passed in R0 will be rounded to 1, 2, 4, 8. Channels are multiplexed into the eight logical channels available. If only one physical channel is available then all eight logical channels will be used for sound.

Similarly if only two physical channels are available, then every other logical channel will be used for each physical channel, ie channel 1 will use logical channels 1 3, 5 and 7, and channel 2 will use logical channels 2, 4, 6 and 8.

Because of this interleaving the channels are multiplexed into one half, quarter or eighth of the sample period. This results in the overall signal level per channel being scaled down by the same amount, so the overall signal peak level for all multi-channel modes remains constant. The more physical channels in operation, the quieter each one becomes!

When you have 16-bit sound configured, the values of R0 and R1 must be such that 8-bit, converted 8-bit and 16-bit sound data can all fit within a page, which is the maximum size of the sound DMA buffer. If not, the number of samples is set to the highest value for which all three types of data will fit. Also, not all sample periods can be provided; in such cases the sample period is set to the closest match. As always, you can check the number of samples and the sample period actually set by calling Sound_Configure with null parameters.

The DMA Buffer Size and Sample Rate (R1, R2)

Generally these settings should not be altered. The sample rate is probably of greatest use as its parameter defines how long each piece of sample data should last. 10000 bytes of sample data played at the default sample rate of 48 microseconds would result in a sound lasting 0.48 seconds. If the sample rate was then changed to 50 microseconds, the sound would last 0.50 seconds. Therefore, if data is sampled at different sample rates, but the same relative pitch needs to be maintained, then this can be achieved by altering the sample rate value.

R1 can be thought of as giving the number of samples per channel for both 8 and 16-bit sound. The two definitions are effectively the same for 8-bit sound, but the new definition also covers 16-bit sound.

R2 sets the sample period for both 8-bit and 16-bit sound. However, the SWI Sound_SampleRate is the preferred way to control sample rates for 16-bit sound.

Sound_Enable (SWI &40141)

This SWI is used by the *AUDIO command and suspends any DMA interrupts. It is important to remember that any subsequent sound commands may be stored, so that when the sound is enabled the stored sounds will be played immediately.

On Entry:
R0=New State
        2 = ON
        1 = OFF
        0 = No change (just read previous state)

On Exit:
R0=Previous state
        2 = ON
        1 = OFF

There is no simple way to flush the sound buffers. The only way to clear the sounds is to detach and then re-attach the voices, or to set the SCCB channel flags for each to two, which will make the Level 0 handler flush the channels. However, doing this is prone to problems, as the Voice Generators will not be informed of the change.

Sound_Speaker (SWI &40143)

This SWI is used by the *SPEAKER command and switches off the mono-mix of the left and right audio channels to the internal loudspeaker amplifier (so really irrelevant on the Raspberry Pi!). Sounds are still processed and DMA interrupts continue. The stereo audio output remains active.

On Entry:
R0=New State
      2 = ON
      1 = OFF
      0 = No change (just read previous state)

On Exit:
R0=Previous state
      2 = ON
      1 = OFF

Sound_Stereo (SWI &40142)

This SWI facilitates the re-positioning of the stereo image of the specified channel. There are seven stereo image positions. Depending on the number of physical channels, the call can be used to either position the physical or logical channels. Repositioning of the logical channels is not advised. This method of moving the logical channels can be used to produce different stereo positions.

On Entry:
R0=Logical / Physical Channel
R1=Image position
      - 128 no change

On Exit:
R0=Preserved
R1=Previous image position

Program 23a. indicates the relative merits of logical channel stereo positioning, as opposed to physical channel positioning and positioning of the channels while a sound is being played. For sensible results this program is best run using speakers or headphones attached to the audio jack or through a pair of HDMI speakers.

The channels affected are n, n+N, n+2N up to channel 8, where N is the number of active voices. The default stereo setting for all channels is zero, ie centre. There are seven discrete stereo positions as listed in Figure 23b.

Range	Position
-127 to -80	Full left
-79 to -48	2/3 left
-47 to -16	1/3 left
-15 to +15	Central
+16 to+47	1/3 right
+48 to+79	2/3 right
+80 to +127	Full right

Figure 23b. The seven discreet stereo sound positions.

Program 23a. Demonstration of stereo sound positioning.

```
10 REM >Prog21a
20 REM Stereo Sound Example
30 REM RPi RISC OS System
40 :
50 PRINT"SWI Sound_Stereo Demonstration"
60 :
70 DIM posn(10)
80 FOR N%=1 TO 7
90 READ posn(N%)
100 NEXT
110 :
120 VOICES1
130 PRINT "Moving stereo posn then playing a sound"
140 SYS "Sound_Stereo",1,0:SOUND 1,-15,1,10
150 FOR P%=1 TO 7
160 PRINT"Stereo ";posn(P%)
170 SYS "Sound_Stereo", 1, posn(P%)
180 SOUND 1,-15,100,10
190 A=INKEY(40)
200 NEXT
210 :
220 PROCpak
230 PRINT"Moving stereo posn while playing a sound"
240 SOUND 1,-15,100,10*6
250 FOR P%=7 TO 1 STEP-1
260 PRINT"Stereo ";posn(P%)
270 SYS "Sound_Stereo", 1, posn(P%)
280 A=INKEY(40)
290 NEXT
```

```
300 :
310 END
320 :
330 DATA -127,-79,-47,0,47,79,127
340 :
350 DEF PROCpak
360 PRINT"Press a key":A=GET:PRINT
370 ENDPROC
380 :
390 DEF FNnum(L%,V%)
400 =RIGHT$(STRING$(L%," ")+STR$V%,L%)
410 :
420 DEF FNhnum(L%, V%)
430 =RIGHT$(STRING$(L%," ")+STR$~V%,L%)
```

Linear Handlers

A linear handler registers itself with SoundDMA by calling the Sound_LinearHandler SWI. When registering, you provide the address of the handler code — which is called to fill the SoundDMA buffer — and a parameter is passed to the handler in R0. Typically the parameter will be a pointer to a data area containing any information the handler may need to perform its task. The address and parameter of the previous linear handler (if any) are returned.

Only one linear handler can be registered with the SoundDMA module. You should therefore only register your linear handler immediately before starting to play sound, and should re-register the previous handler as soon as you have finished. You can find which linear handler is currently registered by calling Sound_LinearHandler0 (PRMs 5a-607).

The address of the SoundDMA buffer is passed to the handler for it to fill with 16-bit linear stereo sound data. Each sample is stored in a word as a pair of signed (two's complement) 16-bit values, with the right channel data in bits 0 - 15, and the left channel data in bits 16 - 31. A flag indicates if the buffer already contains sound data converted from multiple channels in 8-bit μ-law format. The full conditions for entry and exit are as follows:

On Entry:
R0 = parameter passed in R2 to Sound_LinearHandler 1 when registering
R1 = pointer to quadword-aligned sound DMA buffer
R2 = pointer to word immediately after sound DMA buffer
R3 = flags:
    bits 0 - 2 initial buffer content indicator:
    0—data in buffer is invalid and must be overwritten

1—data in buffer has been converted from multiple channels in 8-bit μ-law format, and is not all 0.

2—data in buffer is all 0: if handler would generate silent output; it may simply return.

3-7—reserved

bits 8-31—reserved, and should be ignored

R4 = sample rate for playback, measured in units of 1/1024 Hz; for example 20 kHz (20000 Hz) would be passed as 20000 × 1024, which is 20480000

On Exit:

R0 - R10 may be corrupted

R11, R12, R13 must be preserved

24: Floating Point Model

Since the very first releases of RISC OS, floating point architecture has been available for use, and on the early releases it was supplied in the form of a software emulator. However, the ARM chip has full support for additional circuitry whereby extra functionality can be added in the form of co-processors which supply additional architecture. With this comes a considerable improvement in speed over any software emulation.

The VFP or Vector Floating Point co-processor is included in the Raspberry Pi's System-On-a-Chip (SOC) design and so is already built-in to the Pi's hardware. The additional architecture it provides includes registers and instructions to allow the floating point instruction set to be included in assembly language programs. It conforms to the IEEE 754 definition which standardises the format of floating point numbers across computer platforms. In fact the VFP occupies two slots of the 16 slots available on the Raspberry Pi — CP10 and CP11 — which handle the single and double precision operations respectively.

This chapter provides a very brief overview of the VFP architecture and also looks at some of the functionality provided by the Vector Floating Point Module for the co-processors, which is an essential aspect of any VFP programming on the Raspberry Pi.

VFP Architecture

VFP2 is implemented on the ARM chip fitted to your Raspberry Pi. A third incarnation — VFP3 — is available on later releases of the ARM chip and this provides increased functionality. Whilst a program written for the VFP2 instruction set will run on a VFP3 co-processor the reverse is not true, so ensure that any code you may develop uses only the VFP2 instruction set. (You will sometimes see the word NEON use in conjunction with VFP. NEON technology is a 128-bit SIMD — Single Instruction, Multiple Data- architecture extension for the ARM Cortex™ series of processors — again not applicable with the Raspberry Pi but worth knowing about.)

VFP2 provides support for single precision and double precision numbers. As the name implies the latter can represent numbers in more detail than can the former. A single precision number occupies a word of memory (32-bits or binary32), whilst a double occupies two-words of memory (64-bits or binary64). You will recall that the ARM can use 32-bit numbers for its standard values and this begs the question: are the single precision floating point numbers that are available as big as the integer ones? The answer is: yes they are and they can be much bigger as it boils down to the way in which they are represented. The following are examples of floating point or real numbers:

>0.2345
>546.6735268
>1.001011010
>4E7

At bit level each format is broken down into an exponent and fractional portion. In double precision values (64-bit) the fractional portion occupies more space as illustrated in Figure 25a.

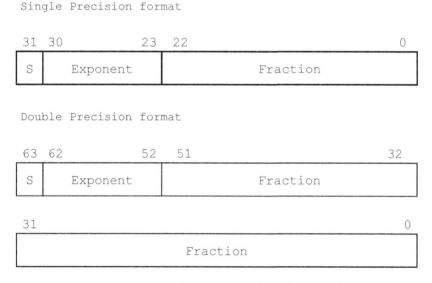

Figure 24a. Construction of single and double precision numbers.

The Register File

The load and store architecture of the ARM chip persists in VFP and to deal with floating point values it provides a set of registers specifically for the purpose. There are 32 in all with the prefix S and numbered S0-S31. These registers are used to hold single precision values as they are all one word wide. For the manipulation of double precision numbers these registers can be paired up to form up to 16 two-word width registers. The prefix D is used to denote this and they are numbered D0-D15. Figure 24b illustrates this principle.

S0	S1	<<	>>	D0
S2	S3			D1
S4	S5			D2
S6	S7			D3
S8	S9			D4
S10	S11			D5
S12	S13			D6
S14	S15			D7
S16	S17			D8
S18	S19			D9
S20	S21			D10
S22	S23			D11
S24	S25			D12
S26	S27			D13
S28	S29			D14
S30	S31			D15

Figure 24b. The VFP Register File. The Sn registers may be used individually or paired to create a double precision register, Dx.

You should be clear that these registers are one and the same, and although the values in registers may be either single or double they can only contain one value at a time. Thus S0 and S1 can be used individually for two single precision values or combined as D0 for a double prevision value. If D0 is loaded with a value then the contents of S0 and S1 are wiped. It is perfectly possible to have single precision value in S0 and S1 and a double precision value in D1 as D1 is composed of S2 and S3.

The VFP2 co-processor provides three system registers. The most important of these from our perspective is the Floating Point Status and Control Register or FPSCR. You can think of this as the CPSR for the normal ARM instruction set, in that it provides flag status information. Indeed the N, Z, C and V flags are all present and have the same function, although conditional test branches are performed to a different set of rules that VFP programmers should be aware of.

Even if you are not considering taking on VFP programming the co-processors can be useful as you can use the 32 single precision registers as additional storage space for your normal programs. This is a rather cheeky way of gaining more register storage if you are pushed for space!

Context Switching

A context switch is a procedure that a computer's processor follows to change from one task to another while ensuring that the tasks do not conflict and data is preserved. In this case the term 'context' refers to the data in the registers and program counter at a specific moment in time. At any one moment in time on the ARM that is a large amount of data. We often deal with this by pushing everything on the stack and then pulling it off before we return to the original task. In some cases we know and are aware (the PRMs tell us) that the data in some places is going to get trashed.

Now refer back to the VFP2 architecture and in particular the register file. That's an awful lot of information — add to this the three system registers and the amount of data we are looking at is growing. Being able to preserve this information as we switch from task to task becomes complex and poses the question: where should it be placed?

This is even more conflicting if, for example, you are trying to run two VFP processes on the Desktop and have the Wimp to deal with at the same time — lots of data and none of it dealt with automatically. There is the additional fact that the two VFP co-processors must be switched on for RISC OS to recognise and use them. This can become an involved process especially given the need to identify whether they are already in use, and are therefore switched on.

The issue is that multiple context switches may be required every second and this starts to impinge on memory and processing time. Things get slow and at the end of the day effective context switching is critical if the system is to provide a user-friendly multitasking interface.

VFP Support Module

The VFP Module supplies a number of SWI calls that will handle and deal with all these issues. Provided all users adhere to this official way of accessing the VFP instruction set then all housekeeping is taken care of for you as is the RISC OS way. It does this by providing a context environment for individual VFP operations to run in, each identified by its own context handle.

The SWI calls provided by the module allow:

- Contexts to be created

- Contexts to be destroyed (removed)

- Switching between existing contexts

- Context features and values to be interrogated

For each run situation you will need to create a context for your VFP program to operate in regardless if it is a standalone routine, an application or a module. Like so many things, it is relatively straightforward once you know how to do it. The various VFPSupport SWIs and functions which start at &58EC0. are summarised below:

VFPSupport_CheckContext

Checks whether it's possible to create a context with the indicated settings, and how much memory is required for the context save area if the application is to manage memory allocation itself.

VFPSupport_CreateContext

Creates and potentially activates a context as defined and set up by the above call.

VFPSupport_DestroyContext

Destroys a context, potentially activating the indicated context if the context being destroyed was the active one.

VFPSupport_ChangeContext

Activates the specified context.

VFPSupport_ExamineContext

Returns in a descriptor block a list of words describing the format of a VFP register dump.

VFPSupport_FastAPI

FastAPI can be used as a fast way of context switching from privileged modes.

VFPSupport_ActiveContext

Returns the currently active context pointer.

VFPSupport_Version

Returns the current module version number * 100. At time of writing the version was 0.02 which is not backwardly compatible with the original version 0.01.

VFPSupport_Features

Returns the values of the FPSID, MVFR0, & MVFR1 registers.

Creating A Context

Two calls are involved in creating a context. First we ensure that the context can be created with the required parameters and then, assuming there are no errors, we create the context. VFPSupport_CheckContext is called first and has the following entry and exit conditions with R0 acting as a flag register:

On Entry:
R0 Flags:
Bit 0:   = 0 User Mode access required.
           = 1 User Mode access not required
Bit 1:   = 0 Context not saved in Application space.

=1 Context saved in application space

Bits2-29 = 0

Bits 30-31 = not used

R1 = Number of double-word registers required (1-16)

On Exit

R0 Number of bytes required to contain context.

All other registers preserved

The following segment of code would check to see if a context could be created that reserved the first two double-word registers for use and at the same time ensured that the VFP co-processors were available for use in User Mode, allowing us to create the context in our own memory space. Bit 0 of R0 allows the programmer to determine where VFP code is executed. By setting this bit you can ensure that VFP code can only be executed when the ARM is in a privileged mode (such as SVC) from the context being created. Bits 30-31 are not used. This is so that you can pre-seed information into these two bits that will be required when the context is created, as outlined shortly.

```
MOV R0, #2
MOV R1, #2
SWI "VFPSupport_CheckContext"
BVS context_error
```

When the call returns R0 will contain the amount of space required for managing the context. This can be saved and used to manually manage the space if required. If the context cannot be created an error is returned.

After checking that the context can be created VFPSupport_CreateContext can be called with the following conditions.

Entry:

R0 Flags:

Bit 0:   = 0 User Mode access required.

         = 1 User Mode access not required

Bit 1:   = 0 Context not saved in Application space.

         = 1 Context saved in application space

Bit 30 = 0 Leave context inactive. =1 Activate lazily

Bit 31 = 0 Leave context inactive. -=1 Activate now

R1 = Number of double-word registers required (1-16)

R2 = Pointer to buffer for use with context, or 0

R3 = Value with which to initialise FPSCR

Exit:

R0 = Context pointer

R1 = Previously active context - if R0 bit 30 or b31 was previously set on entry.

Bits 0 and 1 of R0 have the same function as they do in creating the context. Bits 30 and 31 of R0 are used to determine how the context is activated. If bit31 is set then the context will be activated immediately and the co-processors will be switched in if they are not already active. If bit 30 is set then the context will be activated when a VFP instruction is encountered. Using this so-called 'lazy activation' can provide improved performance in some situations by avoiding redundant save/restore operations, for instance where VFP code might only be executed in certain conditions. It would be a waste of processor time and memory space if those conditions were not met. The set condition of bit 30 supersedes the value of bit 31.

The value in R1 is the same as is passed in creating the context. R2 is a pointer to where the context data should be saved if bit 1 is set. If you are not providing your own memory space then bit 1 of R0 should be clear and R2 can contain 0. If you are creating your own memory buffer then the value returned in R0 by the create context call will need to have been saved. If you do not provide your own space management then the VFP Support module will manage the memory process for you.

The value passed in R3 will be copied to the FPSCR. This allows you to set up any flags and conditions that you might require prior to entering the VFP code. If you have no seeding requirements then this register can be cleared to zero. However there is a caveat here — the VFP support module is still in its infancy and does not provide full software support for all VFP instructions so this can cause it to crash. To ensure that this does not happen, bits 24 and 25 of the FPSCR should be set to place the co-processors in RunFast Mode. Amongst other things, this forces the default result specified by the IEEE 754 standard for actions such as overflow, division by zero and invalid operations that would otherwise require software support to handle. So, in reality, for virtually all instances the results returned will remain accurate.

The segment below shows how a context can be created based on the previous information.

```
MOV R0, #1<<31      ; Activate context immediately flag
ORR R0, R0, #2      ; Allow in user mode & context space
MOV R1, #2          ; Allow D0, D1 and S0, S1, S2, S3
ADR R2, buffer%     ; load address of context buffer
MOV R3, #%11<<25    ; set RunFast Mode
SWI "VFPSupport_CreateContext"
ADR R4, context     ; Save context handle somewhere safe.
STR R0, [R4]        ; save context pointer
```

At this point the VFP instruction set is ready to be utilised. When you have completed your requirements you should remove the context by calling VFPSupport_DestroyContext and the context handle in R1 identifies the context to be removed:

```
LDR R0, [R4]
MOV R1, #0; Null context
SWI "VFPSupport_DestroyContext"
```

The entry and exit conditions are:

On Entry
R0 = Context to destroy
R1 = Context to activate in its place

On Exit
R0 = Context that's now active
All other registers preserved

If the context in R0 is currently active, then the context given in R1 will be activated in its place. Specify 0 to switch to the null context. If the context in R0 is not currently active then R1 is ignored and the active context will not be modified.

You are not required to call VFPSupport_DestroyContext in order to destroy the context if you are managing your own context space, but you should ensure that you have finished all your VFP activity before attempting to reuse any of the context memory, otherwise you will find your data corrupted which could lead to a crash. If the VFP Module is managing space for you then to free up module workspace it is best to destroy the context when you are finished with it.

Demonstration

Program 24a brings together the segments of code discussed above in order to create a program that demonstrates the use of creating and using a context. The lines 250-290 include a few VFP operations to prove that the process works, moving some floating point data around. Note the use of the DCFS directive in line 280 to store a real value in memory. Unfortunately at this stage RISC OS does not support any floating point SWI print equivalent so interrogating data is not as straightforward as it might be unless you include suitable conversion routines with the program for use. If you do want to have a look at the information returned take a note of the address where the .size label is assembled (line 360) and dump the 12 bytes of memory that are there thus:

```
*MEMORY xxxx +12
```

where 'xxxx' is the aforementioned address. Typical output might look like this:

```
00000028 00009400 48BFAE14 48BFAE14
```

Here &28 is the size of the context space required, &9400 is the address of the buffer% space (line 60) and &48BFAE14 is the single precision value 5.99 (line 380)

It is worth saving the program before you run it (if you have not downloaded from the website) as any errors may result in a freeze.

Program 24a. Demonstration of Context Switching

```
 10 REM >Prog24a
 20 REM VFP Test
 30 REM RPi RISC OS Programming
 40 :
 50 DIM code% 512
 60 DIM buffer% 256
 70 FOR pass=0 TO 3 STEP 3
 80 P%=code%
 90 [ OPT pass
100 .start
110 MOV R0, #2
120 MOV R1, #2
130 SWI "VFPSupport_CheckContext"
140 ADR R5, size
150 STR R0, [R5]
160 :
170 MOV R0, #1<<31
180 ORR R0, R0, #2
190 ADR R2, buffer%
200 MOV R3, #%11<<25
210 SWI "VFPSupport_CreateContext"
220 ADR R4, context
230 STR R0, [R4]; save context pointer
240 :
250 ADR R1, value1
260 VLDR S2, [R1]
270 VCVT.F64.F32 D0, S2
280 ADR R1, store
290 VSTR S2, [R1]
300 :
310 LDR R0, [R4]
320 MOV R1, #0; Null context
330 SWI "VFPSupport_DestroyContext"
340 MOV PC, LR
350 :
360 .size EQUD 0
370 .context EQUD 0
380 .value1 DCFS 5.99
```

```
390 .store EQUD 0
400 ]
410 NEXT pass
420 CALL start
```

Summing Up

This chapter is provided to introduce you to one of the most challenging areas of development in floating point use (and abuse) in RISC OS. If you wish to find out more then you should look at the RISC OS Open website and some of the discussions and documentation provided there. The book support pages on the website contain direct links which include a link to the VFP datasheet.

25: GPIO Action

One of the things making the Raspberry Pi so popular is the ability to connect external electronics to it and control them — everything from lights through to complete home automation systems. The sky really is the limit. So it makes sense to examine how we can control those attachments using from RISC OS.

In this chapter we'll look at how the GPIO interface is connected to the Raspberry Pi and how you can use machine code to access that connection, thereby enabling you to read and write to individual GPIO pins. We'll also look at one of the GPIO modules freely available to you if you want to experiment a bit with a proven interface.

While this isn't a primer on the GPIO interface, understanding how it sits with the Raspberry Pi is fundamental to understanding how to program it. Neither am I going to show you how to physically connect devices to your GPIO port.

Figure 25a. The Gertboard in its 'leds' configuration. Jumpers set to output.

There are plenty of other books and articles explaining how to do that and indeed there are dedicated expansion boards that provide a whole range of functionality simply by plugging them onto the GPIO connector. Just for the record, in testing these examples I have used a *Gertboard* which has been configured as described in its manual to run its own 'leds' test file. The photograph in Figure 25a illustrates this configuration. The same result should be achievable with one of the other expansion boards available or even through your own breadboard constructions. .

A far as the GPIO interface goes I would recommend that you download the BCM2835 datasheet, which contains just about everything you would want to know about — not just the GPIO interface but also all the other hardware-orientated aspects of the ARM chip fitted to your Raspberry Pi. The datasheet can be a little daunting if you have not looked at one before, but if you look at it in conjunction with the examples worked below, you will be able to follow it clearly enough, and that will enable you to investigate the numerous other GPIO functions for yourself. You can access a link to this via the Raspberry Pi website or through this book support website.

The GPIO Controller

The GPIO has its own controller and this contains no less than 41 registers. The first five of these registers deal with reading and writing to the 54 GPIO pins. These pins are numbered GPIO 0 through to GPIO 53 although only a handful or so of these are available to us to connect to on the GPIO expansion port itself (this is what the Gertboard and other similar boards connect to). The first five of these registers, their names and the pins they are associated with are listed in Figure 25b.

No	Name	Off	Pins
0	GPIO Function Select 0 (GPSEL0)	#0	0-9
1	GPIO Function Select 1 (GPSEL1)	#4	10-19
2	GPIO Function Select 2 (GPSEL2)	#8	20-29
3	GPIO Function Select 3 (GPSEL3)	#12	30-39
4	GPIO Function Select 4 (GPSEL4)	#16	30-49
5	GPIO Function Select 5 (GPSEL5)	#20	50-53

Figure 25b. GPIO registers and pin control.

It should be noted also that the GPIO Controller pin numbers do not run concurrently on the GPIO main GPIO header connector and may differ again on any expansion board you have attached. Please ensure you familiarise yourself with the system you are using as the pin numbers here relate specifically to the numbers assigned by BCM.

Each of these registers is 32-bits wide and each pin has three bits assigned to it within each register. In GPSEL0 GPIO Pin 0 has bits 0, 1 and 2 assigned to it. GPIO 1 has bits 3, 4 and 5 and so on. In GPSEL1, then the first three bits (0, 1 and 2) are assigned to GPIO 10. In GPSEL2, then the first three bits (0, 1 and 2) are assigned to GPIO 20. Figure 25c illustrates the arrangement for GPSEL2.

(You may have noticed above that not all the bits in Register 5 are used. This is correct. Only the first 12 bits are used and the others are classed as 'reserved'. Likewise bits 30 and 31 in each of the other registers are unused)

Pin 29		Pin 28		Pin 27		Pin 26		Pin 25		Pin 24		Pin 23		Pin 22		Pin 21		Pin 20	
31	30	29	28	27	26	25	24	23	22	21	20	19	18	17	16	15	14	13	12	11	10	9	8	7	6	5	4	3	2	1	0

Figure 25c. Bit association with GPSEL2.

It is important to understand how these bits are assigned as we will need to address them individually at various times to make things happen in their associated registers.

To assign a pin as an input we must store a 0 in the three associated bits (000). To make the same pin an output we must write a 1 in those same three bits (001). For example, to make GPIO 21 an output we must place 001 in bits 3, 4 and 5 (see Figure 25c above). To achieve this we could write the binary value:

```
001000
```

(decimal 8) to GPFEL2. Of course we must preserve and not overwrite any other bits that may be set or clear so we would do this using a bitwise operator as we shall see in due course. (Other bit combinations assign other functions to the pins, so it is important to get this right. The Broadcom datasheet explains these other functions).

The base address for the GPIO controller in RISC OS is &20200000 and this address is where the first register is located — GPSEL0. If we want to get to the second register, GPFEL1, then we need to add four to the controller's base address. Figure 25a also contains a column called 'offset'. This is the number of bytes offset from the GPIO Controller start address where that particular register starts. GPSEL2 has an offset of 8, so its RICS OS address would be 0x20200000+8.

So far we have looked at configuring a pin as an input or an output. To turn the pin on (set) or off (clear) we have to write some values into another register. (In this case I am talking about turning a LED on or turning an LED off.)

There are four registers associated with setting and clearing pins and these are detailed in Figure 25d.

No	Name	Off	Pins
7	GPIO Pin Set 0 (GPSET0)	#28	0-31
8	GPIO Pin Set 1 (GPSET1)	#32	32-53
10	GPIO Output Clear 0 (GPCLR0)	#40	0-31
11	GPIO Ouput Clear 1 (GPCLR1)	#44	32-53

Figure 25d. GPIO registers for setting and clearing.

There is a single bit associated with each pin for the purpose of setting and clearing. For example, to set GPIO 21 we would write a '1' into bit 21 of GPSET0. To clear the same bit we would need to write a '1' into bit 21 of GPCLR0.

If you were to write a 1 to bit21 in GPSET0 but GPIO 21 was defined as an input nothing would happen. If you then set GPIO 21 to an output, an attached LED would light. The last value written to either GPSET0 or GPCLR0 in this case is remembered and actioned when the status of the pin is changed.

As we can see from Figure 25d the offset for GPSET0 is 28 and for GPCLR0 is 40 and this value added to the base address to the GPIO controller is where we need to write to.

Building the Code

That's quite a lot to take in, so let's work through an example. Here we'll assume that we are dealing with GPIO 21. We have an LED attached to it which we want to turn on. Before we can do that we have to initialise the pin by first setting it as an input, then as an output. Finally we can turn the LED on by setting the bit associated with the pin. The toggling of the input/output status of the pin enables it to record what the last action was (by order) when we set or clear its status.

The code segment that follows is pseudo-code just for illustrative purposes — if you try and use it 'as is' it will not work, for reasons which I'll explain shortly!

```
.input
LDR R3, #&2020000          \ get GPIO Base addr
MOV R5, R3                 \ save copy for later use
ADD R3, R3, #8             \ pin 21 in register 2 so add 8
offset
MOV R2, R3                 \ move address into R2
LDR R2, [R2, #0]           \ get value in Register 2
BIC R2, R2, #0b111<,3      \ clear 3 bits assoc with pin 21
```

295

```
    STR R2, [R3, #0]            \ write value back to GPIO Base


  .output
    MOV R2, R3                  \ write GPIO addr to R2
    LDR R2, [R2, #0]            \ get value at R2
    ORR R2, R2, #1<<3           \ set lsb as output for pin 21
    STR R2, [R3, #0]            \ and write to Register 2


  .set
    MOV R3, R5                  \ get base addr
    ADD R3, R3, #28             \ set GPSET0 address for set
    MOV R4, #1                  \ set bit
    MOV  R2, R4, LSL #21        \ rotate to pin 21 and place in
    R2
    STR R2, [R3, #0]            \ write to memory to set
```

The comments should help you follow this through. The key thing to remember here is that, for GPIO 21, we are dealing with Register 2 which has an offset of 8. This means that 8 must be added to the GPIO base address at &20200000. In Register 2 bits 3, 4 and 5 are associated with pin 21. Thus we must shift left any value we want to write into those bits by three places. Take a look at the BIC instruction below which is taken from the input part of the segment:

```
            BIC R2, R2, #%111<<3
```

R2 contains the address of Register 2. If we shift the binary value 111 left by three places we get 111000. The result is that these three bits are cleared when we store this value back in the register. Remember BIC performs a logical bit clear or AND NOT on the value in R2. By effectively placing 000 in the three bits we have assigned the pin as an input. (We have used a slightly different way to perform the LSL here using '<<' which is one of many shortcuts that the BBC BASIC Assembler provides.)

The '.output' routine now programs the same pin as an output by writing a 1 into bits 3, 4 and 5 of Register 2. It does this with:

```
            ORR R2, R2, #1<<3
```

We have now initialised the pin by getting it ready to act as an output.

Now we just have to place a 1 in the bit associated with the pin in the GPSET0 register. GPIO 21 is pin 21 so we have to place a 1 in bit 21 of GPSET0. GPSET0 is offset 28 bytes from the start of the GPIO Controller, so the 28 is added to the base controller address and then the left shifted bit stored there.

As I said, this program won't work, but assuming the LED attached was now illuminated, to turn it off we would use:

```
    MOV R3, R5                  \ get base addr
    ADD R3, R3, #40             \ get GPCLR0 address for set
```

```
MOV R4, #1              \ set bit
MOV  R2, R4, LSL #21    \ rotate to pin 21 and place in
R2
STR R2, [R3, #0]        \ write to memory to set
```

So why won't the program work? Because RISC OS will not allow us to write directly to the GPIO Controller (or other I/O space for that matter)! It is a self-protect mechanism that is built into it to try and ensure we don't correct anything that might otherwise cause it to crash. So we have to get around that.

Virtual Memory

If you look at the BDM datasheet (page 5) the diagram depicts that the I/O block at bus address &7Exxxxxx is mapped to ARM physical address &20xxxxxx. The Raspberry Pi actually has three address spaces – the ARM logical address, the ARM physical address, and the bus physical address. This is because all memory and I/O accesses go through both the ARM's MMU and the VideoCore's MMU before it actually hits the target device.

The way we get around this problem is to use a technique that allows us to create an area of memory that mirrors the protected space we want to access - *virtual memory*. Once we have ascertained what the virtual address is for the GPIO Controller we can read and write to it using a system call. The three calls we use are OS_Memory, OS_EnterOS and OS_LeaveOS.

OS_Memory

This call performs a variety of operations the exact nature of which is defined by a reason code passed in R0. For our purpose we are interested in reason code 13 (&0D) which I used to 'Map in IO permanent'. The entry and exit conditions are:

```
On entry:
R0=13
R1=physical address to map in
```
R2=size to map in
```
On exit:
R0-R2 preserved
```
R3=logical address assigned to R1.

So, R1 will contain &20200000 and R2 we can put &100 as this will more than cover the mapping the registers we need. On exit the address that we can use to access the GPIO Controller will be held in R3. This call can be performed from BASIC using:

```
SYS "OS_Memory",13,&20200000,&100 TO ,,, logical%
```

The variable 'logical%' will hold the logical address for the start of the GPIO Controller. It is this address we must utilise as the GPIO base address.

OS_EnterOS and OS_LeaveOS

The purpose of these calls is to allow the user to enter and leave Supervisor Mode cleanly. There are no register entry and exit conditions, in fact all registers are preserved. Interrupt and Fast Interrupt status is unaltered. Note that SWI calls while in SVC mode will alter R14, and will use R13 as stack.

Pin 21

Program 25a shows how this all comes together for the example we have worked above — GPIO 21. You can run and assembler this one ! Of course it is assumed that you have a Gertboard attached or have made the required changes to select the pins your require (more on this shortly).

Program 25a. Setting GPIO 21 to turn on an attached LED.

```
 10 REM Prog25a
 20 REM GPIO Pin 21 toggle on Gertboard
 30 REM RPi RISC OS Programming
 40 :
 50 DIM code% 256
 60 :
 70 FOR pass=0 TO 3 STEP 3
 80 P%=code%
 90 [
100 OPT pass
110 .start
120 \ First need to get logical address
130 MOV R0, #13
140 LDR R1, gpiobase
150 MOV R2, #&100
160 SWI "OS_Memory"
170 MOV R0, R3
180 \
190 SWI "OS_EnterOS"
200 MOV R5, R3
210 ADD R3, R3, #8
220 MOV R2, R3
230 LDR R2, [R2, #0]
240 BIC R2, R2, #%111<<3
250 STR R2, [R3, #0]
260 :
270 .output
280 MOV R2, R3
290 LDR R2, [R2, #0]
```

```
300 ORR R2, R2, #%1<<3
310 STR R2, [R3, #0]
320 :
330 .set
340 MOV R3, R5
350 ADD R3, R3, #28          \ #40 to run off
360 MOV R4, #1
370 MOV R2, R4, LSL #21
380 STR R2, [R3, #0]
390 :
400 SWI "OS_LeaveOS"
410 MOV PC, R14
420 :
430 .gpiobase
440 EQUD &20200000
450]
460 NEXT pass
470 CALL start
```

Lines 130-160 perform the OS_Memory call and on return the logical address held in R3 is moved into R0 so that the pin action can take place as previously described. As call 13 here performs a permanent map the virtual memory area remains in play until it is 'released' or there is a rebook. Thus we only need to make the call once.

To edit the program so that it turns pin 21 off all you need to do is to edit one line of code as follows:

```
350 ADD R3, R3, #40
```

And assemble again - that simple!

Using and Adapting

I tend to assembler these files into machine code and save them using a name indicative of the pin. For example, for Program 25a I would compile and save the executable using the name, 'on21'. I would also create a complementary file to clear the pin using the filename 'off21'. Creating a pair for each file gives you the immediate ability to set and clear individual pins as you wish:

```
*on21
*off21
```

You only require minimal changes to adapt the program to work on other pins, and you should have more than enough information to do this. If you make the changes listed below to Program 25a then you can have access to GPIO

17. Referring back to Figure 25a we can see that GPIO 17 is in GPIO Function Select 1 (GPSEL1) and the offset here is 4. This is the first change we must make.

Bits 21, 22 and 23 within GPSEL1 are linked to GPIO 17 so the logical shift left value associated with writing %111 and %001 is 21. Finally GPIO 17 is associated with bit 17 in GPSET0 so this is the final shift value we need to change in the assembler.

Program 25b. Changes: adapting for GPIO 17.

```
210 ADD R3, R3, #4          \ 8 is now 4
240 BIC R2, R2, #%111<<21   \ 3 is now 21
300 ORR R2, R2, #%1<<21     \ 3 is now 21
370 MOV R2, R4, LSL #17     \ 21 is now 17
```

Other GPIO Functions

There are a number of other registers that form part of the GPIO Controller that can be used and programmed using these methods. As already mentioned you will need to get a copy of the BCM2835 ARM peripherals datasheet to get the specific detail that you need relating to the other registers, their functions and what you need to do to use them. It is all there.

One final thing in relation to the datasheet: If you look at the memory maps at the start of the document you will see that the ARM peripherals are mapped as starting at &7E000000, whereas in RISC OS they start at &20000000. All operating systems implement their own memory addressing systems which overlay the ones provided by default by the CPU. This allows the OS in question to implement virtual memory mapping — a technique that allows program and applications to use more memory than is actually available to them by swapping data in and out of memory from the SD Card in use or the hard drive attached. From a practical point of view, when you access the Broadcom datasheet you should remember that all the peripheral addresses specified in the text are bus addresses and must be translated into physical addresses. Thus the GPIO Controller start address is given as &7E200000 but we implement as &20200000 in our programs — change the first two numbers from 7E to 20 if you like!

Finally a word of warning. The GPIO pins control a whole host of functions on your Raspberry Pi and if you are not careful you can crash RISC OS causing everything to freeze and necessitating a hard reset. Always save your work before you try to execute any machine code file for the first time.

GPIO Module

You can download a free GPIO Module using PackMan. The module, authored by 'Tank' is well worth investigation even if you plan to program the GPIO directly as demonstrated above. Part of what you can download (there are several items, so download them all to experiment with) includes the source code for the module and will allow you to investigate further — not just how the GPIO is accessed from the module but also how the * commands and SWIs are implemented.

A couple of programs that use the GPIO module are provided below and will help you investigate further any hardware that you have attached to the GPIO. It should work regardless of what board/expansion you are using on the GPIO, and so long as you have LEDs attached to the pins you should see a visual result when you run Program 25d.

Firstly, Program 25c will print information about your GPIO configuration — it uses the GPIO_Info SWI provided by the GPIO module. This will return a block that contains a list of pins located on the expansion port that are tied to the board it's running on. The advantage of this call is that you don't need to know that you are using a particular board and can program without that knowledge.

Program 25c. Access information about your GPIO setup.

```
 10 REM >Prog25c
 20 REM Read GPIO pins available
 30 REM RPi RISC OS Programming
 40 :
 50 SYS "GPIO_Info" TO low%, high%, list%
 60 PRINT ~low%
 70 PRINT ~high%
 80 PRINT ~list%
 90 N%=0
100 end%=FALSE
110 REPEAT
120   pin%=list%?N%
130   PRINT pin%
140   IF pin%=&FF THEN end%=TRUE
150   N%=N%+1
160 UNTIL end%=TRUE
```

Three items of information are returned: low% is the number of the lowest GPIO pin, high% is the highest and list% is the address of a block of memory that holds a byte width table of the pins available. The tables are terminated by &FF and there may be up to five tables — four &FFs (255s) denote the end of the information at any point. The program here assumes just one table block being returned. The loop prints the values in the table. I have used the list it supplied in the Program 25d as information in the DATA statement. You should substitute the numbers here for the ones returned when you ran Program 25c (if they were different).

Program 25d. Cycling LEDs using GPIO Module.

```
10 REM >Prog25d
20 REM LED cycling using GPIO Module
30 REM RPi RISC OS Programming
40 :
50 ON ERROR PRINT REPORT$" at line ";ERL: END
60 :
70 DIM gpio%(17)
80 FOR n%=1 TO 17: READ gpio%(n%): NEXT n%
90 SYS "GPIO_ExpAsGPIO",2: REM Set GPIO as outputs
100 :
110 REPEAT
120 FOR n%=1 TO 17
130   SYS "GPIO_WriteData",gpio%(n%),1
140   a=GET
150   PRINT "Turning On GPIO : "; gpio%(n%)
160   t%=TIME: REPEAT UNTIL TIME=t%+5
170   NEXT n%
180 :
190 FOR n%=17 TO 1 STEP -1
200   SYS "GPIO_WriteData",gpio%(n%),0
210   a=GET
220   PRINT "Turning Off GPIO : "; gpio%(n%)
230   t%=TIME: REPEAT UNTIL TIME=t%+5
240 NEXT n%
250 UNTIL FALSE
260 END
270 :
280 DATA 0,1,4,7,8,9,10,11,14,15,17,18,21,22,23,24,25
```

Line 280 contains the values from the list printed by Program25c. The program uses two loops that utilise the GPIO modules SWI GPIO_WriteData command to turn on an LED by passing a '1' to the pin and to turn the pin off by passing a '0' to it.

Of course there is nothing to stop you combining Program 25c and Program 25d and reading the information directly out of memory and into the array. That is the significance of these two examples — using this technique you are able to create a routine that should work in any situation!

You should also consider adding the following line to you programs to ensure that the GPIO Module is installed:

```
*RMEnsure GPIO 0.00 system.modules.gpio
```

And Finally...

This section marks the end of the book *Raspberry Pi* RISC OS *System Programming. Revealed* There is so much more that could be covered and that fact is supported by the 4000 pages of the Programmers' Reference Manuals. I do encourage you to go to the book support pages on my website where there will be additional information and resources. You can download the program files shown in this book. There will be links to all the sites mentioned and plenty more that you should look at and investigate. If you are enthused then you should certainly read and get involved in the RISC OS forums, where there is not just a wealth of searchable information already but feedback for your own queries and ideas.

If you enjoyed this book and would like to see more then please consider writing a few words on the website where you purchased it and on the RISC OS forums. For indie writer/publishers such as me positive feedback (good and bad) is vital. Remember you can contact me via the Contacts page on my website, and you can follow me on Twitter (@brucefsmith) and also Like me on Facebook: **authorbrucesmith**. I post regularly on these mediums. Please also check out my Blog, *Alan Turing Rocks* (www.brucesmith.info/blog), where I mumble on about all sorts of things.

Sydney, November 2013

Raspberry Pi
RISC OS
SYSTEM

APPENDICES

A: Companion Website

Go to **www.brucesmith.info** and look for the book link to locate additional information and support for the *Raspberry Pi RISC OS System Programming Revealed Hands On Guide*.

The support pages on the website contain the following information:

- BBC BASIC & Assembly Language program files from the book

- Updates to programs and information in the book including corrections and additions.

- Links to websites and additional downloads mentioned in the book.

- Information about RISC OS on the Raspberry Pi

The website also contains details of other books written by Bruce Smith and his Techno Blog – *Alan Turing Rocks*.

B : Hands On Guides

Current and forthcoming titles from BSB. Visit www.brucesmith.info for additional details and information about all Bruce Smith Books. Information is subject to change.

Raspberry Pi Assembly Language RISC OS Beginners

Available in Print and eBook editions.

Available in January 2014 this is the completely revised (and renamed to avoid confusion as to the Operating System being used) edition of the best selling Raspberry Pi Assembly Language Beginners book.

Ideal for the novice, this volume starts from first principles and leads you comfortably through to become an accomplished ARM programmer. It adopts a modular approach with simple examples to get you started. Foundation building early chapters lead you gently into the subject without sacrificing the subtle nuances that make Raspberry Pi Assembly Language special. The tools to do this you may already have, or you can simply download them for free in just seconds. We show you how, quickly and simply. Just some of the many features include:

- Example programs and segments
- Use of the BBC BASIC Assembler
- ARM registers and arrangements
- Data processing
- Branches, shifts and rotates
- Conditional execution
- Addressing modes
- Use of operating system SWI calls
- Macros and look-up tables
- Debugging

NEW chapters for this revised edition include:

- Programming the GPIO
- Floating Point Co-processor programing
- Context Switching
- Using GCC & C

- System on Chip
- Plus more .... see website

Please note that the original volume '*Raspberry Pi Assembly Language Beginners*' will remain on sale for those wishing to purchase it, until this updated volume is available. If you wish to purchase the revised edition please wait until it is available as it will not be possible to refund or upgrade copies.

Note: book contents may change without warning. Please check out **www.brucesmith.info** nearer the release date for full details of final contents.

AMAZON REVIEWS for *Raspberry Pi Assembly Language Beginners*

- Great Introduction. I'd certainly recommend it for anyone interested in learning how to program their Raspberry Pi

- Covers the basic stuff you need to get started and is an easy read, well worth a go if you want to get into assembly

- Assembly Language for Beginners suffers from a few typos, though none critical enough to affect the programs as far I can tell. That minor point aside it is well worth the money, even if you don't consider yourself a beginner. Every RISC OS Pi programmer should be renewing his or her bookshelf with this volume.

- I remember the books of Bruce Smith from the days of the BBC Micro and his reputation for making the technical stuff easy, I am glad to say, hasn't been lost. I hope he continues to write books for the Raspberry Pi. I for one will buy them. The Raspberry Pi is about getting people back into programming-this should be the first book you buy.

- The book is very approachable for novices and anyone who has never programmed before. It takes you through what you need to know in a logical and step by step manner building new knowledge on top of what has been already covered.

- This book is an excellent introduction to coding in ARM assembler on the Raspberry Pi.

Raspberry Pi Assembly Language RASPBIAN Beginners

Available in Print and eBook editions.

Raspberry Pi Assembly Language RASPBIAN Beginners is your hands-on guide to learning to program ARM machine code on your Raspberry Pi. With nothing other than the Raspbian Operating System installed on your Raspberry Pi, this book shows you how to access all the tools that you'll need to create your own machine code programs using assembly language.

Examples are provided that are written using the GCC Compiler running under the Raspbian Operating System on the Raspberry Pi, all of which can be downloaded from the book support website at www.brucesmith.info.

Ideal for the novice, this book starts from first principles and leads you comfortably on your way to become an accomplished programmer. Providing lucid descriptions, award winning author Bruce Smith keeps things simple and includes plenty of program examples you can try for yourself. Ideas and concepts are introduced in the order required so you should never be left wondering. Just some of the many features include:

- 260 pages
- Practical approach with example programs
- GCC assembler and linker
- ARM registers and arrangements
- Addressing modes
- Use of operating system Syscalls
- Debugging with GDB
- Using libc function calls
- Programming the GPIO
- Purchase Print edition and get eBook edition for just 99c/p

Note: book contents may change without warning. Please check out **www.brucesmith.info** for full details.

AMAZON REVIEWS for *Raspberry Pi Assembly Language RASPBIAN Beginners*

- This was just the book I was looking for. Not only does it teach you how about programming the ARM chip it also delves into some of the specifics of the Raspberry Pi itself, and those topics you find unanswered in the forums. This book is worth it for that fact alone providing chapters on things like Thumb Code, Floating Point and programming the GPIO. In summary this is an excellent book which is a must-buy for anyone who wants to learn how to program their Raspberry Pi at the most fundamental level. Well priced and well written, and the print version I have is well-laid out and easy to follow.

  Customer Reviews

  ★★★★★ (3)
  5.0 out of 5 stars

5 star	3	Share you
4 star	0	
3 star	0	Write a
2 star	0	
1 star	0	

  See all 3 customer reviews ›

  Most Helpful Customer Reviews

  3 of 3 people found the following review helpful
  ★★★★★ **Assembly for Pi**
  By tomdkeating on September 11, 2013
  Format: Kindle Edition   Amazon Verified Purchase
  This is a great book for budding programmers who examples and code to learn from and enjoy.

  1 Comment   Was this review helpful to you? Y

- Excellent little book. Uses the linux gcc toolchain rather than the riscos basic assembler, so its easy to try the examples directly under raspbian. I did a lot of X86 assembler coding at one time (ugh!) and had forgotten just how brilliant the ARM instruction set is. Very easy to memorise and get coding. Shows how to interface assembler to C as well. Would thoroughly recommend this to anyone looking to learn ARM assembly language

- This is a great book for budding programmers who want to dig deeper into the Raspberry PI to really understand how the computer works. Great step by step examples and code to learn from and enjoy.

- It is easy to find good books about C# and Java. However, for many more specialized development tools it is hard to find a book that provides what a beginner needs. In many cases, a book thoroughly covers the language commands, but leaves the reader staring a a blank command line wondering "What, exactly, do I need to type to compile and run my program?" Bruce Smith's books do not fall into this trap. Smith provides not only the necessary coaching and instruction in assembly language for the Raspberry Pi's ARM processor, but also gives clear practical instructions for getting everything to work... Whether you are looking just to have some fun learning assembly language with your Raspberry PI or whether you view the PI as a stepping-stone to greater things ARM, Bruce Smith's book definitely belongs on your shelf.

- I'm totally new to Raspberry Pi, Linix, and to Arm processors. This book is clearly written with easy to follow examples. I'm up to chapter 12 so far. I bought the kindle edition and am reading it on my IPad. The formatting, pictures, and text flow are all superb.

NEW: RETRO COMPUTER SERIES

Reviving 8-bit Classic publications for the 6502 for the computer systems that shaped a generation of programmers!

Mastering Interpreters & Compilers
Techniques for the BBC Model B, Master & Electron

"This clear and comprehensive introduction to compilers and interpreters emphasises the practical side of the art. It moves gradually from the idea of a 'wedge' in the BBC Computer's operating system, to a simple interpreter, a simple graphics language, threaded interpretive languages (including FORTH) and, finally, a stand-alone compiler. Listings of the implementations are given.

This book will give anyone with a good knowledge of assembly language the foundation on which to build an interpreter or compiler of their own."

The above description was taken from the back cover of the original BBC Soft publication, published as a BBC Master Guide in 1987. Now close to 30-years on Bruce Smith is republishing this classic guide in its original form complete with BBC BASIC listings.

Available late first quarter 2014. Further details will appear on the website at www.brucesmith.info nearer the time.

C: Alan Turing Rocks

Bruce Smith's occasional blog about computers and technology also includes updates about the projects he is working on. He posts on Facebook and Twitter when he has added a new blog entry.

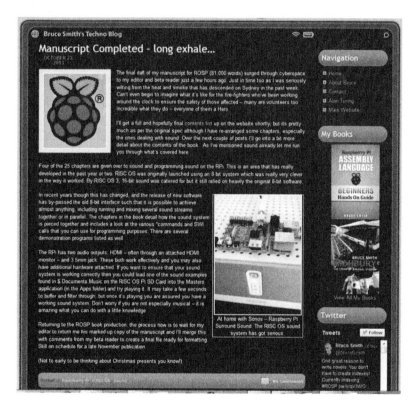

His blog is named after the '*person he would most liked to have met in the world.*' Alan Turing (23 June 1912 – 7 June 1954) was a British mathematician and cryptographer who is considered to be one of the fathers of modern computer science. He never described himself as a philosopher, but his 1950 paper "Computing Machinery and Intelligence" is one of the most frequently cited in modern philosophical literature. It gave a fresh approach to the traditional mind-body problem, by relating it to the mathematical concept of computability. His work can be regarded as the foundation of computer science and of the artificial intelligence program.

Alan Turing's short and extraordinary life has attracted wide interest. It has inspired his mother's memoir (E. S. Turing 1959), a detailed biography (Hodges 1983), a play and television film (Whitemore 1986), and various other works of fiction and art. Alan Turing was arguably one of the greatest minds that ever lived.

Like Bruce Smith at www.facebook.com/authorbrucesmith to receive updates on what Bruce is and has been up to and to ask questions. Follow Bruce on Twitter and to ask questions @brucesfsmith.

Index

%

*

/

16

8

:

<

>

—

A

B

C

I

X

Hands On Guides
Practical Books for Practical People

Want to write or contribute to a book?

If you have a great idea for a great book then email us via www.brucesmith.info

Alan Turing Rocks
www.brucesmith.info/blog

Printed in Great Britain
by Amazon

57578579R00183